HARCOURT SOCIAL Studies

The United States

Reading Support and Intervention

Harcourt

SCHOOL PUBLISHERS

www.harcourtschool.com

ISBN-13: 978-0-15-349432-1
ISBN-10: 0-15-349432-8

1 2 3 4 5 6 7 8 9 10 054 15 14 13 12 11 10 09 08 07 06

Contents

Introduction

Today's students are growing up in the Information Age. Our concept of literacy is expanding and changing. In our technological society, students need to understand and evaluate information in many forms—websites, e-mail, Internet advertisements, trade books, newspapers, and magazines—in addition to their textbooks.

WHY is it important to offer reading support to students in the context of social studies instruction? To succeed in social studies, students must be able to read and make meaning from expository text. The structure of social studies text is very different from the more familiar structure of stories and fiction selections. The organizational pattern of social studies text is likely to be different from texts in other content areas.

Students come to us with varying levels of English proficiency and literacy, as well as a variety of backgrounds and experiences. As we assess and plan for the individual needs of our students in grades 3–6, we identify students who are struggling to comprehend grade-level expository texts. This puts them at a disadvantage. In order for students to learn about the world, past and present, they must be able to connect ideas within a text and also to connect prior knowledge to ideas in a text.

Research shows that we can help students better understand and remember what they read by

- using **direct vocabulary instruction** to teach words that are important to concepts in their reading.
- providing **systematic fluency practice,** through rereadings and feedback, to help students improve their fluency.
- teaching students how and when to **use comprehension strategies** to understand expository text.

HOW can we effectively offer reading support to students in the context of social studies instruction? Teachers need an organized, systematic way to help struggling students access on-grade level texts and materials. *Reading Support and Intervention* gives social studies teachers a practical guide for helping these students. Materials include

- A guide that supplements the *Harcourt Social Studies Teacher Edition* with clear and specific suggestions for supporting struggling readers through-out each lesson.
- Student pages that provide vocabulary and concept words, as well as fluency practice, for each lesson. Graphic organizers are also provided to help students focus on important concepts and monitor their comprehension.
- Procedure Cards for teaching vocabulary, fluency, previewing, and comprehension of expository text.
- Student Cards to guide students in using helpful strategies as they read their social studies text in cooperative learning groups.
- Word Cards that represent the vocabulary words taught in the *Harcourt Social Studies Student Edition,* along with their glossary definitions.

Using *Reading Support and Intervention*

Each lesson in *Reading Support and Intervention* corresponds to lessons in the *Harcourt Social Studies Teacher Edition*. The instructional model presented in this book is best suited for small groups of students who need direct and explicit reading instruction at different times during the social studies lesson. The information presented below will show how to use *Reading Support and Intervention* in conjunction with *Harcourt Social Studies* lessons.

BEFORE . . . starting a new lesson in *Harcourt Social Studies*

Teach Vocabulary Strategies
- *Reading Support and Intervention* lesson
- Procedure Card 1
- *Reading Support and Intervention* student vocabulary/fluency page
- Word Cards

Help Build Fluency
- *Reading Support and Intervention* lesson
- Procedure Card 2
- *Reading Support and Intervention* student vocabulary/fluency page

DURING . . . the lesson in *Harcourt Social Studies*

Support Text Comprehension
- *Reading Support and Intervention* Preview the Lesson
- Procedure Card 3
- *Reading Support and Intervention* Build Comprehension of Expository Text
- *Reading Support and Intervention* student comprehension page
- Procedure Card 4
- Student Cards 1–3

AFTER . . . the lesson in *Harcourt Social Studies*

Facilitate Responses to Expository Text
- *Reading Support and Intervention* student comprehension page
- *Reading Support and Intervention* Summarize/Review and Respond
- Leveled Readers
- Procedure Card 5
- Student Cards 1–3

Teaching Vocabulary

WHAT does research tell us about the importance of direct vocabulary instruction?
As students read expository texts, they are sure to encounter words whose meanings they do not know. Such words may represent key social studies concepts that students are unfamiliar with. Students will not be able to comprehend the text without knowing what the words mean.

Research has shown that the direct teaching of specific words before reading will result in improved reading comprehension. The vocabulary words identified in each *Harcourt Social Studies* lesson are included on the student vocabulary/fluency pages in *Reading Support and Intervention*. Students practice reading aloud vocabulary words along with additional concept words that should be helpful to struggling readers. The program introduces Additional Words that appear in the lesson and that are important to understanding key concepts. Some of these words may be unfamiliar to students who are reading below grade level. Others may be words introduced in earlier lessons in *Harcourt Social Studies* that are also important in the upcoming lesson. Reviewing the meanings of the words and reading them in text-related sentences will help students read the lesson and understand it better.

Word Cards are provided in *Reading Support and Intervention* to aid in direct vocabulary instruction.

Teaching Fluency

WHY do we need to teach fluency in the context of social studies instruction? Fluency is the ability to read a text quickly and with accuracy. Fluent readers recognize words in print and group the words into chunks, such as phrases and clauses. As a result, these students can focus their attention on making connections between concepts and on understanding what they read. By helping less-fluent readers improve their fluency, we help them become better social studies learners.

HOW can we teach fluency? Research tells us that repeated oral readings of a text, with the teacher providing guidance or feedback, helps students improve their fluency and their comprehension. *Reading Support and Intervention* provides sentences with Vocabulary and Additional Words in context, as well as suggestions for fluency practice. The teacher models fluent reading and guides students in oral rereadings.

Previewing the Lesson

HOW can previewing the lesson help struggling readers better understand the text?
Research tells us that good readers intuitively set a purpose for reading. Previewing a lesson helps students become familiar with the text so that they can set a purpose for reading it. After previewing, they read to learn about the topics they have previewed, to find out specific information about those topics, and to answer specific questions.

We also know that students learn by connecting new information to information they already know. Previewing activates students' prior knowledge about concepts they will encounter in the lesson. The preview helps them understand the chronology of historic events and helps them see how these events are related to other events that preceded and followed them.

Building Comprehension of Expository Text

WHAT strategies can students use to increase their understanding of expository text?
Research has identified specific strategies that students can use to improve their reading comprehension. Strategies emphasized in *Reading Support and Intervention* include

- monitoring comprehension.
- using graphic organizers.
- answering questions.

HOW can we help students monitor their comprehension? Students who monitor their understanding as they read are better able to master social studies content. In order to monitor their comprehension, students must learn to think metacognitively. That is, they must learn to think about their thinking. As they read, good readers assess whether or not they understand the content. They choose and use appropriate strategies, such as rereading portions of the text, adjusting their reading rate according to the difficulty of the material, restating passages in their own words, and pausing occasionally to summarize what they have just read.

The Preview the Lesson and the Build Comprehension of Expository Text sections in *Reading Support and Intervention* provide opportunities for you to teach strategies for monitoring comprehension. As you guide students through the lesson and observe where they have problems, you can suggest appropriate strategies to help resolve the difficulty. Explain how the strategy can help them and when to apply it.

Students can also use the KWL, SQ3R or QAR strategy to help them monitor their comprehension as they read. Student Cards are available that provide guidance in using these strategies.

Summarizing the Lesson

WHY is using graphic organizers an important strategy for social studies? Graphic organizers include webs, charts, graphs, and diagrams. The purpose of a graphic organizer is to show how concepts are related. Graphic organizers such as time lines and flowcharts show how events are related chronologically. Other types of graphic organizers show cause-and-effect relationships, comparisons and contrasts between concepts, or how details relate to a main idea.

Completing the *Reading Support and Intervention* graphic organizer for each lesson helps students focus on important concepts in the lesson. Filling in the organizer as they read also helps them monitor their comprehension of the material. The completed organizer gives them a tool that they can use to recall relationships in the text and to summarize what they read.

WHAT does research tell us about the value of answering questions? Having students answer questions about their reading is a traditional strategy that teachers have used to guide and assess learning. Recent research confirms the value of this strategy. Answering questions improves students' comprehension of social studies concepts by

- giving them a purpose for reading the text.
- focusing their attention on the content.
- encouraging them to monitor their comprehension and think metacognitively.
- helping them review what they have learned and relate it to other knowledge.

Support metacognitive thinking and strategy use by asking students to explain how they figured out correct answers or how they can find answers that they do not know.

HOW can Leveled Readers help struggling readers? The Leveled Readers were specifically produced to match the content of *Harcourt Social Studies*. The readers are categorized into three reading levels: Basic, Proficient, and Advanced. These readers can help build fluency when used for small-group reading, shared reading, echo reading, choral reading, or reading at home.

States and Regions

Vocabulary Strategies

Preteach Additional Vocabulary After teaching the Vocabulary words on Student Edition page 14, explain to students that there are several other important words they will see in this lesson. Use Procedure Card 1, along with the suggestions below, to introduce the words.

northernmost	Have students identify the word *north* and suffixes *-ern* and *-most*. Ask students to locate Alaska on the map on page 15 and explain why it is the northernmost state.
similar	Remind students that similar things are alike in some way. *Similar* and *different* are antonyms, or opposites.
culture	Tell students that a culture is a way of life that a group of people share.
area	Explain that the amount of land that makes up a place is called its area. On the map on page 15, have students compare states of noticeably different sizes, such as Texas and Louisiana, and tell which has the greater area.
ranks	Have students use the following context to determine the meaning of *ranks:* "In land area, Canada is the largest country in North America. The United States ranks second."

WORD CARDS To help teach the lesson vocabulary, use the Word Cards on pages 267–268.

Build Fluency

Use page 4 and the steps on Procedure Card 2 to reinforce vocabulary and build fluency. Read each vocabulary word aloud and have students repeat it. Then have students work in pairs to reread the words. Follow a similar procedure with the phrases and sentences. Continue to help students build fluency by having them reread "You Are There" in the Student Edition.

Text Comprehension

BEFORE READING

Preview the Lesson Guide students in previewing the lesson using Procedure Card 3. Point out the following features of the lesson on Student Edition pages 14–19.

- **Pages 14–15** Read the lesson title and the "What to Know" question, and have students predict topics they will learn about in this lesson. Preview the photographs of the Derby Line Library on page 14. Have students locate their state on the map on page 15 and use the key to locate and identify its capital.

- **Pages 16–17** Have students examine the map of the regions of the United States and read the labels. Students should locate their own state and identify the region in which it is located.

- **Pages 18–19** Preview the photographs showing scenes in Canada and Mexico. Have students examine the graph on page 19 and answer the caption questions. Point out that Canada, which is largest in land area, has the smallest population. Then preview the Review questions.

DURING READING

Build Comprehension of Expository Text Present the graphic organizer on page 5. Have students preview the organizer by filling in the lesson title and comparing the two main heads in the organizer with the matching subheads in the Student Edition pages 14–19. Tell students that the section subheads provide additional help with identifying important information. Use Procedure Card 4, the Reading Check questions in *Harcourt Social Studies*, and the directed reading suggestions below.

- **Page 14** After students have read "You Are There," have them locate the border of Vermont and Canada on the map on page 15. Explain that the country of Canada is divided into provinces, as the United States is divided into states.

- **Pages 15–17** Have students read "A Nation of 50 States." Then guide them in filling in the information in the first box of the organizer. Point out the connection to the box with the subhead "Regions of the United States." Tell students that they will find the names of the regions and how states in each region are similar under the section subhead "Regions of the United States" in the text. Then they can write the information in the organizer.

- **Pages 18–19** After students have read "A Country in North America," point out the subheads in the two boxes that match the section subheads in the text. Students can locate and write information about history that Canada shares with the United States and about history that Mexico shares with the United States.

AFTER READING

Summarize Have students use their completed graphic organizers to summarize the lesson. Then have them compare their summaries to the lesson summary on page 19.

Review and Respond Work through the Review questions with students. Use Transparency 1 (Compare and Contrast) to discuss comparisons and contrasts in the lesson.

Draw a Map Suggest that students look at a map of North America to help them draw their own maps. Remind them to give the map a title, to label each country on the map, and to include a compass rose to make clear the relative locations of the countries.

Leveled Readers Use the Leveled Readers and Procedure Card 5 to build fluency and comprehension.

DIRECTIONS Read aloud the words in Part A. Practice reading aloud the phrases and the sentences in Part B.

Part A

Vocabulary Words	Additional Words
contiguous	northernmost
region	similar
relative location	culture
continent	area
population	ranks

Part B

1. Forty-eight states / of the United States / are contiguous, / but Alaska and Hawaii / are separated from the other states.

2. Alaska, / our northernmost state, / shares a border / with the country of Canada.

3. The five regions of the United States / are based on their relative location.

4. The states in each region / often have similar kinds of land, / and the people who live there / often earn their living in similar ways.

5. The states in each region / may also share / a history and culture.

6. The United States / is in the continent of North America.

7. Of the countries in North America, / the United States / ranks second / in land area.

8. In population, / the United States / is the largest country / in North America.

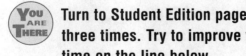 Turn to Student Edition page 14. Practice reading aloud "You Are There" three times. Try to improve your reading each time. Record your best time on the line below.

Number of words ___83___ My Best Time _____ Words per Minute _____

Name _____ Date _____

Lesson Title _____

A Nation of 50 States

Number of contiguous states _____

States that are separated

_____ and _____

Regions of the United States

Names of regions

How states in a region are similar

Canada

Mexico

A Country in North America

**Canada,
Our Northern Neighbor**

Shared history with United States

**Mexico,
Our Southern Neighbor**

Shared history with United States

LESSON 2 **The Land**

Vocabulary Strategies

Preteach Additional Vocabulary After teaching the Vocabulary words on Student Edition page 22, explain to students that there are several other important words they will see in this lesson. Use Procedure Card 1, along with the suggestions below, to introduce the words.

geographer	Point out the root *geo*, meaning "Earth." Discuss the relationship between the words *geography* and *geographer*.
extends	Have students substitute synonyms *stretches* and *reaches* for *extends* in this sentence: "From Florida, the Coastal Plain extends west into Texas and the country of Mexico."
valley	Ask a volunteer to draw a sketch of two mountains and point out the valley between them.
glacier	Tell students that a glacier is a huge mass of ice that very slowly moves across the land.
interior	Point out that the first two letters of this word spell *in*, which can help students remember that *interior* means the inside of a house or the inner part of a body of land, away from the coast.

WORD CARDS To help teach the lesson vocabulary, use the Word Cards on pages 267–268.

Build Fluency

Use page 8 and the steps on Procedure Card 2 to reinforce vocabulary and build fluency. Read each vocabulary word aloud and have students repeat it. Then have students work in pairs to reread the words. Follow a similar procedure with the phrases and sentences. Continue to help students build fluency by having them reread "You Are There" in the Student Edition.

Text Comprehension

BEFORE READING

Preview the Lesson Guide students in previewing the lesson using Procedure Card 3. Point out the following features of the lesson on Student Edition pages 22–29.

• **Pages 22–23** Read the lesson title and discuss the "What to Know" question. Preview the photograph of New York Harbor in the 1890s and the portrait of Robert Louis Stevenson.

• **Pages 24–25** Have students examine the landforms map on page 24 and answer the map skill question. Preview the photograph on page 25, and then have students locate the Appalachian Mountains, the Coastal Plain, and the Interior Plains on the map on page 24.

• **Pages 26–27** Preview the photograph of the Rocky Mountains. Have students read and discuss the Fast Fact.

- **Pages 28–29** Preview the photographs. Have students locate the Central Valley in California on the map on page 24 and identify landforms on the Pacific Coast. Preview the Review questions on page 29.

DURING READING

Build Comprehension of Expository Text Present the graphic organizer on page 9. Have students preview the organizer by filling in the lesson title and comparing the six main heads in the organizer with the matching subheads in the Student Edition pages 22–29. Tell students that the section subheads provide additional help with identifying important information. Use Procedure Card 4, the Reading Check questions in *Harcourt Social Studies,* and the directed reading suggestions below.

- **Page 22** After students have read "You Are There," ask them to show on the map on page 24 the direction in which the great great-grandparents would have traveled across the United States starting from New York City.

- **Page 23** Have students read "Landform Regions." Then guide them in filling in the information in the first box in the organizer. Point out the subhead "A Long Journey" that matches the section subhead in the text.

- **Pages 24–25** After students have read "The Coastal Plain," have them record information in the box with that head in the organizer. Point out the arrow that shows which landform region comes next. Have students read "The Appalachians" and fill in that box. Tell them to use the subhead "A Long Range" to locate information in the text.

- **Pages 26–27** Have students read "The Interior Plains," and write information in that box of the organizer, following the arrow from the previous box. Follow a similar procedure to have them read and write information about "The Rocky Mountains and Beyond."

- **Pages 28–29** After students have read "More Mountains and Valleys," they can complete the last box in the organizer. You may also want to have them list on the reverse side of their organizer sheets the valleys mentioned in this section of the lesson and then write a summary statement about what Stevenson learned on his journey across the United States.

AFTER READING

Summarize Have students use their completed graphic organizers to summarize the lesson. Then have them compare their summaries to the lesson summary on page 29.

Review and Respond If students need additional help with comparing and contrasting, use Focus Skill Transparency 1.

Make Flash Cards Suggest that students go back through the lesson and jot down the names and descriptions of the landform regions. Then they can use these notes to help them make their flash cards. You may want to have students work in pairs to make the flash cards and then use the cards to quiz each other.

Leveled Readers Use the Leveled Readers and Procedure Card 5 to build fluency and

Name _____ Date _____

Part A

Vocabulary Words		Additional Words	
landform region	climate	geographer	glacier
environment	erosion	extends	interior
mountain range	prairie	valley	

Part B

1. To better study the land, / geographers/ often divide it / into landform regions.

2. In the late 1800s, / Robert Louis Stevenson / took a trip / across the United States / that would teach him / about the nation's landforms / and climate.

3. From Florida, / the Coastal Plain / extends west into Texas / and the country of Mexico.

4. The region of valleys and hills / on the eastern side of the Appalachian Mountains / is called the Piedmont.

5. The Appalachians / are a mountain range / running from southern Canada / to central Alabama.

6. Their peaks / were worn down / by glaciers / and by erosion by rain and wind.

7. The eastern part of the Interior Plains / is sometimes called / a prairie.

8. When Stevenson's train / stopped in the middle of Nebraska, / he saw that the environment / was yet again different.

YOU ARE THERE Turn to Student Edition page 22. Practice reading aloud "You Are There" three times. Try to improve your reading each time. Record your best time on the line below.

Number of words ___84___ My Best Time _____ Words per Minute _____

Name _____ Date _____

Lesson Title _____

Landform Regions

Why each is unique _____

_____

A Long Journey Across _____

The Coastal Plain

Description _____

Gets _____ farther _____

The Appalachians

Eastern side _____

Description _____

A Long Range Where _____

_____

Description _____

_____

The Interior Plains

Eastern part _____

Description _____

The Great Plains Description

_____

The Rocky Mountains and Beyond

Part of United States _____

Description _____

The Intermountain Region

Part of this land _____

More Mountains and Valleys

Mountain Ranges to the West

_____

_____

The Journey Ends

Where _____

LESSON 3 **Bodies of Water**

Vocabulary Strategies

Preteach Additional Vocabulary After teaching the Vocabulary words on Student Edition page 30, explain to students that there are several other important words they will see in this lesson. Use Procedure Card 1, along with the suggestions below, to introduce the words.

shape	Point out that *shape* is a noun in phrases such as "the shape of the United States" but is also used as a verb, as in this sentence: "Hundred of bays and sounds also shape the coastline."
offshore	Have students identify the two shorter words that make up this compound word. Explain that an offshore island is located close to the mainland.
source	Tell students that the source of something is where it begins. Have students locate Lake Itasca, the source of the Mississippi River, on the map on page 32.
empty	Discuss the difference between saying that someone empties a bucket of water and saying that a river empties into a larger body of water. The river, unlike the bucket, is still full of water.
continental	Have students identify the word *continent* and suffix *-al*, meaning "about" or "related to." Have them locate the Continental Divide on the map on page 32.

WORD CARDS To help teach the lesson vocabulary, use the Word Cards on pages 267–270.

Build Fluency

Use page 12 and the steps on Procedure Card 2 to reinforce vocabulary and build fluency. Read each vocabulary word aloud and have students repeat it. Then have students work in pairs to reread the words. Follow a similar procedure with the phrases and sentences. Continue to help students build fluency by having them reread "You Are There" in the Student Edition.

Text Comprehension

BEFORE READING

Preview the Lesson Guide students in previewing the lesson using Procedure Card 3. Point out the following features of the lesson on Student Edition pages 30–35.

- **Pages 30–31** Read the lesson title and the "What to Know" question. Encourage students to name familiar bodies of water in the United States. Preview the photograph of Lake Michigan, and have students read the Fast Fact.

- **Pages 32–33** Have students examine the map on page 32 and answer the map skill question. Ask students to point out bodies of water found in or near their own state. Then have students read Children in History on page 33 and discuss the Make It Relevant question. Tell students that Mark Twain wrote *The Adventures of Tom Sawyer.*

- **Pages 34–35** Preview the photograph of the Continental Divide and the Review questions on page 34, and the biography of Marjory Stoneman Douglas on page 35.

DURING READING

Build Comprehension of Expository Text Present the graphic organizer on page 13. Have students preview the organizer by filling in the lesson title and comparing the four main heads in the organizer with the matching subheads in the Student Edition pages 30–34. Tell students that the section subheads provide additional help with identifying important information. Use Procedure Card 4, the Reading Check questions in *Harcourt Social Studies,* and the directed reading suggestions below.

- **Page 30** After students have read "You Are There," point out that the photograph on pages 30–31 shows sailboats on Lake Michigan and also the tall buildings of the city of Chicago.

- **Page 31** Have students read "Inlets and Lakes." Then guide them in filling in the information in the two boxes with the subheads "Gulfs and Inlets" and "Our Largest Lakes" that match the section subheads in the text.

- **Page 32** After students have read "Rivers," point out the box with the subhead "River Systems." Students can write information about the largest river system in the United States in this box.

- **Pages 33–34** Have students read "Rivers in the East" and write information in the box with the subhead "Rivers and Population" that matches the section subhead in the text. Follow a similar procedure to have students read "Rivers in the West" and complete the organizer.

AFTER READING

Summarize Have students use their completed graphic organizers to summarize the lesson. Then have them compare their summaries to the lesson summary on page 34.

Review and Respond If students need additional help with comparing and contrasting, use Focus Skill Transparency 1.

Draw a Poster Provide or point out to students an appropriate map to help them locate the river nearest to your city or town. If students require more information about the river, landforms, nearby cities, or tributaries, suggest or provide helpful sources of information, such as encyclopedias, atlases, or websites.

Leveled Readers Use the Leveled Readers and Procedure Card 5 to build fluency and comprehension.

DIRECTIONS Read aloud the words in Part A. Practice reading aloud the phrases and the sentences in Part B.

Part A

Vocabulary Words		Additional Words	
inlet	river system	shape	empty
gulf	drainage basin	offshore	continental
sound	fall line	source	
tributary			

Part B

1. Hundreds of inlets / along the Atlantic and Pacific coasts / help define the shape / of the United States.

2. The largest gulf bordering the United States / is the Gulf of Mexico.

3. Hundreds of bays and sounds, / which are long inlets / that separate offshore islands / from the mainland, / also shape the coastline.

4. Every river / begins at a source / and ends at a mouth, / where it empties / into a larger body of water.

5. The Mississippi River and its tributaries / create the largest river system / in the United States.

6. The drainage basin / of the Mississippi River system / includes most of the land / between the Rocky and Appalachian Mountains.

7. Many cities / have been built / where rivers flow into oceans, / but other cities / lie inland / along the Fall Line.

8. Rivers that begin east of the Continental Divide / eventually reach the Atlantic Ocean.

YOU ARE THERE Turn to Student Edition page 30. Practice reading aloud "You Are There" three times. Try to improve your reading each time. Record your best time on the line below.

Number of words ___63___   My Best Time _____   Words per Minute _____

Name _____ Date _____

Lesson Title _____

Inlets and Lakes

Gulfs and Inlets

Large gulfs _____

_____

Largest bays and sounds provide

_____

Our Largest Lakes

Known as _____

How many _____

Waterway links _____

_____

Rivers

River Systems Largest in the United States

_____

Rivers in the East

Rivers in the West

Rivers and Population

Where many cities have been built

_____

Where other cities lie _____

_____

How people now use fast-moving

water _____

Rivers and the Continental Divide

Where rivers that begin east of the
Continental Divide eventually reach

_____

Where most rivers that begin west
of the Continental Divide empty

_____

Climate and Vegetation

Vocabulary Strategies

Preteach Additional Vocabulary After teaching the Vocabulary words on Student Edition page 36, explain to students that there are several other important words they will see in this lesson. Use Procedure Card 1, along with the suggestions below, to introduce the words.

orbit	Students may know that the orbit of a planet or an object such as a space station is the path it follows around a larger body in space. Explain that we also use *orbit* as a verb. For example, we say, "Earth orbits the sun."
tilted	Have students use an object such as a book to show the difference between something that is level and something that is tilted.
axis	Use a globe of Earth or the diagram on page 37 to point out the imaginary line that is called Earth's axis. Point out also that Earth is tilted on its axis.
distinct	Discuss the meaning of *distinct* in this sentence: "Some places have four distinct seasons."
precipitation	Tell students that precipitation is moisture that falls to the ground. Precipitation may be in the form of rain, snow, or hail.

WORD CARDS To help teach the lesson vocabulary, use the Word Cards on pages 269–270.

Build Fluency

Use page 16 and the steps on Procedure Card 2 to reinforce vocabulary and build fluency. Read each vocabulary word aloud and have students repeat it. Then have students work in pairs to reread the words. Follow a similar procedure with the phrases and sentences. Continue to help students build fluency by having them reread "You Are There" in the Student Edition.

Text Comprehension

BEFORE READING

Preview the Lesson Guide students in previewing the lesson using Procedure Card 3. Point out the following features of the lesson on Student Edition pages 36–39.

- **Pages 36–37** Read the lesson title and have students recall the meaning of *climate*. Then discuss the "What to Know" question. Preview the photograph of the Rocky Mountains, and ask students to name some other outdoor activities people might do in the mountains. Have students examine the diagram of the four seasons and discuss the question in the caption.

- **Pages 38–39** Have students look at the map of climate regions on page 38 and use the key to find out what climate region they live in. Preview the photograph of desert plants and the Review questions on page 39.

Build Comprehension of Expository Text Present the graphic organizer on page 17. Have students preview the organizer by filling in the lesson title and comparing the two main heads in the organizer with the matching subheads in the Student Edition pages 36–39. Tell students that the section subheads provide additional help with identifying important information. Use Procedure Card 4, the Reading Check questions in *Harcourt Social Studies*, and the directed reading suggestions below.

- **Page 36** After students have read "You Are There," discuss what the paragraph shows about the climate of the Rocky Mountains.

- **Page 37** Before students read "Climate," point out that the organizer has a separate box for each section subhead. Have students use the organizer to set a purpose for reading this section of the lesson. As they read or after reading, students can list in the first box of the organizer three factors affecting climate and then, in the second box, write an effect for each cause.

- **Pages 38–39** Follow a similar procedure to the one used in the previous section. Point out that the information students will write in the first box is found under the main head "Vegetation" in the text, while the information for the second box will be under the section subhead "Vegetation Regions."

AFTER READING

Summarize Have students use their completed graphic organizers to summarize the lesson. Then have them compare their summaries to the lesson summary on page 39.

Review and Respond If students need additional help with comparing and contrasting, use Focus Skill Transparency 1.

Write a Poem Review briefly what students know about writing a poem. Be sure they understand the importance of imagery and rhythmical language and the fact that poems do not have to rhyme. Suggest that students begin by brainstorming words and phrases about the climate and vegetation of your region that they can use in their poems.

Leveled Readers Use the Leveled Readers and Procedure Card 5 to build fluency and comprehension.

DIRECTIONS Read aloud the words in Part A. Practice reading aloud the phrases and the sentences in Part B.

Part A

Vocabulary Words	Additional Words
elevation	orbit
natural vegetation	tilted
arid	axis
tundra	distinct
	precipitation

Part B

1. Factors affecting the climate of a place / include its distance from the equator / and from large bodies of water, / and its elevation.

2. Earth's orbit around the sun / causes changes in seasons / —summer, / autumn, / winter, / and spring.

3. Because Earth is tilted on its axis / as it orbits the sun, / places get different amounts of sunlight and heat / at different times of the year.

4. Some places / have four distinct seasons.

5. The natural vegetation / that grows in a place / varies / depending on the soil.

6. The vegetation / also varies / because of temperature / and precipitation.

7. Only plants that can grow in an arid climate / can grow in deserts.

8. Most of the United States / can be divided / into four main vegetation regions, / which are forest, / grassland, / desert, / and tundra.

YOU ARE THERE Turn to Student Edition page 36. Practice reading aloud "You Are There" three times. Try to improve your reading each time. Record your best time on the line below.

Number of words ___63___ My Best Time _____ Words per Minute _____

Name _____ Date _____

Lesson Title: _____

Climate

Factors Affecting Climate

1. _____

2. _____

3. _____

Earth and the Sun

CAUSE ➡️ EFFECT

Earth's orbit around the sun _____

Earth is tilted on its axis _____

_____

Vegetation

Why natural vegetation varies

1. _____

2. _____

3. _____

Vegetation Regions

Region	Type of Vegetation
1. _____	_____
2. _____	_____
3. _____	_____
4. _____	_____

LESSON 5 # People and the Environment
Vocabulary Strategies

Preteach Additional Vocabulary After teaching the Vocabulary words on Student Edition page 40, explain to students that there are several other important words they will see in this lesson. Use Procedure Card 1, along with the suggestions below, to introduce the words.

route	Tell students that a route is the path or way that people use to travel from one place to another.
alters	Have students substitute the synonym *changes* for *alters* in this sentence: "A human feature is something created by people, such as a building or a road, that alters the land."
ore	Point out that this word, the name for a mineral from which we get a substance such as iron or other metal, is a homonym of *or* and *oar*.
century	Tell students that *century* is from the Latin root *centum*, meaning "hundred." Other words from this root include *cent*, *centimeter*, and *per cent*.
negative	Explain that the root of this word is the Latin *negare*, "to say no." An antonym of *negative* is *positive*.

WORD CARDS To help teach the lesson vocabulary, use the Word Cards on pages 269–272.

Build Fluency

Use page 20 and the steps on Procedure Card 2 to reinforce vocabulary and build fluency. Read each vocabulary word aloud and have students repeat it. Then have students work in pairs to reread the words. Follow a similar procedure with the phrases and sentences. Continue to help students build fluency by having them reread "You Are There" in the Student Edition.

Text Comprehension

BEFORE READING

Preview the Lesson Guide students in previewing the lesson using Procedure Card 3. Point out the following features of the lesson on Student Edition pages 40–45.

- **Pages 40–41** Read the lesson title and the "What to Know" question. Ask students to predict some of the ways that people change the environment. Preview the photographs, and have students read the Fast Fact. Discuss changes that people have made to the environment shown in the photographs.

- **Pages 42–43** Preview the photographs on page 42. Have students identify the oil rig in the smaller photograph and the crop being harvested in the larger one. Then have students examine the map on page 43 and use the map key to answer the map skill question about natural resources where you live.

- **Pages 44–45** Have students examine and discuss the illustration of the Hoover Dam and how it operates. Then preview the Review questions.

Build Comprehension of Expository Text Present the graphic organizer on page 21. Have students preview the organizer by filling in the lesson title and comparing the three main heads in the organizer with the matching subheads in the Student Edition pages 40–45. Tell students that the section subheads provide additional help with identifying important information. Use Procedure Card 4, the Reading Check questions in *Harcourt Social Studies,* and the directed reading suggestions below.

- **Page 40** After students have read "You Are There," point out the connection with the photographs on pages 40–41 and the Fast Fact about the John A. Roebling bridge.

- **Page 41** Have students read "Patterns of Settlement." Then guide them in writing information in the first box of the organizer. Point out the subhead that matches the section subhead in the text.

- **Pages 42–43** After students have read "Patterns of Land Use," call attention to the two boxes below this head in the organizer with subheads that match the section subheads. Students can list in the first box three ways that people use the land. In the second box, they should list two kinds of natural resources and a word that describes the second type of resource.

- **Pages 44–45** Have students read "Changing the Environment" and complete the three boxes with subheads that match the section subheads.

AFTER READING

Summarize Have students use their completed graphic organizers to summarize the lesson. Then have them compare their summaries to the lesson summary on page 45.

Review and Respond If students need additional help with comparing and contrasting, use Focus Skill Transparency 1.

Write a Paragraph Discuss the topic of conserving natural resources and specific things that students can do to help in this effort. You may want to jot down ideas on the board or on chart paper. Tell students to choose one idea to write about. Remind them to begin the paragraph with a topic sentence and then to write two or more additional sentences to give supporting details.

Leveled Readers Use the Leveled Readers and Procedure Card 5 to build fluency and comprehension.

Name _____ Date _____

Read aloud the words in Part A. Practice reading aloud the phrases and the sentences in Part B.

Part A

Vocabulary Words		Additional Words
natural resource	modify	route
renewable	land use	alters
resource	irrigation	ore
nonrenewable	efficiency	century
resource		negative

Part B

1. Settlers / set up communities / where there was farmland, / fresh water, / and transportation routes, / such as rivers.

2. Landforms and climate / can influence land use.

3. A human feature / is something created by people, / such as a building or a road, / that alters the land.

4. Some natural resources / are renewable resources / that can be made again / by people or nature.

5. During the last century, / people began to realize / that the supply of nonrenewable resources, / such as ores, / is limited.

6. Americans use tools / to modify the land / and to gather and use natural resources.

7. Irrigation / can sometimes have negative effects, / such as causing pollution / in waterways.

8. Today, / engineers have learned much / about energy efficiency.

YOU ARE THERE Turn to Student Edition page 40. Practice reading aloud "You Are There" three times. Try to improve your reading each time. Record your best time on the line below.

Number of words ___76___   My Best Time _____   Words per Minute _____

Name _____ Date _____

Lesson Title: _____

Patterns of Settlement

Factors Encouraging Settlement

What can affect where people settle _____

Where people avoided settling _____

How patterns have changed _____

_____

Patterns of Land Use

How People Use the Land

1. _____

2. _____

3. _____

Natural Resources

1. _____

2. _____

Supply is _____.

Changing the Environment

Using Water Changes to the

environment _____

_____

_____

Using the Land How people

modify the environment _____

_____

_____

Balancing the Changes

How _____

Early People

Vocabulary Strategies

Preteach Additional Vocabulary After teaching the Vocabulary words on Student Edition page 52, explain to students that there are several other important words they will see in this lesson. Use Procedure Card 1, along with the suggestions below, to introduce the words.

origin	Tell students that a synonym for *origin* is *beginning*.
descendant	Explain that *descendant* (one who comes later in a family line) is the antonym of *ancestor* (one who came earlier in a family line.)
government	Discuss what students know about government and what governments do.
mound	Ask a volunteer to draw a picture of a mound, a rounded hill of earth.
burial	Tell students that this word is formed from *bury* by changing *y* to *i* and adding the suffix *-al*. Burial is the act of burying a person who has died.

WORD CARDS To help teach the lesson vocabulary, use the Word Cards on pages 273–274.

Build Fluency

Use page 24 and the steps on Procedure Card 2 to reinforce vocabulary and build fluency. Read each vocabulary word aloud and have students repeat it. Then have students work in pairs to reread the words. Follow a similar procedure with the phrases and sentences. Continue to help students build fluency by having them reread "You Are There" in the Student Edition.

Text Comprehension

BEFORE READING

Preview the Lesson Guide students in previewing the lesson using Procedure Card 3. Point out the following features of the lesson on Student Edition pages 52–59.

- **Pages 52–53** Discuss the "What to Know" question. Preview the time line and the illustration. Discuss students' ideas about who these people are and what they are doing. Preview the map of land routes and have students answer the map skill question.

- **Pages 54–55** Preview the illustration on page 54 and have students read and discuss the meaning of the story "How the Robin Got His Red Breast." Call attention to the illustration of a woolly mammoth on page 55, and ask students to describe what is happening in the picture.

- **Pages 56–57** Preview the map of early civilizations, and have students answer the map skill question. On page 57, preview the photograph of Mayan ruins. Have students point out the location of the Mayan civilization on the map on page 56.

- **Pages 58–59** Have students examine the painting of Cahokia. Discuss the caption and how people today may have ideas about what Cahokia looked like. Have students locate Cahokia on the map on page 56. Preview the illustration on page 59, and have students locate Mesa Verde on the map. Then preview the Review questions.

DURING READING

Build Comprehension of Expository Text Present the graphic organizer on page 25. Have students preview the organizer by filling in the lesson title and comparing the five main heads in the organizer with the matching subheads in the Student Edition pages 52–59. Tell students that the section subheads provide additional help with identifying important information. Use Procedure Card 4, the Reading Check questions in *Harcourt Social Studies,* and the directed reading suggestions below.

- **Page 52** After students have read "You Are There," discuss the two different ways it describes that early people obtained food—hunting animals and gathering wild plants.

- **Pages 53–54** Have students read "The Land Bridge Story." Then guide them in summarizing the theory and writing the summary in the first box of the graphic organizer. Next have them read "Other Theories" and write in that box of the organizer why some scientists have other theories and what many Native Americans believe.

- **Page 55** Have students look at the organizer to set a purpose for reading "Early Ways of Life." As they read or after reading, students can fill in the information about how and why early ways of life changed.

- **Pages 56–57** After students have read "The Olmec and the Maya," point out that the subheads in the two smaller boxes in the organizer match the section subheads in the text. Tell students to use the subheads to find and list information about Olmec achievements and Mayan culture.

- **Pages 58–59** As students read "Other Civilizations," or after reading, they can complete the organizer by filling in information about two other civilizations. Tell students that the section subheads can help them identify these civilizations.

AFTER READING

Summarize Have students use their completed graphic organizers to summarize the lesson. Then have them compare their summaries to the lesson summary on page 59.

Review and Respond If students need additional help with comparing and contrasting, use Focus Skill Transparency 1.

Write a Paragraph Suggest that students take notes as they reread passages that tell about theories of how people arrived in the Americas. Remind students to begin the paragraph with a topic sentence and to tell information in their own words.

Leveled Readers Use the Leveled Readers and Procedure Card 5 to build fluency and comprehension.

Name _____ Date _____

DIRECTIONS Read aloud the words in Part A. Practice reading aloud the phrases and the sentences in Part B.

Part A

Vocabulary Words		Additional Words
ancestor	civilization	origin
theory	tradition	descendant
migration	class	government
artifact		mound
		burial

Part B

1. Scientists / have several theories / to explain how the ancestors / of present-day Native Americans / arrived in North America.

2. Many scientists believe / that a migration / took place / across a land bridge / from Asia / to North America.

3. Native American origin stories / have come from descendants / of early people / in the Americas.

4. Artifacts / can tell scientists / a great deal / about life long ago.

5. The Mayan civilization / was influenced / by Olmec traditions.

6. The Maya / were divided into social classes / and had no central government.

7. The earliest civilization of Mound Builders, / the Adena, / built large earth mounds that they used for burials.

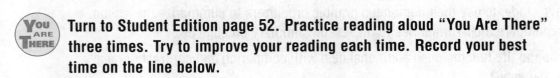 **Turn to Student Edition page 52. Practice reading aloud "You Are There" three times. Try to improve your reading each time. Record your best time on the line below.**

Number of words ____85____ My Best Time _____ Words per Minute _____

Name _____ Date _____

Lesson Title: _____

The Land Bridge Story

Theory

Other Theories

Why

What many Native Americans believe

Early Ways of Life

How ways of life changed

Why ways of life changed

The Olmec and the Maya

The Olmec Civilization Achievements

The Mayan Civilization Culture

Other Civilizations

Who

What they built

Who

What their houses were like

LESSON 2 **The Eastern Woodlands**

Vocabulary Strategies

Preteach Additional Vocabulary After teaching the Vocabulary words on Student Edition page 62, explain to students that there are several other important words they will see in this lesson. Use Procedure Card 1, along with the suggestions below, to introduce the words.

shelter	Give examples of shelters, such as a tent and an apartment building. Have students give other examples.
moccasin	Tell students that this name for a type of leather shoe made by Native Americans comes from an Algonquian language.
goods	Point out that this word looks and sounds like the familiar adjective *good* with *s* added. Explain that *goods* is a noun often used to means items that are bought and sold.
dispute	Tell students that a synonym for *dispute* is *disagreement*. Ask students to suggest other synonyms.
dome	Display a picture of the United States Capitol in Washington, D.C. or another building with a dome. Have students draw and label dome shapes.

WORD CARDS To help teach the lesson vocabulary, use the Word Cards on pages 273–276.

Build Fluency

Use page 28 and the steps on Procedure Card 2 to reinforce vocabulary and build fluency. Read each vocabulary word aloud and have students repeat it. Then have students work in pairs to reread the words. Follow a similar procedure with the phrases and sentences. Continue to help students build fluency by having them reread "You Are There" in the Student Edition.

Text Comprehension

BEFORE READING

Preview the Lesson Guide students in previewing the lesson using Procedure Card 3. Point out the following features of the lesson on Student Edition pages 62–67.

- **Pages 62–63** Read the "What to Know" question and discuss students' ideas about how the geography and climate of the Eastern Woodlands might have affected the Native Americans there. Preview the illustration of Iroquois youngsters playing lacrosse, and have students read the Fast Fact. Preview the photograph of the Eastern Woodlands and ask what resource it shows.

- **Pages 64–65** Have students examine the illustration of an Iroquois village and read the labels. Then have them answer the question in the caption.

- **Pages 66–67** Preview the engraving and discuss how it helps us learn about the Algonquian people. On page 67, preview the picture of an Algonquian bowl and then the Review questions.

Build Comprehension of Expository Text Present the graphic organizer on page 29. Have students preview the organizer by filling in the lesson title and comparing the three main heads in the organizer with the matching subheads in the Student Edition pages 62–67. Tell students that the section subheads provide additional help with identifying important information. Use Procedure Card 4, the Reading Check questions in *Harcourt Social Studies*, and the directed reading suggestions below.

- **Page 62** After students have read "You Are There," ask whether they think they would enjoy playing this Iroquois game and why or why not.

- **Page 63** Have students read "Life in the Eastern Woodlands." Tell them to write in each box in the organizer a way that the people of the Eastern Woodlands used trees as a natural resource.

- **Pages 64–65** After students have read about the Iroquois, have them write information for each category below the heading "The Iroquois" in the graphic organizer. Point out that the section subheads in the text can help students locate information.

- **Pages 66–67** After students have read about the Algonquians, have them write information for each category below the heading "The Algonquians" in the organizer. Discuss similarities and differences that the organizer shows between the Iroquois and the Algonquians.

AFTER READING

Summarize Have students use their completed graphic organizers to summarize the lesson. Then have them compare their summaries to the lesson summary on page 67.

Review and Respond If students need additional help with comparing and contrasting, use Focus Skill Transparency 1.

Give a Speech Have students recall what the Iroquois League was and why it was formed, rereading passages in the lesson as necessary. Remind students that speakers will need to state their opinions clearly and give strong reasons to support those opinions.

Leveled Readers Use the Leveled Readers and Procedure Card 5 to build fluency and comprehension.

Name _____ Date _____

DIRECTIONS Read aloud the words in Part A. Practice reading aloud the phrases and the sentences in Part B.

Part A

Vocabulary Words		Additional Words
division of labor	wampum	shelter
palisade	confederation	moccasin
longhouse	wigwam	goods
		dispute
		dome

Part B

1. Native Americans of the Eastern Woodlands / used trees / to make canoes / and shelters.

2. The women / used animal skins / to make clothing / and moccasins.

3. Division of labor / made it possible / for people to produce more goods.

4. To protect against enemies, / many Iroquois / built palisades around their villages, / where they lived in shelters / called longhouses.

5. Like many other Native Americans, / the Iroquois / traded wampum for goods.

6. The Five Nations / formed a confederation / called the Iroquois League.

7. The league / set up a Grand Council / to settle disputes among the people.

8. Some Algonquians / built wigwams / by bending and tying trunks of small trees / into dome shapes.

 Turn to Student Edition page 62. Practice reading aloud "You Are There" three times. Try to improve your reading each time. Record your best time on the line below.

Number of words ____71____ My Best Time _____ Words per Minute _____

Name _____ Date _____

Lesson Title: _____

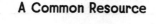

Life in the Eastern Woodlands

A Common Resource

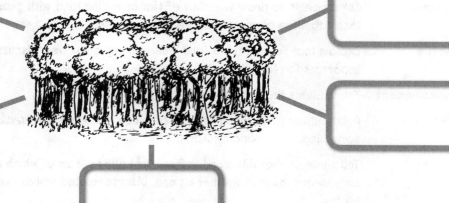

[empty box]   [empty box]

[empty box]   [empty box]

[empty box]

The Iroquois		The Algonquians	
Where _____		Where _____	
Language _____		Language _____	
Villages _____		Villages _____	
Shelters _____		Shelters _____	
Food _____		Food _____	
Government _____		Government _____	
_____		_____	
_____		_____	

LESSON 3 **The Plains**

Vocabulary Strategies

Preteach Additional Vocabulary After teaching the Vocabulary words on Student Edition page 70, explain to students that there are several other important words they will see in this lesson. Use Procedure Card 1, along with the suggestions below, to introduce the words.

prairie	Ask students to draw sketches of flat or rolling land with grass and wildflowers. Have them label the pictures with the word *prairie*.
fertile	Explain that fertile land is land where crops grow well. Discuss why fertile land is important for farming.
independent	Tell students that a synonym for *independent* is *free*.
decision	Point out the similarity in spelling between this word and *decide*. When we decide something, we make a decision.
unity	Tell students that this word is from the Latin root *unus*, which means "one." The word *unity* means joining together as one. Discuss related words such as *united* in United States.

WORD CARDS To help teach the lesson vocabulary, use the Word Cards on pages 275–276.

Build Fluency

Use page 32 and the steps on Procedure Card 2 to reinforce vocabulary and build fluency. Read each vocabulary word aloud and have students repeat it. Then have students work in pairs to reread the words. Follow a similar procedure with the phrases and sentences. Continue to help students build fluency by having them reread "You Are There" in the Student Edition.

Text Comprehension

BEFORE READING

Preview the Lesson Guide students in previewing the lesson using Procedure Card 3. Point out the following features of the lesson on Student Edition pages 70–75.

- **Pages 70–71** Read the "What to Know" question. Discuss what students know about the geography and climate of the Plains. Preview the illustration and have students read the Fast Fact. Have them examine the diagram of a buffalo, read the labels, and answer the question in the caption.

- **Pages 72–73** Have students examine the illustration of Great Plains Life, read the captions, and identify activities they see in the illustration.

- **Pages 74–75** Have students read the Primary Sources feature and discuss the document-based question. Preview the illustration of a tribal leader and the Review questions.

Build Comprehension of Expository Text Present the graphic organizer on page 33. Have students preview the organizer by filling in the lesson title and comparing the four main heads in the organizer with the matching subheads in the Student Edition pages 70–75. Tell students that the section subheads provide additional help with identifying important information. Use Procedure Card 4, the Reading Check questions in *Harcourt Social Studies,* and the directed reading suggestions below.

- **Page 70** After students have read "You Are There," discuss the reasons that the buffalo hunt was so important to these people.

- **Page 71** Have students read "Life on the Plains." Then have them list in the first diagram in the organizer ways that the Plains Indians used the different parts of the buffalo. Tell students to use information from the text and from the diagram in this section of the lesson.

- **Page 72** After students have read "Farmers and Hunters," have them list in the Farming box the important crops grown by Plains groups. In the Hunting box, students should list the names of animals that Plains groups hunted.

- **Page 73** Have students read "A Nomadic Society." Then tell them to write labels below the two pictures in the organizer that show important items made by people of the Great Plains.

- **Pages 74–75** After students have read "Plains Cultures," have them write in the organizer important details from this section of the lesson. Point out that the subheads "Government" and "Traditions and Religious Beliefs" match the section subheads in the text.

Summarize Have students use their completed graphic organizers to summarize the lesson. Then have them compare their summaries to the lesson summary on page 75.

Review and Respond If students need additional help with comparing and contrasting, use Focus Skill Transparency 1.

Draw a Building Plan Suggest that students look back at information in the lesson and the illustration on pages 72–73 to help them write accurate instructions. You might provide one or more samples of directions with lists of materials and numbered steps for students to use as models for formats and style. Remind them to write the instructions in their own words.

Leveled Readers Use the Leveled Readers and Procedure Card 5 to build fluency and comprehension.

Name _____ Date _____

Part A

Vocabulary Words		Additional Words
lodge	travois	prairie
sod	council	fertile
scarce	ceremony	independent
tepee		decision
		unity

Part B

1. Millions of buffalo / once roamed / the dry prairie land / of the Plains region.

2. Native American groups of the Central Plains / farmed / in the fertile valleys of the Missouri River / and the Platte River.

3. They built / large round earthen lodges, / sometimes covered by sod.

4. Wood was scarce / in the western part / of the Interior Plains.

5. The Great Plains Indians / built shelters called tepees.

6. They carried goods / on a travois / pulled by a dog.

7. The ten groups of Cheyenne / were independent of each other / in many ways, / but each group / sent its leaders / to meet in a council of chiefs.

8. All the Cheyenne groups / had to follow / the council's decisions.

9. Ceremonies / such as the sun dance / showed the people's respect for nature / and helped build a sense of unity.

YOU ARE THERE Turn to Student Edition page 70. Practice reading aloud "You Are There"
three times. Try to improve your reading each time. Record your best
time on the line below.

Number of words ____87____ My Best Time _____ Words per Minute _____

Lesson Title _____

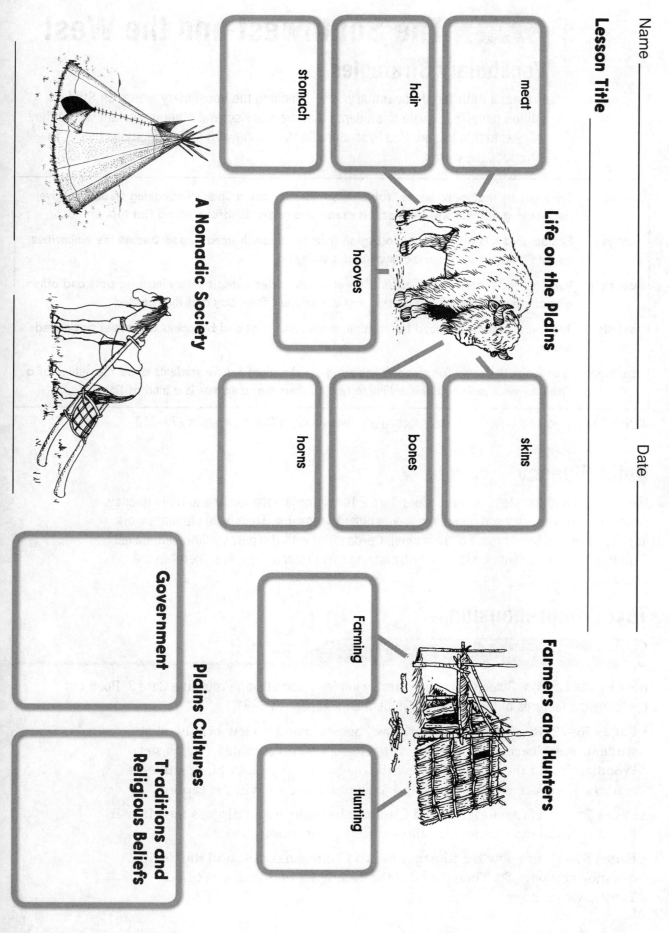

Life on the Plains

meat

hair

stomach

hooves

skins

bones

horns

A Nomadic Society

Farmers and Hunters

Farming

Hunting

Plains Cultures

Government

Traditions and Religious Beliefs

LESSON 4 **The Southwest and the West**

Vocabulary Strategies

Preteach Additional Vocabulary After teaching the Vocabulary words on Student Edition page 76, explain to students that there are several other important words they will see in this lesson. Use Procedure Card 1, along with the suggestions below, to introduce the words.

mesa	Tell students that *mesa* means "table" in Spanish, or ask a Spanish-speaking student to give the meaning. Discuss why this name is used for a raised landform with a flat top.
canyon	Explain that this word came into English from the Spanish word *cañón*. Discuss the similarities and differences between a canyon and a valley.
pottery	Point out the shorter word *pot* in this word. Tell students that pottery includes pots and other objects, such as vases and plates, that are shaped from clay and then heated.
brush	Tell students that this word has multiple meanings. Twigs and branches are sometimes called brush.
salmon	Pronounce the word for students, pointing out the silent *l*. Have students draw the outline of a fish and write *salmon* in the outline to remind them that a salmon is a kind of fish.

WORD CARDS To help teach the lesson vocabulary, use the Word Cards on pages 275–278.

Build Fluency

Use page 36 and the steps on Procedure Card 2 to reinforce vocabulary and build fluency. Read each vocabulary word aloud and have students repeat it. Then have students work in pairs to reread the words. Follow a similar procedure with the phrases and sentences. Continue to help students build fluency by having them reread "You Are There" in the Student Edition.

Text Comprehension

BEFORE READING

Preview the Lesson Guide students in previewing the lesson using Procedure Card 3. Point out the following features of the lesson on Student Edition pages 76–81.

- **Pages 76–77** Read the "What to Know" question and review briefly what students have learned about effects of geography and climate in the Eastern Woodlands and the Plains. Preview the diagram of a pueblo. Have students read the Fast Fact and the labels and answer the question in the caption.

- **Pages 78–79** Have students read Children in History and discuss the Make It Relevant question. Preview the illustrations and captions.

- **Pages 80–81** Preview the illustration of a Chumash couple and the Review questions on page 80. Then preview the biography of Navajo poet Luci Tapahonso on page 81.

Build Comprehension of Expository Text Present the graphic organizer on page 37. Have students preview the organizer by filling in the lesson title and comparing the three main heads in the organizer with the matching subheads in the Student Edition pages 76–80. Tell students that the section subheads provide additional help with identifying important information. Use Procedure Card 4, the Reading Check questions in *Harcourt Social Studies,* and the directed reading suggestions below.

- **Page 76** After students have read "You Are There," remind them that they learned about the Ancient Puebloans in Lesson 1.

- **Page 77** Have students read "The Southwest" and fill in important details in the first box of the organizer. Point out that the subhead "Adapting to the Southwest" matches the section subhead and can help students locate information.

- **Page 78** After students have read "Pueblo Culture," have them fill in the next box in the organizer. Point out the subhead "Religion and Government" and the arrows between this box and the one above. Explain that the two-headed arrows show a direct connection between the information in these two sections of the lesson.

- **Pages 79–80** Have students read "Groups to the West." Tell them to summarize the ways of life of the three groups under the section subhead "Ways of Life" in the organizer and then to fill in the information under the subhead "Trading for Needed Goods."

AFTER READING

Summarize Have students use their completed graphic organizers to summarize the lesson. Then have them compare their summaries to the lesson summary on page 80.

Review and Respond If students need additional help with comparing and contrasting, use Focus Skill Transparency 1.

Draw a Map Suggest that students reread parts of the lesson to find clues about the areas where the people of the Southwest and West lived. Then students can use that information to shade in those areas on their maps.

Leveled Readers Use the Leveled Readers and Procedure Card 5 to build fluency and comprehension.

Name _____ Date _____

Part A

Vocabulary Words		Additional Words	
adapt	adobe	mesa	brush
staple	hogan	canyon	salmon
surplus	trade network	pottery	

Part B

1. The Pueblo peoples / of the desert Southwest / were able to adapt their ways of life / to a land of mesas, / canyons, / cliffs, / and mountains.

2. Even in the dry environment, / the Pueblo people / were able to grow their staple foods / of corn, / beans, / and squash.

3. They found ways / to collect water / and to store / a surplus of food.

4. The Navajo / built hogans / by covering wooden frames / with mud or adobe.

5. The Pueblo and the Navajo / sometimes traveled far / to trade their pottery and baskets / with other tribes.

6. The Shoshone / lived part of the year / in the Great Basin / and built shelters with dry brush.

7. The Nez Perce, / who lived to the northwest, / made long spears and nets / to catch salmon.

8. Native Americans / in the Plateau, / Great Basin, / and California cultural regions / formed large trade networks / to get goods / from faraway places.

YOU ARE THERE Turn to Student Edition page 76. Practice reading aloud "You Are There" three times. Try to improve your reading each time. Record your best time on the line below.

Number of words ___98___ My Best Time _____ Words per Minute _____

Name _____ Date _____

Lesson Title: _____

The Southwest

Land _____

Adapting to the Southwest

Staple foods _____

Also grew _____ used to weave _____

Pueblo Culture

What shaped their lives _____

What they depended on for resources not found nearby _____

Religion and Government

Who led Navajo ceremonies _____

What had a strong role in the government of the Pueblo _____

Groups to the West

Ways of Life

People _____ Way of Life _____

People _____ Way of Life _____

People _____ Way of Life _____

Trading for Needed Goods

What people formed _____ Why _____

LESSON 5 # The Northwest and the Arctic

Vocabulary Strategies

Preteach Additional Vocabulary After teaching the Vocabulary words on Student Edition page 82, explain to students that there are several other important words they will see in this lesson. Use Procedure Card 1, along with the suggestions below, to introduce the words.

stranded	Point out the *-ed* ending. Explain that a strand is a strip of land along the edge of a body of water. The word *stranded* can mean "washed up on shore."
rank	Tell students that synonyms include *position* and *level*. Give examples, such as higher and lower ranks in the armed forces.
totem pole	Point out the totem poles in the illustration on page 85, and discuss their significance.
unique	Tell students that this word, like *unity* and *unite*, is from the Latin root *unus*, meaning "one." *Unique* describes something that is the only one of its kind.
caribou	Ask if students know what a reindeer is. Explain that *caribou* is another name for *reindeer*, large deer that live in northern regions.

WORD CARDS To help teach the lesson vocabulary, use the Word Cards on pages 277–278.

Build Fluency

Use page 40 and the steps on Procedure Card 2 to reinforce vocabulary and build fluency. Read each vocabulary word aloud and have students repeat it. Then have students work in pairs to reread the words. Follow a similar procedure with the phrases and sentences. Continue to help students build fluency by having them reread "You Are There" in the Student Edition.

Text Comprehension

BEFORE READING

Preview the Lesson Guide students in previewing the lesson using Procedure Card 3. Point out the following features of the lesson on Student Edition pages 82–87.

- **Pages 82–83** Read the "What to Know" question and ask how students think these regions may differ from those they have learned about previously. Discuss how the artifacts and the scene shown in the illustration differ from those of other regions.

- **Pages 84–85** Have students examine the illustration of a Northwest Coast village, read the labels, and answer the question in the caption.

- **Pages 86–87** Preview the illustrations of Inuit life. Discuss how these scenes of the Arctic are like and unlike those of the Pacific Northwest on the preceding pages. Then preview the Review questions.

Build Comprehension of Expository Text Present the graphic organizer on page 41. Have students preview the organizer by filling in the lesson title and comparing the three main heads in the organizer with the matching subheads in the Student Edition pages 82–87. Tell students that the section subheads provide additional help with identifying important information. Use Procedure Card 4, the Reading Check questions in *Harcourt Social Studies,* and the directed reading suggestions below.

- **Page 82** After students have read "You Are There," talk about why whales may have been an important resource for peoples of the Northwest and the Arctic.

- **Page 83** Have students read "A Region of Plenty" and fill in information about the land of the Northwest Coast. Tell students they can locate information about groups and their food sources under the section subhead "People of the Northwest Coast." Guide students in recording that information in the organizer.

- **Pages 84–85** After students have read "Resources and Trade," explain that the two-headed arrows between the first two boxes in the organizer show that both sections of the lesson are about the same region. Point out that the organizer box is structured the same way as the section in the text. Students should write in the organizer information from the introductory paragraph and from each of the three subsections.

- **Pages 86–87** Have students read "Lands of the North" and complete the organizer, using the subheads to help them locate information.

AFTER READING

Summarize Have students use their completed graphic organizers to summarize the lesson. Then have them compare their summaries to the lesson summary on page 87.

Review and Respond If students need additional help with comparing and contrasting, use Focus Skill Transparency 1.

Write a Poem Discuss how poetry uses colorful language to express ideas in an interesting way. You may want to read several short poems as examples. Suggest that students begin by listing ideas, words, and phrases to include in their poems. Remind them that poems do not have to rhyme.

Leveled Readers Use the Leveled Readers and Procedure Card 5 to build fluency and comprehension.

Name _____ Date _____

Part A

Vocabulary Words		Additional Words	
harpoon	potlatch	stranded	unique
clan	kayak	rank	caribou
economy	igloo	totem pole	
barter			

Part B

1. Most Pacific Northwest groups / captured only whales / that had become stranded / on the shore.

2. Makah clans, / in which each person / held a specific rank, / made important decisions / about village life.

3. The people of the Northwest Coast / made almost everything from wood, / including totem poles.

4. Trading / was a large part / of the region's economy.

5. The Chinook / developed a unique language / that allowed them to barter goods / on behalf of two groups / who spoke very different languages.

6. Northwest Coast groups / expressed their good fortune / through a potlatch.

7. The Inuit and the Aleut / in the Arctic region / hunted foxes, / caribou, / and polar bears.

8. They also used / harpoons and kayaks /to hunt seals, / walruses, / and whales.

9. During the winter, / some Inuit / lived in igloos.

YOU ARE THERE Turn to Student Edition page 82. Practice reading aloud "You Are There" three times. Try to improve your reading each time. Record your best time on the line below.

Number of words ___76___   My Best Time _____   Words per Minute _____

Name _____ Date _____

Lesson Title: _____

| A Region of Plenty | ⟷ | Resources and Trade |

Land _____

People of the Northwest Coast

Groups _____

_____

Important resources _____

_____

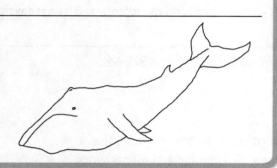

Important resource

_____

Family Shelters

Type _____

Who lived their _____

The Dalles

What it was _____

Best-known traders _____

A Potlatch

What it was _____

Lands of the North

Arctic Groups

_____ and _____

Life in the Arctic

Resources _____

_____

Houses _____

_____

Life in the Sub-Arctic

Where _____

People _____

Resources _____

| CAUSE | → | EFFECT |
| | | farming not possible |

LESSON 1　Exploration and Technology

Vocabulary Strategies

Preteach Additional Vocabulary After teaching the Vocabulary words on Student Edition page 108, explain to students that there are several other important words they will see in this lesson. Use Procedure Card 1, along with the suggestions below, to introduce the words.

compass	Explain that a compass is a tool used for finding direction. If possible, display a compass and demonstrate its use.
astrolabe	Read this context clue: "They used the astrolabe to figure out the positions of the sun, moon, and stars." Discuss how knowing the positions of objects in the sky can help sailors figure out where they are on the sea.
longitude	Have students identify lines of longitude on a map or globe.
latitude	Have students identify lines of latitude on a map or globe.
risky	Point out the root word *risk* with the suffix *-y* added to form an adjective. Give synonyms, such as *dangerous* and *uncertain*.

WORD CARDS To help teach the lesson vocabulary, use the Word Cards on pages 279–280.

Build Fluency

Use page 44 and the steps on Procedure Card 2 to reinforce vocabulary and build fluency. Read each vocabulary word aloud and have students repeat it. Then have students work in pairs to reread the words. Follow a similar procedure with the phrases and sentences. Continue to help students build fluency by having them reread "You Are There" in the Student Edition.

Text Comprehension

BEFORE READING

Preview the Lesson Guide students in previewing the lesson using Procedure Card 3. Point out the following features of the lesson on Student Edition pages 108–115.

- **Pages 108–109** Read the "What to Know" question. Discuss the difficulties of traveling long distances by land hundreds of years ago. Preview the time line and the illustrations of the explorer Marco Polo and the first printing press.

- **Pages 110–111** Preview the illustration of a caravel on pages 110–111. Discuss why people may have wanted faster ships.

- **Pages 112–113** Preview the map on page 112 and the painting on page 113. Ask students to explain what each of these illustrations shows.

- **Pages 114–115** Preview the illustration, and have students read Children in History. Discuss the Make It Relevant question. Then preview the Review questions on page 115.

Build Comprehension of Expository Text Present the graphic organizer on page 45. Have students preview the organizer by filling in the lesson title and comparing the four main heads in the organizer with the matching subheads in the Student Edition pages 108–115. Tell students that the section subheads provide additional help with identifying important information. Use Procedure Card 4, the Reading Check questions in *Harcourt Social Studies,* and the directed reading suggestions below.

- **Page 108** After students have read "You Are There," discuss how the invention of the printing press made a difference in people's lives.

- **Page 109** Have students read "A Rush of New Ideas." Then guide them in locating and filling in the information in the web at the top left of the graphic organizer.

- **Pages 110–111** As students read "The World Awaits," have them fill in the information in the next part of the organizer. Then discuss briefly other important concepts, making sure students understand that Europeans at that time did not know that North America or South America even existed.

- **Pages 112–115** Have students read "The Business of Exploring" and fill in brief details about Christopher Columbus. Before students read the final section, ask what they think the subhead "Two Worlds Meet" means, and what the two worlds were. After reading, students should complete the organizer.

AFTER READING

Summarize Have students use their completed graphic organizers to summarize the lesson. Then have them compare their summaries to the lesson summary on page 115.

Review and Respond Work through the Review questions with students. Use Transparency 2 (Main Idea and Details) to discuss main ideas and details mentioned in the lesson.

Write a Conversation Discuss with students how the cultures of a Spanish sailor and a Taino leader in 1492 may have differed. You may want to have students work with partners to write and then act out their conversations.

Leveled Readers Use the Leveled Readers and Procedure Card 5 to build fluency and comprehension.

Name _____ Date _____

Part A

Vocabulary Words		Additional Words	
technology	entrepreneur	compass	latitude
navigation	cost	astrolabe	risky
expedition	benefit	longitude	
empire	Reconquista		

Part B

1. In the 1400s, / Europeans / wanted to buy and then resell / Asian goods, / but they lacked the technology / to travel to Asia / by sea.

2. Prince Henry of Portugal / started a school / with the aim of making better ships, / maps, / and tools for navigation.

3. Prince Henry / hired scientists / to improve two navigational tools / —the compass and the astrolabe.

4. Sailors used the compass / to help them find their longitude, / and the astrolabe / to help them find their latitude.

5. Europeans / made expeditions to Asia / and also traded with rich empires / in North Africa.

6. Explorers / had to be entrepreneurs / and persuade others that the cost / was worth the risk / of an expedition.

7. The benefit / was the chance / of finding riches / worth many times the cost.

8. Christopher Columbus's idea / of sailing west to reach Asia / was risky, / but after the Reconquista, / Spain's king and queen / agreed to help him.

YOU ARE THERE Turn to Student Edition page 108. Practice reading aloud "You Are There" three times. Try to improve your reading each time. Record your best time on the line below.

Number of words ___86___ My Best Time _____ Words per Minute _____

Name _____ Date _____

Lesson Title: _____

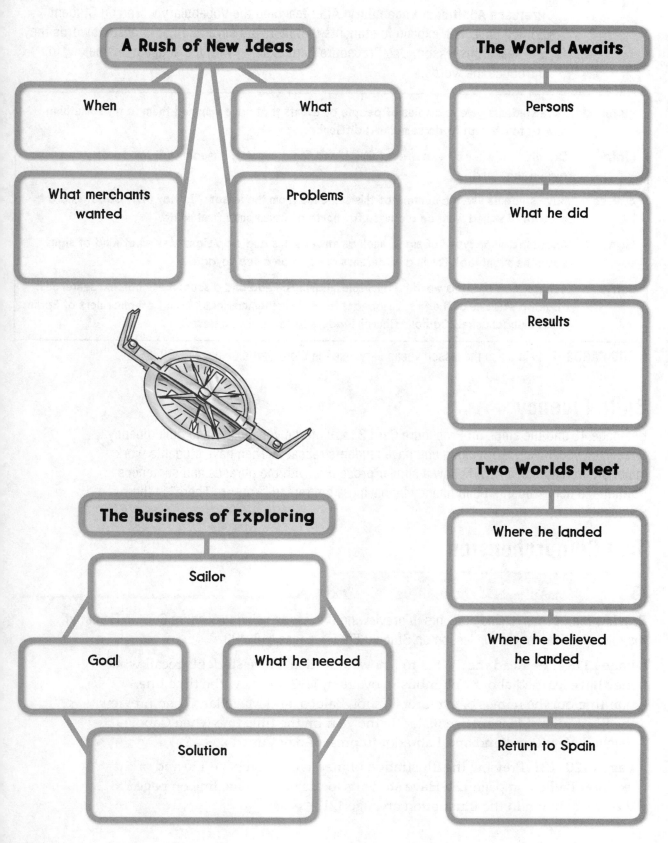

A Rush of New Ideas

When

What

What merchants wanted

Problems

The Business of Exploring

Sailor

Goal

What he needed

Solution

The World Awaits

Persons

What he did

Results

Two Worlds Meet

Where he landed

Where he believed he landed

Return to Spain

LESSON 2 **A Changing World**

Vocabulary Strategies

Preteach Additional Vocabulary After teaching the Vocabulary words on Student Edition page 118, explain to students that there are several other important words they will see in this lesson. Use Procedure Card 1, along with the suggestions below, to introduce the words.

inspired	Have students give examples of people or events that have inspired them to try something new or to attempt to do something difficult.
claim	Explain that when an explorer claimed land for a country, it meant that the country now owned that land.
course	Have students use the context of this sentence from the lesson: "In May 1497, Cabot and a crew of 18 sailed west on a course far north of Columbus's first route."
sign	Discuss familiar types of signs, such as street signs and stop signs. Ask what kind of signs someone might look for in a wilderness area or on a sea voyage.
settle	Tell students that this word has multiple meanings. Read and discuss these context sentences: "Balboa was one of the first Europeans to settle in the Americas." "The Catholic rulers of Spain and Portugal asked Catholic Church leaders to settle such a case."

WORD CARDS To help teach the lesson vocabulary, use the Word Cards on pages 279–280.

Build Fluency

Use page 48 and the steps on Procedure Card 2 to reinforce vocabulary and build fluency. Read each vocabulary word aloud and have students repeat it. Then have students work in pairs to reread the words. Follow a similar procedure with the phrases and sentences. Continue to help students build fluency by having them reread "You Are There" in the Student Edition.

Text Comprehension

BEFORE READING

Preview the Lesson Guide students in previewing the lesson using Procedure Card 3. Point out the following features of the lesson on Student Edition pages 118–123.

- **Pages 118–119** Read the "What to Know" question. Have students recall what they have learned about Columbus's voyage in 1492. Preview the time line, pointing out the names of explorers Cabot, Balboa, and Magellan. Then preview the illustrations. Have students locate the year on the time line when Cabot reached Newfoundland and Labrador in present-day Canada.

- **Pages 120–121** Preview the illustration of mapmakers on page 120 and of the explorer Balboa on page 121. Have students locate on the time line on page 118 the event shown in the illustration on page 121.

• **Pages 122–123** Have students examine the map showing voyages of exploration. Have them answer the map skill question. Then preview the illustration of Spanish coins and the Review questions on page 123.

During Reading

Build Comprehension of Expository Text Present the graphic organizer on page 49. Have students preview the organizer by filling in the lesson title and comparing the four main heads in the organizer with the matching subheads in the Student Edition pages 118–123. Tell students that the section subheads provide additional help with identifying important information. Use Procedure Card 4, the Reading Check questions in *Harcourt Social Studies,* and the directed reading suggestions below.

• **Page 118** After students have read "You Are There," ask how they think the mystery may be solved.

• **Page 119** Have students read "England Explores." Then guide them in writing in the organizer important information about John Cabot's expedition.

• **Page 120** After students have read "A New Map of the World," discuss what Vespucci realized and why it was important. Then have students complete the next box in the organizer.

• **Page 121** Before students read "Reaching the Pacific," set a purpose for reading—to find out who reached the Pacific and how. Have students fill in the organizer as they read or after reading.

• **Pages 122–123** Either as they read or after reading "A New View of the World," students can fill in the information to complete the organizer.

After Reading

Summarize Have students use their completed graphic organizers to summarize the lesson. Then have them compare their summaries to the lesson summary on page 123.

Review and Respond If students need additional help identifying main ideas and details, use Focus Skill Transparency 2.

Make a Table of Explorers Tell students to look back over the lesson and write down names of explorers and the areas they explored. Discuss how to make a chart with headings such as "Explorer" and "Area Explored." Have students display their charts, trace the routes on the map, and describe the distances to classmates.

Leveled Readers Use the Leveled Readers and Procedure Card 5 to build fluency and comprehension.

Name _____   Date _____

Read aloud the words in Part A. Practice reading aloud the phrases and the sentences in Part B.

Part A

Vocabulary Words	Additional Words	
isthmus	inspired	sign
treaty	claim	settle
	course	

Part B

1. Columbus's trips to the Indies / inspired several European rulers / to send ships west.

2. The rulers / were eager to claim lands / and riches / of their own.

3. In May, 1497, / John Cabot and a crew of 18 / sailed west / on a course / far north of Columbus's first route.

4. Amerigo Vespucci / sailed down the coast / of South America, / looking for signs / that he had reached Asia.

5. The Spanish explorer Balboa / was one the first Europeans / to settle in the Americas.

6. He and other explorers / crossed the Isthmus of Panama / and reached / the Pacific Ocean.

7. Spain and Portugal / both claimed the same land, / so they asked Catholic Church leaders / to settle the case.

8. Later, / Spain and Portugal / signed a treaty / to move the dividing line / that the leaders / had drawn.

YOU ARE THERE Turn to Student Edition page 118. Practice reading aloud "You Are There" three times. Try to improve your reading each time. Record your best time on the line below.

Number of words ___83___   My Best Time _____   Words per Minute _____

Name _____ Date _____

Lesson Title: _____

England Explores

Explorer _____ Year _____

What he thought he had found _____

What he actually may have found _____

⬇

A New Map of the World

Explorer _____ Where he sailed _____

What he realized _____

What was named for him _____

⬇

Reaching the Pacific

Explorer _____ Year _____

What he did _____

_____

⬇

A New View of the World

Explorer _____ What he named _____

Sailors on one of his ships were _____.

New lands were divided between _____.

LESSON 3 **Spanish Explorations**

Vocabulary Strategies

Preteach Additional Vocabulary After teaching the Vocabulary words on Student Edition page 126, explain to students that there are several other important words they will see in this lesson. Use Procedure Card 1, along with the suggestions below, to introduce the words.

convert	Explain that to convert people is to cause them to change their religion.
encouraged	Point out the root word *courage* and prefix *en-*, meaning "put into." To encourage someone is to put courage into them. The *-ed* ending shows that the action took place in the past.
fountain	Students may have seen fountains in parks or other public places. Explain that a fountain may also be a natural source of water flowing from the earth.
Protestant	Point out the word *protest* and suffix *-ant*. Tell students that a Protestant was someone who protested against leaders of the Catholic Church. Help students pronounce *Protestant* correctly.
banned	Point out that this past-tense verb is a homophone of *band*. Tell students that to ban something is to forbid it.

WORD CARDS To help teach the lesson vocabulary, use the Word Cards on pages 279–282.

Build Fluency

Use page 52 and the steps on Procedure Card 2 to reinforce vocabulary and build fluency. Read each vocabulary word aloud and have students repeat it. Then have students work in pairs to reread the words. Follow a similar procedure with the phrases and sentences. Continue to help students build fluency by having them reread "You Are There" in the Student Edition.

Text Comprehension

BEFORE READING

Preview the Lesson Guide students in previewing the lesson using Procedure Card 3. Point out the following features of the lesson on Student Edition pages 126–133.

• **Pages 126–127** Read the "What to Know" question, making sure that students understand the word *conquer*. Have students recall why earlier European explorers came to the Americas. Preview the time line and the painting on page 126. Have students locate on the time line the event mentioned in the caption for the illustration on page 127.

• **Pages 128–129** Have students examine the illustrations of the Spanish conquistador and Aztec warrior, read the labels, and discuss the question in the caption. Then preview the map showing the movement of conquistadors in North America, and have students answer the map skill question.

- **Pages 130–133** Preview the illustration of de Soto's expedition. On page 134, preview the illustration of Saint Ignatius and the Review questions. Then preview the biography of the explorer Estevanico on page 135.

DURING READING

Build Comprehension of Expository Text Present the graphic organizer on page 53. Have students preview the organizer by filling in the lesson title and comparing the four main heads in the organizer with the matching subheads in the Student Edition pages 126–132. Tell students that the section subheads provide additional help with identifying important information. Use Procedure Card 4, the Reading Check questions in *Harcourt Social Studies*, and the directed reading suggestions below.

- **Page 126** After students have read "You Are There," ask whether they think the soldiers will find a Fountain of Youth, and why or why not.

- **Page 127** Have students read "The Spanish Explore Florida." Then guide them in summarizing and writing information in the organizer. Point out that the section subhead in the text can help them find this information.

- **Pages 128–129** After students have read "Early Conquistadors," have them summarize in the organizer what Cortés wanted and what he did, and then what Coronado wanted and what he did.

- **Page 130** Have students read "Expeditions Continue" and add information about Pizarro and de Soto to the organizer, using the section subheads in the text to help them locate information about each of these conquistadors.

- **Pages 131–132** Before students read "Missionaries to America," point out that the previous sections of this lesson have all been about conquistadors. Now students will read about a different group who came to America. After reading, have students complete the final box in the organizer.

AFTER READING

Summarize Have students use their completed graphic organizers to summarize the lesson. Then have them compare their summaries to the lesson summary on page 132.

Review and Respond If students need additional help identifying main ideas and details, use Focus Skill Transparency 2.

Write a Journal Tell students to choose one of the explorers from this lesson and reread passages that tell about the places that person explored. Then students can write journal entries written from the point of view of someone traveling with the explorer.

Leveled Readers Use the Leveled Readers and Procedure Card 5 to build fluency and comprehension.

Name _____ Date _____

DIRECTIONS Read aloud the words in Part A. Practice reading aloud the phrases and the sentences in Part B.

Part A

Vocabulary Words		Additional Words
grant	conquistador	convert
reform	missionary	encouraged
Reformation		fountain
Counter-Reformation		Protestant
		banned

Part B

1. Some Spanish explorers / came to the Americas / to find adventure and riches, / while others / wanted to convert Native Americans / to Christianity.

2. The King of Spain / encouraged the explorers / and offered grants / to those who led expeditions.

3. Juan Ponce de León / set out to find / a so-called Fountain of Youth, / but instead / he landed in what is now / the state of Florida.

4. The conquistador Cortés / conquered the Aztecs / in what is now / Mexico.

5. During the Reformation, / Martin Luther and other Protestants / called for reforms / in the Catholic Church.

6. The Catholic Church / tried to keep its power / through the Counter-Reformation, / and banned books / that went against its teachings.

7. The Church / sent missionaries / to convert Native Americans / to the Catholic religion.

YOU ARE THERE Turn to Student Edition page 126. Practice reading aloud "You Are There" three times. Try to improve your reading each time. Record your best time on the line below.

Number of words ___89___   My Best Time _____   Words per Minute _____

Name _____ Date _____

Lesson Title: _____

The Spanish Explore Florida

Explorer _____ Set out to find _____

What he did _____

_____

Early Conquistadors

What Cortés wanted _____

What Cortés did _____

What Coronado wanted _____

What Coronado did _____

_____

Expeditions Continue

What Pizarro did _____

What de Soto did _____

_____

Missionaries to America

What happened in Europe _____

Why the Church sent missionaries _____

_____

LESSON 4 **Other Nations Explore**

Vocabulary Strategies

Preteach Additional Vocabulary After teaching the Vocabulary words on Student Edition page 136, explain to students that there are several other important words they will see in this lesson. Use Procedure Card 1, along with the suggestions below, to introduce the words.

waterway	Have students identify the two shorter words that make up this compound word. Tell students that a river is one kind of waterway.
navigator	Write *navigate, navigation,* and *navigator,* and have students compare them. Explain that the suffix *-or* often shows that a person performs an action, as in a sailor who sails, or an actor who acts.
inland	On a map, have students point out inland areas, or areas away from coasts.
rapids	Cover final *s* and ask what the adjective *rapid* means. (fast, quick) Explain that adding *s* creates a noun that means a stretch of fast-moving water in a river or stream.
adrift	Tell students that something set adrift moves or drifts along wherever the wind or water takes it. A synonym for *adrift* is *afloat.*

WORD CARDS To help teach the lesson vocabulary, use the Word Cards on pages 281–282.

Build Fluency

Use page 56 and the steps on Procedure Card 2 to reinforce vocabulary and build fluency. Read each vocabulary word aloud and have students repeat it. Then have students work in pairs to reread the words. Follow a similar procedure with the phrases and sentences. Continue to help students build fluency by having them reread "You Are There" in the Student Edition.

Text Comprehension

BEFORE READING

Preview the Lesson Guide students in previewing the lesson using Procedure Card 3. Point out the following features of the lesson on Student Edition pages 136–141.

- **Pages 136–137** Read the "What to Know" question and preview the time line. Discuss what the time line shows about what explorers found. Preview the illustrations of Henry Hudson and of a ship searching for the Northwest Passage.

- **Pages 138–139** Preview the illustration of the St. Lawrence River. Have students read and discuss the Fast Fact.

- **Pages 140–141** Have students examine the time line on page 140 and answer the question in the caption. Have students compare this time line with the time line on page 136. Then preview the illustration and the Review questions on page 141.

Build Comprehension of Expository Text Present the graphic organizer on page 57. Have students preview the organizer by filling in the lesson title and comparing the three main heads in the organizer with the matching subheads in the Student Edition pages 136–141. Tell students that the section subheads provide additional help with identifying important information. Use Procedure Card 4, the Reading Check questions in *Harcourt Social Studies*, and the directed reading suggestions below.

- **Page 136** After students have read "You Are There," call attention to the illustration on this page and discuss its connection with the information in the paragraph.

- **Page 137** Have students read "The Northwest Passage." Then guide them in filling in the information about the Northwest Passage in the organizer.

- **Pages 138–139** After students have read "Verrazano and Cartier," have them write information about each of these explorers in the organizer. Point out that there is not enough space to write every detail, so students will need to summarize.

- **Pages 140–141** Have students read "Hudson's Voyages" and complete the organizer. Point out that the three explorers made many voyages and searched for the Northwest Passage over a wide area, but none of them was able to find it.

Summarize Have students use their completed graphic organizers to summarize the lesson. Then have them compare their summaries to the lesson summary on page 141.

Review and Respond If students need additional help identifying main ideas and details, use Focus Skill Transparency 2.

Write a Scene Tell students to choose one of the explorers and to use information from the lesson to help them write their scenes. Point out that students may find information in "You Are There," in captions for illustrations, and from the Fast Fact on page 139, as well as from passages in the text.

Leveled Readers Use the Leveled Readers and Procedure Card 5 to build fluency and comprehension.

Name _____ Date _____

DIRECTIONS Read aloud the words in Part A. Practice reading aloud the phrases and the sentences in Part B.

Part A

Vocabulary Words	Additional Words	
Northwest Passage mutiny	waterway navigator inland	rapids adrift

Part B

1. Explorers in the 1500s / began searching / for a route they called / the Northwest Passage.

2. The first country to find this waterway / would control an important new trade route / between Europe and Asia / and gain great riches.

3. Giovanni da Verrazano / searched the coastlines / of North America and South America / but did not find / the Northwest Passage.

4. Jacques Cartier, / a French navigator, / traveled up the St. Lawrence River / and went inland / as far as what is now Montreal.

5. Instead of reaching the Pacific, / Cartier reached river rapids / that his boat could not pass.

6. An English explorer / named Henry Hudson / made four voyages / in search of the Northwest Passage.

7. After a cold winter / and much suffering, / Hudson's crew / mutinied.

8. They set Hudson / and eight others / adrift / in a small boat.

You ARE THERE Turn to Student Edition page 136. Practice reading aloud "You Are There" three times. Try to improve your reading each time. Record your best time on the line below.

Number of words ___70___ My Best Time _____ Words per Minute _____

Name _____ Date _____

Lesson Title: _____

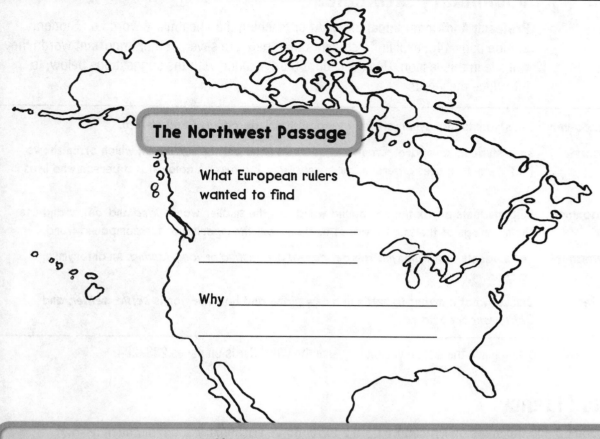

The Northwest Passage

What European rulers
wanted to find

_____

_____

Why _____

_____

Verrazano and Cartier	
Giovanni da Verrazano	**Jacques Cartier**
What he did _____	What he did _____
_____	_____
_____	_____
What he did not find _____	What he did not find _____

Hudson's Voyages

Explorer _____ How many voyages _____

What he did _____

_____

What he did not find _____

LESSON 1 **The Spanish Colonies**

Vocabulary Strategies

Preteach Additional Vocabulary After teaching the Vocabulary words on Student Edition page 146, explain to students that there are several other important words they will see in this lesson. Use Procedure Card 1, along with the suggestions below, to introduce the words.

overpower	Tell students that synonyms for *overpower* include *conquer* and *defeat*.
colonist	Have students compare *colony* and *colonist*. Point out the suffix *-ist*, which often shows that the noun names a person, as in *artist* and *guitarist*. A colonist is a person who lives in a colony.
landowner	Help students break the compound word into the smaller words *land* and *owner* and use the meanings of the smaller words to figure out the meaning of the compound word.
permanent	Tell students that synonyms for *permanent* are *lasting* or *long-lasting*. An antonym is *temporary*.
settlement	Discuss what it means to settle in a new place and how the words *settle*, *settler*, and *settlement* are related.

WORD CARDS To help teach the lesson vocabulary, use the Word Cards on pages 283–284.

Build Fluency

Use page 60 and the steps on Procedure Card 2 to reinforce vocabulary and build fluency. Read each vocabulary word aloud and have students repeat it. Then have students work in pairs to reread the words. Follow a similar procedure with the phrases and sentences. Continue to help students build fluency by having them reread "You Are There" in the Student Edition.

Text Comprehension

BEFORE READING

Preview the Lesson Guide students in previewing the lesson using Procedure Card 3. Point out the following features of the lesson on Student Edition pages 146–151.

- **Pages 146–147** Read the "What to Know" question and have students recall how Spain claimed land in the Americas. Preview the time line and the illustration of a Spanish fort.

- **Pages 148–149** Preview the illustration of a sugar mill in Brazil. Have students examine the map of New Spain and answer the map skill question.

- **Pages 150–151** Have students study the graph. Explain that it shows how the number of Europeans in the Western Hemisphere changed over time. Have students answer the question in the caption. Then preview the Review questions on page 150 and the biography of Bartolomé de Las Casas on page 151.

Build Comprehension of Expository Text Present the graphic organizer on page 61. Have students preview the organizer by filling in the lesson title and comparing the three main heads in the organizer with the matching subheads in the Student Edition pages 146–150. Tell students that the section subheads provide additional help with identifying important information. Use Procedure Card 4, the Reading Check questions in *Harcourt Social Studies*, and the directed reading suggestions below.

- **Page 146** After students have read "You Are There," ask who they think the newcomers are and what animals they ride. Invite students to predict what will happen.

- **Page 147** Have students read "New Spain." Then guide them in writing a sentence in the "Effect" box in the organizer to tell what happened as a result of Spain's wish to protect the lands it had claimed in the Americas.

- **Page 148** After students have read "Slavery in the Americas," have them write sentences in the boxes to tell what happened because Spain and Portugal needed workers in their colonies, and then what happened that caused colonists to capture Africans to be enslaved workers.

- **Pages 149–150** Have students read "Settling the Borderlands" and then write sentences about three kinds of places that were built in the Americas as a result of Spain's wish to protect its empire by settling the borderlands.

Summarize Have students use their completed graphic organizers to summarize the lesson. Then have them compare their summaries to the lesson summary on page 150.

Review and Respond If students need additional help identifying main ideas and details, use Focus Skill Transparency 2.

Write a Report Tell students that their textbook is one resource they can use for information on the topic of why Spain set up missions. You may also wish to suggest or provide additional research materials for students to use. Remind students to take notes as they read and to write the information in their reports in their own words.

Leveled Readers Use the Leveled Readers and Procedure Card 5 to build fluency and comprehension.

Name _____ Date _____

Part A

Vocabulary Words		Additional Words
colony	presidio	overpower
plantation	mission	colonist
slavery	hacienda	landowner
borderlands		permanent
		settlement

Part B

1. Spain, / which claimed / large parts of the Americas, / also tried to overpower Native American tribes / and take their lands.

2. Spain / formed the colony of New Spain / in 1535 / to protect its lands / and to govern the people there.

3. Many colonists / came to New Spain / to start plantations.

4. Both Spain and Portugal / forced Native Americans into slavery / to grow crops / and to mine gold and silver.

5. Bartolomé de Las Casas / was a landowner / who spoke out in favor of better treatment / of the Native Americans.

6. Spanish soldiers / built presidios / to protect the borderlands.

7. In 1565, / Spanish settlers / built the first permanent European settlement / in what is now / the United States.

8. Spanish missionaries / built missions / in the borderlands, / and some settlers / built haciendas.

YOU ARE THERE Turn to Student Edition page 146. Practice reading aloud "You Are There" three times. Try to improve your reading each time. Record your best time on the line below.

Number of words ___75___   My Best Time _____   Words per Minute _____

Name _____ Date _____

Lesson Title: _____

New Spain

Cause	Spain wanted to protect its lands in the Americas.	→	Effect	

Slavery in the Americas

Cause	Spain and Portugal needed many workers.	→	Effect	

Cause		→	Effect	The colonists began to capture Africans to be enslaved workers.

Effect	

Settling the Borderlands

Cause	Spain wanted to protect its empire by settling the borderlands.	→	Effect	

Effect	

LESSON 2 **The Virginia Colony**

Vocabulary Strategies

Preteach Additional Vocabulary After teaching the Vocabulary words on Student Edition page 152, explain to students that there are several other important words they will see in this lesson. Use Procedure Card 1, along with the suggestions below, to introduce the words.

lumber	Ask whether students have ever been to a lumberyard, where wood is sold in the form of boards used to build things. Explain that after trees have been cut down and sawed into pieces, the wood is called lumber.
merchant	Tell students that someone who buys and sells goods is called a merchant. This word is from the Latin root *mercari*, meaning "trade." Other words with this root include *market* and *merchandise*.
company	Discuss known meanings. Be sure students understand that a business can also be called a company. Give examples of well-known businesses that have the word *company* in their names.
governor	Ask students to name the governor of their state. Explain that a governor is the leader of a government. Point out the similarity between the words *governor* and *government*.

WORD CARDS To help teach the lesson vocabulary, use the Word Cards on pages 283–286.

Build Fluency

Use page 64 and the steps on Procedure Card 2 to reinforce vocabulary and build fluency. Read each vocabulary word aloud and have students repeat it. Then have students work in pairs to reread the words. Follow a similar procedure with the phrases and sentences. Continue to help students build fluency by having them reread "You Are There" in the Student Edition.

Text Comprehension

BEFORE READING

Preview the Lesson Guide students in previewing the lesson using Procedure Card 3. Point out the following features of the lesson on Student Edition pages 152–157.

- **Pages 152–153** Read the "What to Know" question. Discuss whether English settlers may have had the same reasons as Spanish settlers in New Spain. Preview the time line and the illustrations of Queen Elizabeth I and of the Lost Colony.

- **Pages 154–155** Preview the portrait of John Smith and the photograph of the reconstruction of Jamestown. On page 155, preview the illustration of Africans arriving in Jamestown.

- **Pages 156–157** Preview the illustration of the Powhatan defending their land and the Review questions on page 156. Have students look at the biography of Pocahontas on page 157. Explain that students may have heard from other sources, some of them partly fiction, about this Native American young woman.

DURING READING

Build Comprehension of Expository Text Present the graphic organizer on page 65. Have students preview the organizer by filling in the lesson title and comparing the three main heads in the organizer with the matching subheads in the Student Edition pages 152–156. Tell students that the section subheads provide additional help with identifying important information. Use Procedure Card 4, the Reading Check questions in *Harcourt Social Studies*, and the directed reading suggestions below.

- **Page 152** After students have read "You Are There," invite them to tell what they think may happen to this group of settlers.

- **Page 153** Have students read "England Attempts a Colony." Call attention to the structure of the organizer, which is a sequence chart with events in time order. Guide students in recording and summarizing in the organizer information about the first English colony, the next colony, and then about the Virginia Company. Point out that the subheads in the boxes match the section subheads in the text, which will help students locate information.

- **Page 154** After students have read "Jamestown," have them complete the next section in the organizer. Point out the two subheads that match the section subheads in the text.

- **Pages 155–156** After reading "Growth and Government," students can complete the graphic organizer, using the three section subheads to locate information.

AFTER READING

Summarize Have students use their completed graphic organizers to summarize the lesson. Then have them compare their summaries to the lesson summary on page 156.

Review and Respond If students need additional help identifying main ideas and details, use Focus Skill Transparency 2.

Construct a Time Line Suggest that students review the lesson and jot down events and dates to include on their time line. Then they can plan and construct a time line that is neat and easy to read.

Leveled Readers Use the Leveled Readers and Procedure Card 5 to build fluency and comprehension.

DIRECTIONS Read aloud the words in Part A. Practice reading aloud the
phrases and the sentences in Part B.

Part A

Vocabulary Words		Additional Words
raw material	stock	lumber
represent	legislature	merchant
royal colony	cash crop	company
indentured	profit	governor
servant		

Part B

1. England's rulers / knew they would benefit / from the lumber /
   and other raw materials / that colonies in America / would provide.

2. In the early 1600s, / a group of English merchants / set up the Virginia
   Company / to start a new colony / in Virginia.

3. In return for money / to set up the company, / owners received stock.

4. Colonists in Jamestown / began growing tobacco / as a cash crop.

5. The Virginia Company / sold tobacco / all over Europe / and made
   huge profits.

6. Growing tobacco / required many workers, / so the Virginia Company /
   brought indentured servants / to Virginia.

7. Colonists / set up a legislature, / called the House of Burgesses, /
   and elected members / to represent them.

8. In 1624, / King James I / made Virginia a royal colony / and picked
   a governor, / who shared power / with the House of Burgesses.

YOU ARE THERE Turn to Student Edition page 152. Practice reading aloud "You Are There"
three times. Try to improve your reading each time. Record your best
time on the line below.

Number of words ___76___ My Best Time _____ Words per Minute _____

Name _____ Date _____

Lesson Title: _____

England Attempts a Colony

The Lost Colony

First colony   When _____

Where _____

What happened _____

_____

Next Colony   When _____

What happened _____

_____

The Virginia Company

When _____

Who _____

What they wanted _____

_____

_____

Jamestown

England's First Permanent Colony

Leader _____

What happened _____

The Powhatan Confederacy

What happened _____

Growth and Government

Leader _____   Cash crop _____

Newcomers Arrive Who _____ _____

The House of Burgesses When _____

What it was _____

The Powhatan Wars What happened _____

_____

LESSON 3 **The Plymouth Colony**

Vocabulary Strategies

Preteach Additional Vocabulary After teaching the Vocabulary words on Student Edition page 158, explain to students that there are several other important words they will see in this lesson. Use Procedure Card 1, along with the suggestions below, to introduce the words.

passage	Tell students that this word has multiple meanings. Discuss meanings that students know, and explain that *passage* can also mean "journey," especially a journey by sea or by air.
site	Give *place* and *location* as synonyms for *site.* Point out that *site* is a homophone of the familiar word *sight.*
benefited	Identify the base word *benefit* from the Latin *bene* + *facere*, meaning "to do good." Other words from the root *bene* include *beneficial*, *benefactor*, *beneficiary*, and *benevolent.*
cooperation	Explain that cooperation means working together. Discuss recent examples of cooperation in your classroom.
prosper	Tell students that to prosper is to succeed or to do well. This word is from the Latin *prosperus*, which means "favorable."

WORD CARDS To help teach the lesson vocabulary, use the Word Cards on pages 285–286.

Build Fluency

Use page 68 and the steps on Procedure Card 2 to reinforce vocabulary and build fluency. Read each vocabulary word aloud and have students repeat it. Then have students work in pairs to reread the words. Follow a similar procedure with the phrases and sentences. Continue to help students build fluency by having them reread "You Are There" in the Student Edition.

Text Comprehension

BEFORE READING

Preview the Lesson Guide students in previewing the lesson using Procedure Card 3. Point out the following features of the lesson on Student Edition pages 158–163.

- **Pages 158–159** Read the "What to Know" question. Ask students why they think an area of North America came to be called New England. Preview the time line and the painting of Pilgrims boarding the *Mayflower* to sail from England to America.

- **Pages 160–161** Preview the illustration on page 160, discussing briefly how women's rights have changed since the time of the Plymouth colony. Then preview the illustration on page 161, and have students read the Fast Fact.

• **Pages 162–163** Have students look at the painting on page 162. Discuss the caption question about how the artist viewed the Pilgrims' first Thanksgiving. Preview the photograph of the Plymouth Plantation Historical Site and the Review questions on page 163.

DURING READING

Build Comprehension of Expository Text Present the graphic organizer on page 69. Have students preview the organizer by filling in the lesson title and comparing the four main heads in the organizer with the matching subheads in the Student Edition pages 158–163. Tell students that the section subheads provide additional help with identifying important information. Use Procedure Card 4, the Reading Check questions in *Harcourt Social Studies*, and the directed reading suggestions below.

• **Page 158** After students have read "You Are There," ask how they would feel about taking such a voyage. What might make it worthwhile for them?

• **Page 159** Have students read "The Pilgrims' Journey." Point out that the section subhead "Seeking Religious Freedom" explains why these people made their journey. Guide students in filling in the information under this same subhead in the organizer

• **Pages 160–161** After students have read "The Mayflower Compact," have them complete the next section in the organizer. Point out the subhead that matches the section subhead in the text. Follow the same procedure for "Building a Colony." Tell students to list under "How" several ways that the colonists were helped.

• **Pages 162–163** Tell students to read "Plymouth Grows" and then to complete the graphic organizer, using the section subheads to locate information.

AFTER READING

Summarize Have students use their completed graphic organizers to summarize the lesson. Then have them compare their summaries to the lesson summary on page 163.

Review and Respond If students need additional help identifying main ideas and details, use Focus Skill Transparency 2.

Write a Speech Discuss with students why the Mayflower Compact was written and what it said. Encourage them to look back at the text to recall details. Tell students to choose a position, either in favor of signing the Mayflower Compact or against it. Remind them to make clear statements of their opinions and supporting reasons in their speeches.

Leveled Readers Use the Leveled Readers and Procedure Card 5 to build fluency and comprehension.

Name _____ Date _____

Read aloud the words in Part A. Practice reading aloud the
phrases and the sentences in Part B.

Part A

Vocabulary Words	Additional Words
pilgrim	passage
compact	site
self-government	benefited
majority rule	cooperation
	prosper

Part B

1. A group of English people / who had moved to the Netherlands / to follow their religious beliefs / came to be known as Pilgrims.

2. The Virginia Company / agreed to pay / the Pilgrims' passage to North America / on a ship called the *Mayflower*.

3. Because they arrived / in a place with no government, / the men aboard the *Mayflower* / signed a compact.

4. The Mayflower Compact / included a very new idea, / self-government, / and also / the idea of majority rule.

5. The settlers / chose a site / on a harbor, / with fresh water / and good land for growing crops / nearby.

6. The colonists / lived in peace with the Wampanoag, / and both groups / benefited from their cooperation.

7. After the colony's leaders / decided to divide the land / among the colonists, / the colonists / began to prosper from their farming.

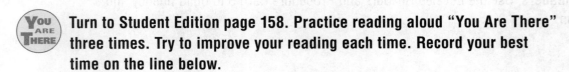 Turn to Student Edition page 158. Practice reading aloud "You Are There" three times. Try to improve your reading each time. Record your best time on the line below.

Number of words ____84____ My Best Time _____ Words per Minute _____

Name _____ Date _____

Lesson Title: _____

The Pilgrims' Journey

Seeking Religious Freedom

Who _____ Going where _____

When _____ Ship _____

The Mayflower Compact

Self-Government

What the signers agreed _____

Two important ideas _____

Building a Colony

Help from Native Americans

Who helped the colonists _____

How _____

_____

_____

Plymouth Grows

Growing Prosperity

How colonists prospered _____

Trouble Starts

When _____ Why _____

_____

LESSON 4 # The French and the Dutch

Vocabulary Strategies

Preteach Additional Vocabulary After teaching the Vocabulary words on Student Edition page 166, explain to students that there are several other important words they will see in this lesson. Use Procedure Card 1, along with the suggestions below, to introduce the words.

partnership	Point out the root word *partner* and suffix *-ship*, meaning "state or condition." Other words with this suffix include *friendship* and *leadership*.
warehouse	Have students identify the elements of this compound word. (*ware* + *house*) Explain that *ware* means goods or articles for sale, and that a warehouse is a building used to store these goods.
mouth	Tell students that this word has multiple meanings. Draw a river growing wider and emptying into the sea. Label the mouth of the river.
hardship	Have students identify the root word *hard* and suffix *-ship,* and recall the meaning of the suffix. Discuss examples of hardships that colonists faced.
levee	Use this context sentence: "Settlers built levees, or earthen walls, to protect the low-lying town from flood water."

WORD CARDS To help teach the lesson vocabulary, use the Word Cards on pages 285–286.

Build Fluency

Use page 72 and the steps on Procedure Card 2 to reinforce vocabulary and build fluency. Read each vocabulary word aloud and have students repeat it. Then have students work in pairs to reread the words. Follow a similar procedure with the phrases and sentences. Continue to help students build fluency by having them reread "You Are There" in the Student Edition.

Text Comprehension

BEFORE READING

Preview the Lesson Guide students in previewing the lesson using Procedure Card 3. Point out the following features of the lesson on Student Edition pages 166–173.

- **Pages 166–167** Read the "What to Know" question. Review briefly what students have learned about why Spain and England set up colonies. Preview the time line and the illustrations showing French and Huron traders and the statue of Samuel de Champlain, founder of Quebec. Have students examine the map on page 167 and answer the map skill question.

- **Pages 168–169** Have students examine the illustration showing the Dutch settlement of New Amsterdam in the 1640s. Then have them read the Fast Fact. Explain that the site where New Amsterdam was located is today part of New York City.

- **Pages 170–171** Preview the photograph of the statue on page 170 and the illustrated map on page 171. Have students read the captions and trace the explorers' routes shown on the map.

- **Page 172–173** Preview the illustration and map of New Orleans on page 172. Call attention to the table on page 173, and discuss the question in the caption. Then preview the Review questions.

DURING READING

Build Comprehension of Expository Text Present the graphic organizer on page 73. Have students preview the organizer by filling in the lesson title and comparing the four main heads in the organizer with the matching subheads in the Student Edition pages 166–173. Tell students that the section subheads provide additional help with identifying important information. Use Procedure Card 4, the Reading Check questions in *Harcourt Social Studies,* and the directed reading suggestions below.

- **Page 166** After students have read "You Are There," discuss the relationship it portrays between the French and the Huron.

- **Page 167** Have students read "New France." Discuss the aims of the French merchants and the king. Then guide students in writing in the organizer facts about New France and the first French settlement. Point out how the section subhead in the text can help students locate important information.

- **Pages 168–169** Have students read about the Dutch colony of New Netherland and fill in information about New Netherland in the organizer.

- **Pages 170–171** After students have read "Exploring New France," encourage them to refer to the section subheads as they add information to the organizer about explorers and what the explorers did.

- **Pages 172–173** Tell students to read "Louisiana" and complete the graphic organizer.

AFTER READING

Summarize Have students use their completed graphic organizers to summarize the lesson. Then have them compare their summaries to the lesson summary on page 173.

Review and Respond If students need additional help identifying main ideas and details, use Focus Skill Transparency 2.

Draw a Map Tell students to use the chart on page 173 and information and maps from Lessons 2 and 3, as well as from this lesson, to help them create their maps of European land claims in North America.

Leveled Readers Use the Leveled Readers and Procedure Card 5 to build fluency and comprehension.

Name _____ Date _____

Part A

Vocabulary Words	Additional Words	
demand	partnership	levee
supply	warehouse	
ally	mouth	
proprietary colony	hardship	

Part B

1. Jacques Cartier / started a trading partnership / with the Huron people / in the region / that became known as New France.

2. The demand for furs / was high, / so the Dutch / set up the colony / of New Netherland / in order to profit / from the fur trade.

3. Trade with Native Americans / added to the supply of fur.

4. By the 1630s, / the Dutch settlement of New Amsterdam / had about 200 people, / 30 houses, / and warehouses / for storing food and furs.

5. When fighting over the fur trade / broke out, / the Huron / were allies with the French.

6. In 1684, / La Salle / tried to start a settlement / near the mouth of the Mississippi River, / but hardships / led to disagreements / among the settlers.

7. In 1712, / the French king / made Louisiana / a proprietary colony.

8. Settlers in New Orleans, / Louisiana's capital, / built levees / to protect the low-lying town / from floodwater.

YOU ARE THERE Turn to Student Edition page 166. Practice reading aloud "You Are There" three times. Try to improve your reading each time. Record your best time on the line below.

Number of words ___82___ My Best Time _____ Words per Minute _____

Name _____ Date _____

Lesson Title: _____

New France

What French merchants wanted _____

What the French king wanted merchants to do _____

First French settlement in North America _____ Founder _____

When it was founded _____ How New France grew _____

New Netherland

Where _____

What the Dutch wanted _____

What they believed they had bought _____

Name of settlement _____ Location good for _____

Results of conflicts _____

Exploring New France

Explorers _____ and _____ found the _____.

Explorer _____ claimed the _____ for _____.

What he named the region _____ What happened _____

Louisiana

The French king made Louisiana a _____ in _____.

Capital _____ What happened _____

LESSON 1 **The New England Colonies**

Vocabulary Strategies

Preteach Additional Vocabulary After teaching the Vocabulary words on Student Edition page 178, explain to students that there are several other important words they will see in this lesson. Use Procedure Card 1, along with the suggestions below, to introduce the words.

pure	Point out that some products, such as bottled water, use the word *pure* in their advertising. Something that is pure is clean and not mixed with anything else.
sermon	Explain that a sermon is a speech, often one that is given by a religious leader.
strict	Ask students what the phrase *strict rules* means to them. Discuss the idea that some rules may be interpreted differently depending on circumstances, but strict rules are very exact and usually do not allow for exceptions.
require	Tell students that this word can mean "need." For example, plants require water to grow. It can also mean "demand" or "insist on." For example, voting laws require people to be 18 years old in order to vote.
common	Have students tell meanings they know for this word. Call attention to the common in the illustration on page 181. Explain that many towns in New England still have a grassy area like a park in the center of town that is called a common.

WORD CARDS To help teach the lesson vocabulary, use the Word Cards on pages 287–288.

Build Fluency

Use page 76 and the steps on Procedure Card 2 to reinforce vocabulary and build fluency. Read each vocabulary word aloud and have students repeat it. Then have students work in pairs to reread the words. Follow a similar procedure with the phrases and sentences. Continue to help students build fluency by having them reread "You Are There" in the Student Edition.

Text Comprehension

BEFORE READING

Preview the Lesson Guide students in previewing the lesson using Procedure Card 3. Point out the following features of the lesson on Student Edition pages 178–185.

- **Pages 178–179** Discuss the "What to Know" question. Review briefly what students know about the geography of New England. Preview the time line and the illustrations of the Plymouth colony and of the Puritan migration.

- **Pages 180–181** Have students examine the map of New England colonies and answer the map skill question. Preview the illustration of Roger Williams and explain that he started his own colony after he was expelled for disagreeing with Puritan leaders. Have students examine and discuss the illustration of a New England town.

- **Pages 182–183** Preview the illustration of whalers, and explain that whaling was an important industry in New England. Have students examine the map on page 183, identify the triangles formed by the trade routes, and answer the map skill question.

- **Pages 184–185** Point out the illustration showing conditions on a slave ship, and then preview the Review questions. Call attention to the biography of Anne Hutchinson on page 185. Tell students that she, like Roger Williams, was expelled from the Massachusetts Bay Colony and started her own colony.

DURING READING

Build Comprehension of Expository Text Present the graphic organizer on page 77. Have students preview the organizer by filling in the lesson title and comparing the five main heads in the organizer with the matching subheads in the Student Edition pages 178–184. Tell students that the section subheads provide additional help with identifying important information. Use Procedure Card 4, the Reading Check questions in *Harcourt Social Studies,* and the directed reading suggestions below.

- **Page 178** After students have read "You Are There," have them recall the challenges faced by the Pilgrims in the early years of the Plymouth Colony.

- **Page 179** Have students read "The Puritans Arrive" and write in the graphic organizer the name of the new colony.

- **Pages 180–181** After students have read "Change and Conflict," have them fill in the next section of the organizer. Point out the subhead "King Philip's War" that matches the section subhead in the text. Then have students read "Life in New England" and use the subheads to help them as they continue to fill in information about New England.

- **Pages 182–184** Have students read "New England's Economy" and complete the next section of the organizer, using section subheads to locate information. Then students can read "The Middle Passage" and fill in the last box.

AFTER READING

Summarize Have students use their completed graphic organizers to summarize the lesson. Then have them compare their summaries to the lesson summary on page 184.

Review and Respond Work through the Review questions with students. If students need additional help with main ideas and details, use Focus Skill Transparency 2.

Write a Letter Suggest that students reread passages from the lesson and jot down information they may want to include in their letters. Remind them to use the correct form for a friendly letter.

Leveled Readers Use the Leveled Readers and Procedure Card 5 to build fluency and comprehension.

DIRECTIONS Read aloud the words in Part A. Practice reading aloud the phrases and the sentences in Part B.

Part A

Vocabulary Words		Additional Words	
dissent	exports	pure	require
expel	triangular	sermon	common
industry	trade route	strict	
imports	Middle Passage		

Part B

1. English settlers / who wanted to make the Church of England / more "pure" / were called Puritans.

2. John Winthrop / described a "city upon a hill" / in a sermon / and led a group of Puritans / to Massachusetts.

3. He and other leaders / thought that dissent / might hurt their society.

4. When Roger Williams / disagreed with them, / they voted / to expel him.

5. Most New England colonies / required towns / to have schools.

6. Houses in small towns / were built around the common.

7. Shipbuilding / was a leading industry / in New England.

8. The colonies had to follow / strict rules / about exports and imports.

9. Many colonial trading ships / followed triangular trade routes.

10. Millions of enslaved Africans / were forced to travel / across the Atlantic Ocean / on a journey called the Middle Passage.

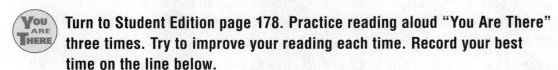 **Turn to Student Edition page 178. Practice reading aloud "You Are There" three times. Try to improve your reading each time. Record your best time on the line below.**

Number of words ___79___ My Best Time _____ Words per Minute _____

Name _____ Date _____

Lesson Title: _____

<table>
<tr><td colspan="2" align="center">**The Puritans Arrive**</td></tr>
<tr><td>**A City on the Hill**   Colony _____</td></tr>
</table>

Change and Conflict

Who disagreed with leaders _____

What they did _____

King Philip's War   Between _____

Life in New England

Religion and Education   Lived by _____

Towns required to have _____

Town and Home   Where most people lived _____

How decisions were made _____

New England's Economy

Farming and Fishing   Important industries _____

Colonial Trade   Leaders in _____

Triangular Trade Routes   Connected _____

The Middle Passage

Was part of _____

Working Against Slavery   Who _____

LESSON 2 # The Middle Colonies

Vocabulary Strategies

Preteach Additional Vocabulary After teaching the Vocabulary words on Student Edition page 186, explain to students that there are several other important words they will see in this lesson. Use Procedure Card 1, along with the suggestions below, to introduce the words.

outnumbered	Have students identify the elements *out*, *number*, and *-ed*. Divide students into groups containing different numbers of people, and have them tell which is outnumbered by the other.
social	Explain that this word is from the Latin root *socius*, meaning "companion," also the root of *society* and *associate*.
breadbasket	Have students identify the two shorter words, *bread* and *basket*, that make up this compound word. Tell students that bread is sometimes served in a basket called a *breadbasket*.
gristmill	Point out the illustration of a gristmill on page 190 and have students explain what happens there.
general store	Tell students that general stores sold a variety of goods that people needed. However, the stores were not large or divided into different departments as modern stores are.

WORD CARDS To help teach the lesson vocabulary, use the Word Cards on pages 287–290.

Build Fluency

Use page 80 and the steps on Procedure Card 2 to reinforce vocabulary and build fluency. Read each vocabulary word aloud and have students repeat it. Then have students work in pairs to reread the words. Follow a similar procedure with the phrases and sentences. Continue to help students build fluency by having them reread "You Are There" in the Student Edition.

Text Comprehension

BEFORE READING

Preview the Lesson Guide students in previewing the lesson using Procedure Card 3. Point out the following features of the lesson on Student Edition pages 186–191.

• **Pages 186–187** Discuss the "What to Know" question. Review briefly what students have learned about how geography affected life and the economy in New England. Preview the time line and the illustration of the New York colony. Tell students that this colony was first settled by the Dutch.

- **Pages 188–189** Have students examine the map of the Middle Colonies and answer the map skill question. Preview the illustrations of William Penn and farm life in the Middle Colonies.

- **Pages 190–191** Have students examine and discuss the illustration of a town in the Middle Colonies and answer the question in the caption. Preview the Review questions.

DURING READING

Build Comprehension of Expository Text Present the graphic organizer on page 81. Have students preview the organizer by filling in the lesson title and comparing the four main heads in the organizer with the matching subheads in the Student Edition pages 186–191. Tell students that the section subheads provide additional help with identifying important information. Use Procedure Card 4, the Reading Check questions in *Harcourt Social Studies,* and the directed reading suggestions below.

- **Page 186** After students have read "You Are There," ask whether they have heard of Wall Street in New York City. Explain that today it is a famous street where some of the nation's important financial business is done.

- **Page 187** Have students read "Settling the Middle Colonies" and fill in information in the graphic organizer. Point out the two subheads that match the section subheads in the text.

- **Pages 188–189** After students have read "Pennsylvania," have them fill in the next section of the organizer. Point out the subhead "Government and Diversity" that matches the section subhead in the text. Then have students read "Life in the Middle Colonies" and use the subheads to help them as they continue to fill in information about the Middle Colonies.

- **Pages 190–191** Have students read "The Breadbasket Colonies" and complete the organizer, using section subheads to locate information.

AFTER READING

Summarize Have students use their completed graphic organizers to summarize the lesson. Then have them compare their summaries to the lesson summary on page 191.

Review and Respond Work through the Review questions with students. If students need additional help with main ideas and details, use Focus Skill Transparency 2.

Write a Letter Suggest that students reread the section of the lesson that gives information about artisans and apprentices. Explain that students can add details from their imaginations when they write their letters but should base their ideas on information from the lesson.

Leveled Readers Use the Leveled Readers and Procedure Card 5 to build fluency and comprehension.

Name _____ Date _____

DIRECTIONS Read aloud the words in Part A. Practice reading aloud the phrases and the sentences in Part B.

Part A

Vocabulary Words		Additional Words	
refuge	diversity	outnumbered	gristmill
proprietor	religious	social	general
trial by jury	toleration	breadbasket	store
immigrant	apprentice		

Part B

1. Dutch settlers in New Netherland / were outnumbered, / and England took over / the colony.

2. A religious group known as the Quakers / found a refuge / in New Jersey.

3. William Penn, / the proprietor of Pennsylvania, / gave people the right / to a trial by jury.

4. Immigrants from many parts of the world / created diversity / and made the region / an interesting place.

5. As a result / of the religious movement / called the Great Awakening, / religious toleration grew.

6. Religion / was a major part of social life / in the Middle Colonies.

7. Farmers grew so many crops / used in making bread / that the Middle Colonies came to be called / the "breadbasket" colonies.

8. Every market town / had a gristmill / and a general store.

9. Young people / learned skills needed to be an artisan / by becoming an apprentice.

You ARE THERE Turn to Student Edition page 186. Practice reading aloud "You Are There" three times. Try to improve your reading each time. Record your best time on the line below.

Number of words ___65___ My Best Time _____ Words per Minute _____

Name _____ Date _____

Lesson Title: _____

Settling the Middle Colonies

Dutch Settlement Who took over the colony _____

New Jersey Early settlers _____ Hoped to find _____

Pennsylvania

Government and Diversity Proprietor_____

What he wanted _____

_____

Life in the Middle Colonies

The Great Awakening Results _____

_____

Religion and Social Life

Major part of social life _____

The Breadbasket Colonies

Farms and Ports Main crops _____

Important port _____ Busiest port _____

Colonial Jobs What many colonists worked in _____

The Southern Colonies

Vocabulary Strategies

Preteach Additional Vocabulary After teaching the Vocabulary words on Student Edition page 194, explain to students that there are several other important words they will see in this lesson. Use Procedure Card 1, along with the suggestions below, to introduce the words.

assembly	Have students define the word in this context: "Maryland and Virginia both had governors and elected assemblies." Point out that the plural is formed by changing *y* to *i* and adding *-es*.
labor	Tell students that synonyms include *work* and *effort*.
sugarcane	Point out the two shorter words that make up this compound word. Explain that sugarcane is a plant from which sugar is made. A cane is a hollow stem.
dye	Point out that this word, which means "a substance that causes a change in color," is a homophone of *die*.
clipper	Explain that a clipper was a type of fast sailing ship. Clippers were usually long and slender with tall masts and large sails.

WORD CARDS To help teach the lesson vocabulary, use the Word Cards on pages 289–290.

Build Fluency

Use page 84 and the steps on Procedure Card 2 to reinforce vocabulary and build fluency. Read each vocabulary word aloud and have students repeat it. Then have students work in pairs to reread the words. Follow a similar procedure with the phrases and sentences. Continue to help students build fluency by having them reread "You Are There" in the Student Edition.

Text Comprehension

BEFORE READING

Preview the Lesson Guide students in previewing the lesson using Procedure Card 3. Point out the following features of the lesson on Student Edition pages 194–201.

• **Pages 194–195** Discuss the "What to Know" question. Review briefly what students have learned about how geography affected life and the economy in other colonies. Preview the time line and the illustration of Chesapeake Bay on page 194. Have students read the Fast Fact. Preview the illustration of growing tobacco. Tell students that it was an important cash crop.

• **Pages 196–197** Have students examine the map of the Southern Colonies and answer the map skill question. Preview the portrait of James Oglethorpe, the founder of Georgia. Have students read the Primary Sources feature and discuss the document-based question.

- **Pages 198–199** Preview and discuss the illustrations that show how enslaved people kept their culture alive. Then have students examine the illustration of a Southern plantation. Discuss the statements in the caption.

- **Pages 200–201** Preview the illustration on page 200. Ask students how they can tell that it shows Baltimore long ago and not today. Preview the illustration on page 201, and discuss whether it shows shipping today or long ago. Then preview the Review questions.

DURING READING

Build Comprehension of Expository Text Present the graphic organizer on page 85. Have students preview the organizer by filling in the lesson title and comparing the six main heads in the organizer with the matching subheads in the Student Edition pages 194–201. Tell students that the section subheads provide additional help with identifying important information. Use Procedure Card 4, the Reading Check questions in *Harcourt Social Studies,* and the directed reading suggestions below.

- **Page 194** After students have read "You Are There," have them tell what they learned from it about the Maryland Colony.

- **Page 195** Have students read "Maryland and Virginia" and list in the organizer things that these two colonies had in common. Discuss differences between the two colonies.

- **Pages 196–197** After reading "The Carolinas and Georgia," have students fill in the next section of the organizer. Point out the subheads that match the section subheads in the text. Then have students read "Heading West" and use the subheads to guide them as they continue to fill in the organizer.

- **Pages 198–199** Have students read and discuss "Slavery in the Colonies." After filling in this section in the organizer, students can read "Life in the South" and write information for each of the subheads in the next box.

- **Pages 200–201** After students read "The Southern Economy," have them use the subheads to help them list cash crops and then other industries that were part of the economy of the Southern Colonies.

AFTER READING

Summarize Have students use their completed graphic organizers to summarize the lesson. Then have them compare their summaries to the lesson summary on page 201.

Review and Respond Work through the Review questions with students. If students need additional help with main ideas and details, use Focus Skill Transparency 2.

Write a Diary Entry Have students reread the part of the lesson that tells about Eliza Lucas Pinckney. Remind them to write from Eliza's point of view and to include facts as well as Eliza's ideas and feelings.

Leveled Readers Use the Leveled Readers and Procedure Card 5 to build fluency and comprehension.

Name _____ Date _____

Read aloud the words in Part A. Practice reading aloud the phrases and the sentences in Part B.

Part A

Vocabulary Words		Additional Words	
constitution	indigo	assembly	dye
debtor	broker	labor	clipper
planter	naval stores	sugarcane	

Part B

1. Maryland and Virginia, / which had much in common, / both had governors / and elected assemblies.

2. Carolina / had a constitution, / but most power / remained with the king / and the proprietors.

3. James Oglethorpe / wanted debtors to settle / the Georgia Colony.

4. Some Native Americans / were captured / and sent to work / on sugarcane plantations / in the West Indies.

5. The cash crops / produced by the labor of enslaved workers / made some planters / the richest people / in the Southern Colonies.

6. Indigo, / a plant / that produces a blue dye / used to color clothing, / became the major cash crop/ in South Carolina.

7. Brokers / took the crops to market to sell / and bought the goods / the planters wanted.

8. Southern colonists / built sawmills / and made naval stores.

9. Over time, / shipbuilders / developed the Baltimore clipper, / one of the fastest sailing ships.

YOU ARE THERE Turn to Student Edition page 194. Practice reading aloud "You Are There" three times. Try to improve your reading each time. Record your best time on the line below.

Number of words ___78___   My Best Time _____   Words per Minute _____

Name _____ Date _____

Lesson Title: _____

The Carolinas and Georgia

Life in Maryland and Virginia   What they had in common _____

_____

The Carolinas and Georgia

Carolina Split into _____ and _____

Georgia Why economy grew _____

Heading West

Settling the Backcountry When _____

Conflicts with Native Americans Why _____

_____

Slavery in the Colonies

Slavery and Society Where slavery was legal _____

Life in the South

Farm Life Two kinds of farms _____ _____

Southern Cities What port cities did _____

The Southern Economy

Cash Crops and Exports Cash crops _____

Other Industries _____

LESSON 1 # Fighting for Control

Vocabulary Strategies

Preteach Additional Vocabulary After teaching the Vocabulary words on Student Edition page 222, explain to students that there are several other important words they will see in this lesson. Use Procedure Card 1, along with the suggestions below, to introduce the words.

conflicting	Point out the head "Conflicting Claims" on page 223. Explain that the base word *conflict* is a verb accented on the second syllable. It is a homograph of the noun *conflict*, accented on the first syllable. Two countries that claim the same land have conflicting claims.
union	Discuss the relationship between this word and the known words *united* and *unity*.
favor	Discuss familiar meanings. Then discuss this context: "Britain sent more troops and supplies to the colonies, and the war slowly turned in its favor."
molasses	Explain that molasses is a kind of brown syrup that comes from sugar during processing. It is used for cooking.
objected	Tell students that synonyms for this word are *opposed* and *disagreed*. Point out the base word *object*, accented on the second syllable, a homograph of the noun *object*.

WORD CARDS To help teach the lesson vocabulary, use the Word Cards on pages 291–292.

Build Fluency

Use page 88 and the steps on Procedure Card 2 to reinforce vocabulary and build fluency. Read each vocabulary word aloud and have students repeat it. Then have students work in pairs to reread the words. Follow a similar procedure with the phrases and sentences. Continue to help students build fluency by having them reread "You Are There" in the Student Edition.

Text Comprehension

BEFORE READING

Preview the Lesson Guide students in previewing the lesson using Procedure Card 3. Point out the following features of the lesson on Student Edition pages 222–227.

- **Pages 222–223** Read the "What to Know" question. Explain that the French and Indian War was not between the French and Native Americans but between Britain and France, with Native Americans fighting for both sides. Preview the time line and the map of North America, and have students answer the map skill question. Then have students look at the illustration of Fort Necessity, read the Fast Fact, and locate the date of the Battle of Fort Necessity on the time line.

- **Pages 224–225** Preview the illustration and the map of the French and Indian War. Have students answer the map skill question.

- **Pages 226–227** Preview the illustration of a frontier settlement and the portrait of Pontiac. Then preview the Review questions on page 227.

Build Comprehension of Expository Text Present the graphic organizer on page 89. Have students preview the organizer by filling in the lesson title and comparing the four main heads in the organizer with the matching subheads in the Student Edition pages 222–227. Tell students that the section subheads provide additional help with identifying important information. Use Procedure Card 4, the Reading Check questions in *Harcourt Social Studies,* and the directed reading suggestions below.

• **Page 222** After students have read "You Are There," have them look at the illustration on pages 222 and 223 and describe in their own words the events taking place at Fort Necessity.

• **Page 223** Have students read "Conflicting Claims." Ask them to identify the region claimed by two different countries. Then guide students in filling in the first box of the organizer. Point out that the organizer is a sequence chart. The events described in the chart are in time order.

• **Page 224** After students have read "The French and Indian War Begins," they can fill in the information in the next part of the organizer. On the first line, they should explain briefly who formed alliances.

• **Pages 225–227** Have students read "The War Expands." Discuss and have students summarize orally the information in the subsections "Early Defeats for Britain" and "Britain Wins Control." Tell students to add information from the subsection "The Treaty of Paris" to the organizer. Then they can read "More Troubles" and list in the organizer two reasons for more troubles in the colonies.

Summarize Have students use their completed graphic organizers to summarize the lesson. Then have them compare their summaries to the lesson summary on page 227.

Review and Respond Work through the Review questions with students. Use Focus Skill Transparency 3, Cause and Effect, to identify causes and effects in the lesson.

Write a Newspaper Story Remind students that a newspaper story answers the questions When, Where, Who, What, and Why. Suggest that students write these five questions as headings on scrap paper and jot down information under each heading as they skim or reread passages in the lesson. Then they can use their notes as a basis for writing their articles.

 Leveled Readers Use the Leveled Readers and Procedure Card 5 to build fluency and comprehension.

Name _____ Date _____

Read aloud the words in Part A. Practice reading aloud the phrases and the sentences in Part B.

Part A

Vocabulary Words		Additional Words	
alliance	proclamation	conflicting	molasses
delegate	budget	union	objected
Parliament		favor	

Part B

1. Conflicting claims / to the Ohio Valley region / were made by Britain and France.

2. By the mid-1700s, / both France and Britain / had formed alliances / with many of the Native American tribes / in the Ohio Valley.

3. Seven colonies / sent delegates to Albany in 1754, / but they did not approve / Benjamin Franklin's / Albany Plan of Union.

4. Parliament / sent an army to the colonies / to help fight the French / and their Native American allies.

5. After early defeats, / Britain sent more troops and supplies / to the colonies, / and the war / slowly turned in its favor.

6. After the French and Indian War, / Britain's king / made a proclamation / that all lands west of the Appalachian Mountains / belonged to Native Americans.

7. British leaders / looked at their budget / and decided that the colonists / should help pay off / the cost of the war.

8. Many merchants / objected to the Sugar Act, / which taxed the sugar and molasses / brought into the colonies from the West Indies.

YOU ARE THERE Turn to Student Edition page 222. Practice reading aloud "You Are There" three times. Try to improve your reading each time. Record your best time on the line below.

Number of words ___72___ My Best Time _____ Words per Minute _____

Name _____ Date _____

Lesson Title _____

Conflicting Claims

Region _____ Who claimed it _____

What France did _____

What the British decided _____

⬇

The French and Indian War Begins

Alliances _____

Meeting When _____ Where _____ Who _____

What they talked about _____

Start of French and Indian War When _____ Where _____

⬇

The War Expands

When war ended _____ Treaty of Paris gave Britain _____

_____

⬇

More Troubles

Why

1. _____

2. _____

LESSON 2 **Colonists Speak Out**

Vocabulary Strategies

Preteach Additional Vocabulary After teaching the Vocabulary words on Student Edition page 230, explain to students that there are several other important words they will see in this lesson. Use Procedure Card 1, along with the suggestions below, to introduce the words.

document	Tell students that a document is a formal piece of writing. Other kinds of documents may include computer files, photographs, videos, and audio recordings. Ask students which kind of documents their text most likely refers to when telling about events that took place in 1765.
taxation	Point out the root word *tax* and suffix *-ation,* meaning "act or process." Have students define *taxation* in their own words.
liberty	Give *freedom* and *independence* as synonyms for *liberty.*
massacre	Point out that authors sometimes give definitions to help readers understand a text. Use this sentence from the lesson as an example: "A massacre is the killing of many people who cannot defend themselves."

WORD CARDS To help teach the lesson vocabulary, use the Word Cards on pages 291–292.

Build Fluency

Use page 92 and the steps on Procedure Card 2 to reinforce vocabulary and build fluency. Read each vocabulary word aloud and have students repeat it. Then have students work in pairs to reread the words. Follow a similar procedure with the phrases and sentences. Continue to help students build fluency by having them reread "You Are There" in the Student Edition.

Text Comprehension

BEFORE READING

Preview the Lesson Guide students in previewing the lesson using Procedure Card 3. Point out the following features of the lesson on Student Edition pages 230–237.

- **Pages 230–231** Read the "What to Know" question. Have students recall how colonists felt about the Sugar Act. Preview the time line and explain that the Stamp Act and Townshend Acts were new taxes on the colonists. After previewing the illustration of the British Parliament on page 230, have students read the Primary Sources feature about the Stamp Act Cartoon and discuss the document-based question.

- **Pages 232–233** Have students examine the diagram and answer the questions in the captions. Discuss methods that people use today to exchange information rapidly, such as e-mail and instant messaging.

- **Pages 234–235** Have students read Children In History and discuss the Make It Relevant question. Preview the paintings and captions on page 235.
- **Pages 236–237** Preview the engraving on page 236. Ask students if they have heard of Paul Revere and what they know about him. Preview the Review questions. Call attention to the biography of Patrick Henry on page 237. Explain that Henry was one of the leaders of the colonists who protested against British rule.

DURING READING

Build Comprehension of Expository Text Present the graphic organizer on page 93. Have students preview the organizer by filling in the lesson title and comparing the four main heads in the organizer with the matching subheads in the Student Edition pages 230–236. Tell students that the section subheads provide additional help with identifying important information. Use Procedure Card 4, the Reading Check questions in *Harcourt Social Studies*, and the directed reading suggestions below.

- **Page 230** After students have read "You Are There," have them predict what Parliament will do and why.
- **Page 231** Have students read about the Stamp Act. Discuss the colonists' reactions, including Patrick Henry's speech to the House of Burgesses, and the Stamp Act Congress. Then guide students in filling in the first box of the organizer.
- **Pages 232–233** After students have read "Colonists Work Together," have them write information in the organizer. Tell students that the section subheads will help them identify important information.
- **Page 234–236** Have students read about the Townshend Acts and add to the organizer. Then they can read "The Boston Massacre" and complete the organizer by writing a brief summary of the events that took place.

AFTER READING

Summarize Have students use their completed graphic organizers to summarize the lesson. Then have them compare their summaries to the lesson summary on page 236.

Review and Respond Work through the Review questions with students. If students need additional help with causes and effects, use Focus Skill Transparency 3.

Draw a Cartoon Discuss the use of political cartoons to try to persuade people to believe or act in a certain way. You may want to display and discuss examples of political cartoons, pointing out symbolism, the use of caricatures, and labels or other text that helps viewers understand the cartoonist's point of view. Provide appropriate art materials for students to use in creating their own cartoons.

Leveled Readers Use the Leveled Readers and Procedure Card 5 to build fluency and comprehension.

Name _____ Date _____

DIRECTIONS Read aloud the words in Part A. Practice reading aloud the phrases and the sentences in Part B.

Part A

Vocabulary Words		Additional Words
representation	repeal	document
imperial policy	treason	taxation
congress	protest	liberty
boycott		massacre

Part B

1. In 1765, / Parliament approved / the Stamp Act, / which put a tax on paper documents / in the colonies.

2. Some members of the Virginia House of Burgesses / accused Patrick Henry of treason / when he said that Parliament / did not represent the colonies.

3. After the Stamp Act Congress / met in New York City / in 1765, / people began to repeat these words /—no taxation / without representation.

4. Some colonists / began to boycott / all British goods.

5. Groups called the Sons of Liberty / and the Daughters of Liberty / took action / against the Stamp Act.

6. By 1766, / so many colonists / opposed the Stamp Act / that Parliament voted to repeal it.

7. Committees of Correspondence / were organized to protest / British imperial policies.

8. In 1770, / British soldiers / killed five colonists / in a fight / that became known as the Boston Massacre.

You ARE There Turn to Student Edition page 230. Practice reading aloud "You Are There" three times. Try to improve your reading each time. Record your best time on the line below.

Number of words ___87___ My Best Time _____ Words per Minute _____

Name _____ Date _____

Lesson Title _____

The Stamp Act

When _____ What it was _____

What people said about it _____

↓

Colonists Work Together

What colonists wanted _____

Groups who took action _____

What happened as a result _____

What the colonists formed _____

Why _____

What they asked people to do _____

↓

The Townshend Acts

When passed _____ What they were _____

What colonists did _____

What Parliament did _____

_____

↓

The Boston Massacre

When _____ What happened _____

_____

LESSON 3 **Disagreements Grow**

Vocabulary Strategies

Preteach Additional Vocabulary After teaching the Vocabulary words on Student Edition page 238, explain to students that there are several other important words they will see in this lesson. Use Procedure Card 1, along with the suggestions below, to introduce the words.

competition	Have students use the meanings of the base word *compete* and suffix *-ition* ("act or process") to define *competition*.
set	Discuss known meanings for this multiple-meaning word. Point out the phrases *set sail* on page 239 and *set of laws* on page 240 in the text.
coercive	Explain that a law or action that is coercive forces people to do something they do not want to do.
intolerable	Give these synonyms: *unacceptable, unbearable*.
weapon	Students may know the meaning of this word but not recognize the word in print. Give examples of other words in which *ea* has the short *e* sound, such as *bread*, *threat*, and *feather*.

WORD CARDS To help teach the lesson vocabulary, use the Word Cards on pages 293–294.

Build Fluency

Use page 96 and the steps on Procedure Card 2 to reinforce vocabulary and build fluency. Read each vocabulary word aloud and have students repeat it. Then have students work in pairs to reread the words. Follow a similar procedure with the phrases and sentences. Continue to help students build fluency by having them reread "You Are There" in the Student Edition.

Text Comprehension

BEFORE READING

Preview the Lesson Guide students in previewing the lesson using Procedure Card 3. Point out the following features of the lesson on Student Edition pages 238–243.

• **Pages 238–239** Read the "What to Know" question. Have students recall what the colonists did to protest the Stamp Act and the Townshend Acts. Preview the time line and the illustration of the Boston Tea Party. Have students read the Fast Fact and locate the date of the Boston Tea Party on the time line.

• **Pages 240–241** Have students look at the illustration on page 240 and read the caption. Explain that colonists were forced to give food and housing to British soldiers. Discuss how students and their families might feel if they were in the colonists' position. Then have students examine the illustrated time line on page 241 and answer the Time Line question.

- **Pages 242–243** Call attention to the map of Lexington and Concord, and have students answer the map skill question. Preview the photograph of the statue of Paul Revere in Boston, and the Review questions.

DURING READING

Build Comprehension of Expository Text Present the graphic organizer on page 97. Have students preview the organizer by filling in the lesson title and comparing the four main heads in the organizer with the matching subheads in the Student Edition pages 238–243. Tell students that the section subheads provide additional help with identifying important information. Use Procedure Card 4, the Reading Check questions in *Harcourt Social Studies,* and the directed reading suggestions below.

- **Page 238** After students have read "You Are There," ask why they think colonists might want to protest British rule.

- **Page 239** Have students read about the Boston Tea Party and then turn to the graphic organizer. Point out that the organizer is a sequence diagram. Guide students in writing information in the first box. Explain that the date they should write in the organizer is the date that the Boston Tea Party took place.

- **Pages 240–241** After students have read "The Coercive Acts," have them record information in the organizer. Then do the same with "The First Continental Congress." Point out that students should list three actions taken by the First Continental Congress.

- **Pages 242–243** Have students read "Lexington and Concord" and complete the organizer by writing the date and a brief summary of the events that took place.

AFTER READING

Summarize Have students use their completed graphic organizers to summarize the lesson. Then have them compare their summaries to the lesson summary on page 243.

Review and Respond Work through the Review questions with students. If students need additional help with causes and effects, use Focus Skill Transparency 3.

Write a Poem Remind students that poems do not have to rhyme but should use colorful language and images to describe the battle scenes. You may want to read aloud to students the first verse of Ralph Waldo Emerson's poem "Concord Hymn" and discuss Emerson's use of poetic language to create an image of the scene in readers' minds.

Leveled Readers Use the Leveled Readers and Procedure Card 5 to build fluency and comprehension.

DIRECTIONS   Read aloud the words in Part A. Practice reading aloud the phrases and the sentences in Part B.

Part A

Vocabulary Words		Additional Words	
monopoly	petition	competition	intolerable
blockade	Minutemen	set	weapon
quarter	revolution	coercive	

Part B

1. In 1773, / Parliament passed the Tea Act, / giving Britain's East India Company / a monopoly on tea.

2. Because there was no competition, / colonists had to buy their tea / from the East India Company / and pay the tax.

3. After colonists / threw more than 300 chests of tea / into Boston Harbor, / Parliament / passed a new set of laws.

4. To enforce these laws /, which colonists called / the Coercive Acts, / Parliament / ordered the British navy / to blockade Boston Harbor.

5. Britain / also ordered the colonists / to quarter British soldiers.

6. Many colonists / said the new laws / were intolerable.

7. In 1774, / the First Continental Congress / sent a petition to the king / to remind him / of the colonists' basic rights / as British citizens.

8. In April 1775, / the British General Gage / sent over 700 soldiers / to arrest the leaders of the Sons of Liberty / and take their weapons.

9. Fighting between British soldiers and the Minutemen / was the beginning of a long war / called the American Revolution.

YOU ARE THERE   Turn to Student Edition page 238. Practice reading aloud "You Are There" three times. Try to improve your reading each time. Record your best time on the line below.

Number of words ___73___   My Best Time _____   Words per Minute _____

Name _____ Date _____

Lesson Title _____

The Boston Tea Party

Date _____ Reason _____

Who did it _____ What they did _____

_____

↓

The Coercive Acts

Date _____ What they were _____

Purpose _____

These laws united colonists _____.

↓

The First Continental Congress

Date of meeting _____ Place _____

Who _____

What they did

1. _____

2. _____

3. _____

↓

Lexington and Concord

Date _____ What happened _____

_____

_____

UNIT 3

Chapter 6

LESSON 4 # The Road to War

Vocabulary Strategies

Preteach Additional Vocabulary After teaching the Vocabulary words on Student Edition page 244, explain to students that there are several other important words they will see in this lesson. Use Procedure Card 1, along with the suggestions below, to introduce the words.

currency	Have students use this context clue from page 245: "Congress also decided to print its own paper money, which became known as Continental currency."
bill	Discuss known meanings for this multiple-meaning word, including its use as a name for paper money, such as a one-dollar bill or a ten-dollar bill.
cannon	Have students point out the cannon in the picture of George Washington on page 244.
retreat	Tell students that an antonym of *retreat* is *advance*. Ask volunteers to demonstrate advancing and retreating.
rebellion	Explain that a rebellion is an attempt to overthrow a government by the use of force. Discuss related words such as *rebel* (noun accented on first syllable), *rebel* (verb accented on second syllable) and *rebellious*.

WORD CARDS To help teach the lesson vocabulary, use the Word Cards on pages 293–294.

Build Fluency

Use page 100 and the steps on Procedure Card 2 to reinforce vocabulary and build fluency. Read each vocabulary word aloud and have students repeat it. Then have students work in pairs to reread the words. Follow a similar procedure with the phrases and sentences. Continue to help students build fluency by having them reread "You Are There" in the Student Edition.

Text Comprehension

BEFORE READING

Preview the Lesson Guide students in previewing the lesson using Procedure Card 3. Point out the following features of the lesson on Student Edition pages 244–248.

- **Pages 244–245** Read the "What to Know" question. Explain that Britain was a nation with a powerful army and navy, while the colonists lived in separate colonies with only part-time militias. Ask students to predict how the colonists may have prepared for war with Britain. Preview the time line and the illustrations. Have students locate the date of the Second Continental Congress on the time line.

- **Pages 246–247** Have students examine the illustration of the Battle of Bunker Hill and read the labels. Then have them examine the inset map and discuss the Illustration question.

- **Pages 248–249** Preview the portrait of King George III and the Review questions on page 248. Call attention to the biography of the poet Phillis Wheatley on page 249.

DURING READING

Build Comprehension of Expository Text Present the graphic organizer on page 101. Have students preview the organizer by filling in the lesson title and comparing the three main heads in the organizer with the matching subheads in the Student Edition pages 244–248. Tell students that the section subheads provide additional help with identifying important information. Use Procedure Card 4, the Reading Check questions in *Harcourt Social Studies*, and the directed reading suggestions below.

- **Page 244** After students have read "You Are There," have them tell what they know about the kind of person Washington was.

- **Page 245** Have students look at the organizer to set a purpose for reading "The Second Continental Congress." Point out that they will need to list four actions taken by Congress. Students can fill in the information as they read or after reading.

- **Pages 246–247** Have students use the organizer to set a purpose for reading "The Battle of Bunker Hill." Point out that they will need to locate and record information about when and where the battle was fought, the names of the colonial commanders, and the outcome of the battle.

- **Page 248** Have students read "Trying for Peace" and complete the organizer by writing the date and a brief summary of the events that took place.

AFTER READING

Summarize Have students use their completed graphic organizers to summarize the lesson. Then have them compare their summaries to the lesson summary on page 248.

Review and Respond Work through the Review questions with students. If students need additional help with causes and effects, use Focus Skill Transparency 3.

Conduct an Interview Suggest that students reread passages in the lesson to find information that can help them write good questions and accurate answers. Remind students that Washington was chosen as the army's commander in chief partly because he had served in the French and Indian War. An interviewer might ask questions about his background and experience.

Leveled Readers Use the Leveled Readers and Procedure Card 5 to build fluency and comprehension.

Name _____ Date _____

Part A

Vocabulary Words	Additional Words
commander in chief	currency
earthwork	bill
olive branch	cannon
	retreat
	rebellion

Part B

1. The Second Continental Congress / formed an army / and chose George Washington / as the army's commander in chief.

2. Congress / also printed its own paper money, / which became known as / Continental currency.

3. Congress paid the soldiers / in bills called Continentals.

4. After sunset on June 16, 1775, / colonial commanders / ordered their soldiers / to build earthworks on Breed's Hill / near Boston.

5. The nearby city of Charlestown / was hit and set on fire / by cannons shooting from British ships / in the harbor.

6. On Breed's Hill, / the colonists / ran out of ammunition / and had to retreat.

7. Congress / sent King George III another petition, / which became known as the Olive Branch Petition / because it asked for peace.

8. King George III / promised to do / whatever was necessary / to crush the rebellion.

You ARE There Turn to Student Edition page 244. Practice reading aloud "You Are There" three times. Try to improve your reading each time. Record your best time on the line below.

Number of words ___70___ My Best Time _____ Words per Minute _____

Name _____ Date _____

Lesson Title: _____

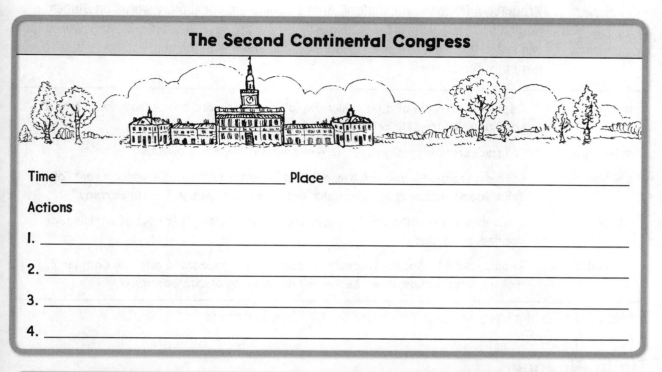

The Second Continental Congress

Time _____ Place _____

Actions

1. _____

2. _____

3. _____

4. _____

The Battle of Bunker Hill

Time _____ Actual place _____

Colonial commanders _____

Outcome _____

Trying for Peace

Time _____ Events _____

_____

LESSON 5 **Declaring Independence**

Vocabulary Strategies

Preteach Additional Vocabulary After teaching the Vocabulary words on Student Edition page 252, explain to students that there are several other important words they will see in this lesson. Use Procedure Card 1, along with the suggestions below, to introduce the words.

pamphlet	Display an example of a pamphlet. Explain that this word comes from the title of a Latin poem of the 12th century, *Pamphilus seu De Amore*.
self-evident	Tell students that synonyms for *self-evident* are *clear* and *obvious*.
unalienable	Point out the prefix *un-*, which means "not," and the suffix *-able*, which means "able." Tell students that *unalienable* means "not able to be changed or taken away."
pursuit	Students may know the word *pursue*. Explain that pursuit is the act of pursuing, or seeking, something.
confederation	Remind students that the Iroquois League, which they learned about in Chapter 2, was a confederation. Have them recall the meaning of *confederation*.

WORD CARDS To help teach the lesson vocabulary, use the Word Cards on pages 293–296.

Build Fluency

Use page 104 and the steps on Procedure Card 2 to reinforce vocabulary and build fluency. Read each vocabulary word aloud and have students repeat it. Then have students work in pairs to reread the words. Follow a similar procedure with the phrases and sentences. Continue to help students build fluency by having them reread "You Are There" in the Student Edition.

Text Comprehension

BEFORE READING

Preview the Lesson Guide students in previewing the lesson using Procedure Card 3. Point out the following features of the lesson on Student Edition pages 252–259.

- **Pages 252–253** Read the "What to Know" question and have students predict how the colonies will cut their ties with Britain. Preview the time line and the illustration of Thomas Paine and *Common Sense*. Have students locate on the time line the date that the pamphlet was published. Preview the illustration on page 253 and explain that Thomas Jefferson was chosen to write the words of the Declaration of Independence.

- **Pages 254–255** Preview the mural on page 254. Then have students examine the Primary Sources feature about the Declaration of Independence on page 255 and discuss the document-based question.

- **Pages 256–257** Preview and discuss the paintings of historic events. Point out that photography had not yet been invented in the 1700s, so works of art such as drawings and paintings are the only way for people today to see how people, places, and events may have looked.

- **Pages 258–259** Preview the illustrations of John Dickinson and the Articles of Confederation and of early money. Then preview the Review questions.

DURING READING

Build Comprehension of Expository Text Present the graphic organizer on page 105. Have students preview the organizer by filling in the lesson title and comparing the four main heads in the organizer with the matching subheads in the Student Edition pages 252–259. Tell students that the section subheads provide additional help with identifying important information. Use Procedure Card 4, the Reading Check questions in *Harcourt Social Studies,* and the directed reading suggestions below.

- **Page 252** After students have read "You Are There," discuss reasons the pamphlet might have given to make colonists want to be free of Britain.

- **Page 253** Have students read "Moving Toward Independence." Then guide them in filling in the information in the first box in the organizer.

- **Pages 254–255** After students have read "The Declaration of Independence," have them record information about the Declaration in the graphic organizer. Point out the key words *rights* and *grievances* in the section subhead on page 254.

- **Pages 256–259** Have students read "Congress Approves the Declaration" and fill in the next box in the organizer. Then they can read "Forming a New Government" and complete the organizer. Explain that students should write a brief summary of the weaknesses of the new plan of government. Point out the section subhead "Weaknesses of the Article" in the text.

AFTER READING

Summarize Have students use their completed graphic organizers to summarize the lesson. Then have them compare their summaries to the lesson summary on page 259.

Review and Respond Work through the Review questions with students. If students need additional help with causes and effects, use Focus Skill Transparency 3.

Write a Persuasive Letter Have students discuss the reasons that colonists had for wanting to become independent. Remind students of the difference between fact and opinion. Tell them to be sure and support their opinions with facts, including information and examples. Provide a model of the correct format for a business letter.

Leveled Readers Use the Leveled Readers and Procedure Card 5 to build fluency and comprehension.

Name _____ Date _____

Part A

Vocabulary Words	Additional Words
independence	pamphlet
resolution	self-evident
grievance	unalienable
declaration	pursuit
preamble	confederation

Part B

1. In his pamphlet *Common Sense,* / Thomas Paine wrote / that the colonists should rule themselves.

2. Many colonists / began to call for independence.

3. At the Second Continental Congress / on June 7, 1776, / Richard Henry Lee of Virginia / called for a resolution of independence.

4. In the preamble / to the Declaration of Independence, / Thomas Jefferson / explained why the colonies / had the right to form a new nation.

5. The next part of the Declaration / describes the colonists' main ideas about government / and says that certain truths / are self-evident.

6. Jefferson wrote / that people have / "certain unalienable Rights," / including "Life, / Liberty, / and the pursuit of Happiness."

7. The longest part of the Declaration / lists the colonists' grievances / against King George III and Parliament.

8. A committee headed by John Dickinson / wrote the country's first plan of government, / the Articles of Confederation.

You Are There **Turn to Student Edition page 252. Practice reading aloud "You Are There" three times. Try to improve your reading each time. Record your best time on the line below.**

Number of words ___73___ My Best Time _____ Words per Minute _____

Name _____ Date _____

Lesson Title: _____

Moving Toward Independence

Pamphlet title _____

Author _____

What people began to call for _____

What Lee called for _____

The Declaration of Independence

States that all people have certain

_____.

Longest part lists the colonists'

_____

States that the colonies were

_____ states

Congress Approves the Declaration

Accepted on _____

Signed by _____

_____

The Declaration has inspired people around the world to work for

_____ and _____.

Forming a New Government

Committee head _____ Plan _____

National legislature _____

Weaknesses _____

_____.

LESSON 1 **Americans and the Revolution**

Vocabulary Strategies

Preteach Additional Vocabulary After teaching the Vocabulary words on Student Edition page 268, explain to students that there are several other important words they will see in this lesson. Use Procedure Card 1, along with the suggestions below, to introduce the words.

personal	Tell students that *personal* and related words such as *person, impersonate,* and *personality* are from the Latin word *persona,* which means "person" and also "an actor's mask" or "a character in a play."
shortage	Students may be familiar with the concept of a water shortage due to a lack of rain. Explain that a shortage occurs when people run short of, or lack, something.
hoard	Discuss the idea that during a shortage, people may try to hoard, or save up and hide away, items that are in short supply.
recognized	Have students offer a familiar meaning or meanings. Then discuss the meaning in this context: "She became the first woman veteran to be recognized by Congress."
reward	Ask students to give examples of how people earn rewards, such as returning a lost wallet or rescuing someone from danger.
divided	Point out that things can be divided by cutting or breaking them into parts. Discuss how groups of people can be divided by having different ideas or opinions.

WORD CARDS To help teach the lesson vocabulary, use the Word Cards on pages 297–298.

Build Fluency

Use page 108 and the steps on Procedure Card 2 to reinforce vocabulary and build fluency. Read each vocabulary word aloud and have students repeat it. Then have students work in pairs to reread the words. Follow a similar procedure with the phrases and sentences. Continue to help students build fluency by having them reread "You Are There" in the Student Edition.

Text Comprehension

BEFORE READING

Preview the Lesson Guide students in previewing the lesson using Procedure Card 3. Point out the following features of the lesson on Student Edition pages 268–273.

• **Pages 268–269** Read the "What to Know" question. Ask students to imagine what it was like for American colonists to live with a war going on around them. Preview the time line and the illustration of British soldiers below the text, and have students read the Fast Fact. Preview the illustration of British soldiers burning a home, and discuss how the war affected the lives of these colonists.

- **Pages 270–271** Have students examine the graph of American imports from Britain and answer the question in the caption. Then preview the illustrations. Tell students that the women pictured on page 271 were some of the women they will read about who played important roles in the war.

- **Pages 272–273** Preview the illustrations of African American soldiers and of Thayendanegea. Explain that different groups of people had their own reasons for supporting either the Patriots or the British. Then preview the Review questions.

DURING READING

Build Comprehension of Expository Text Present the graphic organizer on page 109. Have students preview the organizer by filling in the lesson title and comparing the five main heads in the organizer with the matching subheads in the Student Edition pages 268–273. Tell students that the section subheads provide additional help with identifying important information. Use Procedure Card 4, the Reading Check questions in *Harcourt Social Studies,* and the directed reading suggestions below.

- **Page 268** After students have read "You Are There," discuss how the war has affected the lives of the people in the family it describes.

- **Pages 269–270** Have students read "Personal Hardships." Discuss and identify the main idea. Then have students write a main idea sentence for this section in the organizer. Tell students that the section subhead can help them identify an important personal hardship. Follow the same procedure for "Economic Hardships." Point out the arrows showing how these two sections of the lesson are related.

- **Pages 271–273** Point out in the organizer that the next three sections of the lesson are about particular groups of people and how each group was affected by the war. Have students read "Women and the War" and write a main idea sentence in the organizer. Follow the same procedure for "African Americans, Free and Enslaved," and for "People in the West."

AFTER READING

Summarize Have students use their completed graphic organizers to summarize the lesson. Then have them compare their summaries to the lesson summary on page 273.

Review and Respond Work through the Review questions with students. If students need additional help with causes and effects, use Focus Skill Transparency 3.

Write a Conversation Tell students that each speaker in the conversation should express an opinion and use facts to support that opinion. Explain that students can use information from this lesson and from previous lessons to support the speakers' opinions. Help students set up their written conversations in a script format. Students might like to take turns with a classmate reading aloud their completed conversations.

Leveled Readers Use the Leveled Readers and Procedure Card 5 to build fluency and comprehension.

Name _____ Date _____

Read aloud the words in Part A. Practice reading aloud the phrases and the sentences in Part B.

Part A

Vocabulary Words		Additional Words	
Patriot	inflation	personal	recognized
Loyalist	profiteering	shortage	reward
neutral	veteran	hoard	divided

Part B

1. Colonists who supported independence / called themselves Patriots, / while those who remained loyal to the king / were called Loyalists.

2. About one-third of the colonists / stayed neutral.

3. Colonists / faced personal and economic hardships / during the war.

4. British ships / set up blockades, / causing a shortage / of imported goods.

5. As the shortage of goods grew worse, / Americans also faced inflation.

6. Laws were passed / to limit profiteering / and to make it illegal / for people to hoard large amounts of goods.

7. Women / such as Margaret Corbin, / the first woman veteran to be recognized by Congress, / took on new roles.

8. Some enslaved African Americans / fought for the Continental Army, / and many were promised / their freedom as a reward.

9. Native Americans / were divided by the war.

YOU ARE THERE **Turn to Student Edition page 268. Practice reading aloud "You Are There" three times. Try to improve your reading each time. Record your best time on the line below.**

Number of words ___94___   My Best Time _____   Words per Minute _____

Name _____ Date _____

Lesson Title _____

Hardships

Personal Hardships

Main Idea _____

_____

_____

_____

Economic Hardships

Main Idea _____

_____

_____

_____

Groups of people affected by the war

Women and the War

Main Idea _____

_____

_____

_____

African Americans, Free and Enslaved

Main Idea _____

_____

_____

_____

People in the West

Main Idea _____

_____

_____

_____

LESSON 2 **Fighting for Independence**

Vocabulary Strategies

Preteach Additional Vocabulary After teaching the Vocabulary words on Student Edition page 274, explain to students that there are several other important words they will see in this lesson. Use Procedure Card 1, along with the suggestions below, to introduce the words.

everyday	Explain that the compound word *everyday* is an adjective, used to describe a noun, as in the phrase "his everyday clothes." However, in the phrase "the clothes he wears every day," *every* and *day* are written as two separate words.
experienced	Discuss the kinds of knowledge and skills an experienced soldier might have, and how a soldier would acquire them.
loss	Have students offer known meanings for *loss,* such as a win or loss in a game, or a loss of appetite. Then discuss this context: "The Americans suffered great losses at the Battle of Long Island."
rowboat	Have students identify the two shorter words *row* and *boat.* Point out the rowboat in the illustration on page 276 and have students describe how it moves through the water.

WORD CARDS To help teach the lesson vocabulary, use the Word Cards on pages 297–298.

Build Fluency

Use page 112 and the steps on Procedure Card 2 to reinforce vocabulary and build fluency. Read each vocabulary word aloud and have students repeat it. Then have students work in pairs to reread the words. Follow a similar procedure with the phrases and sentences. Continue to help students build fluency by having them reread "You Are There" in the Student Edition.

Text Comprehension

BEFORE READING

Preview the Lesson Guide students in previewing the lesson using Procedure Card 3. Point out the following features of the lesson on Student Edition pages 274–281.

- **Pages 274–275** Read the "What to Know" question. Have students recall important events that led up to the Revolutionary War. Preview the time line and illustrations. Have students compare the British soldier and American soldier and answer the question in the caption.

- **Pages 276–277** Preview the paintings and the illustration of the medal. Tell students that the battle that followed the crossing of the Delaware was the Battle of Trenton, an American victory. Have students determine from the caption on page 277 the outcome of the Battle of Saratoga. Then have them locate the dates for both of these battles on the time line on page 274.

- **Pages 278–281** Preview the illustration of the march to Valley Forge and the portrait of von Steuben. On page 280, preview the portrait of Jorge Farragut and the Review questions. Call attention to the biography of Bernardo de Gálvez on page 281. Tell students that Gálvez was a leader who helped the Americans during the American Revolution.

DURING READING

Build Comprehension of Expository Text Present the graphic organizer on page 113. Have students preview the organizer by filling in the lesson title and comparing the five main heads in the organizer with the matching subheads in the Student Edition pages 274–280. Tell students that the section subheads provide additional help with identifying important information. Use Procedure Card 4, the Reading Check questions in *Harcourt Social Studies*, and the directed reading suggestions below.

- **Page 274** After students read "You Are There," discuss the hardships that Washington's army faced. Tell students that they will read more about the Marquis de Lafayette in the lesson.

- **Page 275** Have students have read "Comparing Armies." Then guide them in writing four details about each army in the graphic organizer.

- **Pages 276–277** After students have read "Early Battles in the North," have them discuss and fill in the information in the organizer. Follow the same procedure for "An Important Victory."

- **Pages 278–280** Have students read "Winter at Valley Forge." Tell them to write in the organizer a brief description of conditions at Valley Forge and the names of two people from other countries who helped Washington and the Continental Army. Point out that the section subheads can help students locate this information. Then have students read "Contributions from Other Nations" and complete the organizer by listing four contributions.

AFTER READING

Summarize Have students use their completed graphic organizers to summarize the lesson. Then have them compare their summaries to the lesson summary on page 280.

Review and Respond Work through the Review questions with students. If students need additional help with causes and effects, use Focus Skill Transparency 3.

Write a Speech Suggest that students reread sections of the lesson and make notes about events that might have cheered the soldiers at Valley Forge, such as battles they had already won, and help they were receiving. Students can practice their speeches by reading to a partner or by making and playing back a recording.

Leveled Readers Use the Leveled Readers and Procedure Card 5 to build fluency and comprehension.

Name _____ Date _____

DIRECTIONS **Read aloud the words in Part A. Practice reading aloud the phrases and the sentences in Part B.**

Part A

Vocabulary Words		Additional Words
enlist	turning point	everyday
mercenary	negotiate	experienced
campaign		loss
		rowboat

Part B

1. When George Washington / took command of the Continental Army, / the soldiers had no uniforms / —only their everyday clothes.

2. Many of the soldiers / were farmers / who had enlisted in the army.

3. The British army, / one of the most powerful armies in the world, / was made up of experienced soldiers / and mercenaries.

4. The Americans / suffered great losses / at the Battle of Long Island / in the spring of 1776.

5. On Christmas night, / 1776, / Patriot troops / crossed the icy Delaware River in rowboats / and won a victory / that gave them hope for the future.

6. In 1777, / the British army / planned a new campaign, / but the British loss at Saratoga / was a turning point in the war.

7. While the war raged on / in North America, / Benjamin Franklin / was in France, / negotiating with the French government.

 Turn to Student Edition page 274. Practice reading aloud "You Are There" three times. Try to improve your reading each time. Record your best time on the line below.

Number of words ___60___ My Best Time _____ Words per Minute _____

Name _____ Date _____

Lesson Title _____

Comparing Armies

Continental Army	British Army
_____	_____
_____	_____
_____	_____
_____	_____

Early Battles in the North

Where	Outcome
_____	_____
_____	_____

An Important Victory

Where _____

Why it was important

_____

Winter at Valley Forge

What it was like _____

Who helped _____, _____

Contributions from Other Nations

1. _____

2. _____

3. _____

4. _____

LESSON 3 **Winning Independence**

Vocabulary Strategies

Preteach Additional Vocabulary After teaching the Vocabulary words on Student Edition page 284, explain to students that there are several other important words they will see in this lesson. Use Procedure Card 1, along with the suggestions below, to introduce the words.

hanged	Tell students that *hanged* is often used as the past tense of *hang* in the context of executing a human being by hanging. In other contexts, we often use *hung*, as in "We hung up our jackets."
volunteer	Explain that a volunteer is a person who offers to do a job that he or she is not required to do.
betrayed	Tell students that *betray* comes from the Latin *tradere*, "to hand over." The words *traitor* and *treason* are from the same root.
surrounded	Explain that *surround* means "to encircle."
accept	Students may know this word in the context of accepting a gift. Explain that it can also mean to allow or approve of something.
retired	Ask whether students know of an older family member or acquaintance who has retired from his or her job.

WORD CARDS To help teach the lesson vocabulary, use the Word Cards on pages 297–300.

Build Fluency

Use page 116 and the steps on Procedure Card 2 to reinforce vocabulary and build fluency. Read each vocabulary word aloud and have students repeat it. Then have students work in pairs to reread the words. Follow a similar procedure with the phrases and sentences. Continue to help students build fluency by having them reread "You Are There" in the Student Edition.

Text Comprehension

BEFORE READING

Preview the Lesson Guide students in previewing the lesson using Procedure Card 3. Point out the following features of the lesson on Student Edition pages 284–289.

- **Pages 284–285** Read the "What to Know" question. Have students recall what they learned in Lesson 2 about the fight for independence, and ask them to predict how the Americans will win the war. Preview the time line and the illustrations of a naval battle and of Mary McCauley, who carried water to American troops during a battle.

- **Pages 286–287** Have students examine the map of major battles and answer the map skill question. Then preview the illustration of the Battle of Cowpens and have students locate Cowpens on the map.

- **Pages 288–289** Preview the illustrations of the surrender at Yorktown and of Washington retiring. Have students use their prior knowledge to predict what Washington will do after the war. Then preview the Review questions.

DURING READING

Build Comprehension of Expository Text Present the graphic organizer on page 117. Have students preview the organizer by filling in the lesson title and comparing the three main heads in the organizer with the matching subheads in the Student Edition pages 284–289. Tell students that the section subheads provide additional help with identifying important information. Use Procedure Card 4, the Reading Check questions in *Harcourt Social Studies*, and the directed reading suggestions below.

- **Page 284** After students have read "You Are There," explain that John Paul Jones was a hero of the Revolution. Have students tell why he might have been called a hero.

- **Page 285** Have students look at the graphic organizer to set a purpose for reading "Revolutionary Heroes." Either as they read or after reading the section, students can fill in the names of four heroes and tell what each did.

- **Pages 286–287** Follow a similar procedure for "The War Moves" as for the previous section, having students record in the chart the places where four battles took place in the South and the outcome of each battle. Point out that the section subhead "Battles in the South" in the text matches a subhead in the organizer. Tell students that if they are not sure from the text which side won a battle, they can also refer to the map on page 286.

- **Pages 288–289** Have students read "The War Ends" and complete the organizer. Point out that the three subheads in the organizer match the section subheads in the text and can help students locate information.

AFTER READING

Summarize Have students use their completed graphic organizers to summarize the lesson. Then have them compare their summaries to the lesson summary on page 289.

Review and Respond Work through the Review questions with students. If students need additional help with causes and effects, use Focus Skill Transparency 3.

Draw a Medal Tell students to choose one of the Patriot heroes they read about in this lesson. Explain that students will then need to choose a symbol that represents the hero's contribution and will also make an attractive design for a medal. Tell students they may include words on their medals.

Leveled Readers Use the Leveled Readers and Procedure Card 5 to build fluency and comprehension.

DIRECTIONS   Read aloud the words in Part A. Practice reading aloud the
phrases and the sentences in Part B.

Part A

Vocabulary Words	Additional Words	
civilian	hanged	surrounded
traitor	volunteer	accept
	betrayed	retired

Part B

1. During the Revolutionary War, / the Continental Army and Navy /
   received help / from many civilians.

2. Nathan Hale / was a teacher / who served as an American spy /
   and was hanged by the British.

3. As word of the fight for freedom spread, / more volunteers came.

4. Benedict Arnold, / a former Continental Army officer / who had become
   a traitor, / led British attacks on Virginia towns.

5. He betrayed his country / because he was not happy / with his rank
   and salary.

6. At the Battle of Yorktown, / in 1781, / British General Charles Cornwallis /
   finally gave up / after being surrounded for weeks.

7. The Americans who went to Paris / to negotiate a peace treaty / wanted
   Britain to accept / American independence.

8. After British troops left the country, / George Washington / retired as
   leader of the army, / telling Congress / that his work was done.

You ARE THERE   **Turn to Student Edition page 284. Practice reading aloud "You Are
There" three times. Try to improve your reading each time. Record your
best time on the line below.**

Number of words ___57___   My Best Time _____   Words per Minute _____

Name _____ Date _____

Lesson Title _____

Revolutionary Heroes

Hero	What he or she did
_____	_____
_____	_____
_____	_____
_____	_____

The War Moves

Battles in the South	Outcome
_____	_____
_____	_____
_____	_____
_____	_____

The War Ends

Victory at Yorktown

When _____ What happened _____

_____

_____

The Treaty of Paris

When it was signed _____ What it did _____

_____

After the War

What happened _____

LESSON 4 **Effects of the War**

Vocabulary Strategies

Preteach Additional Vocabulary After teaching the Vocabulary words on Student Edition page 292, explain to students that there are several other important words they will see in this lesson. Use Procedure Card 1, along with the suggestions below, to introduce the words.

press	Discuss the phrase "freedom of the press." Explain that this meaning for *press* developed from the name of the printing press, which made it possible to publish newspapers.
antislavery	Identify the familiar word *slavery* and the prefix *anti-,* which means "against." Students may know other words with this prefix, such as *antiwar* or *antibacterial.*
sued	Point out the *-ed* ending. Tell students that to sue is to seek justice in a court of law. The word *sue* is from the Latin root *sequi,* meaning "to follow." Other words with this root include *sequence* and *sequel.*
acre	Tell students that an acre is a unit of area that is used to measure land. Students may want to look up the number of square feet in an acre.

WORD CARDS To help teach the lesson vocabulary, use the Word Cards on pages 299–300.

Build Fluency

Use page 120 and the steps on Procedure Card 2 to reinforce vocabulary and build fluency. Read each vocabulary word aloud and have students repeat it. Then have students work in pairs to reread the words. Follow a similar procedure with the phrases and sentences. Continue to help students build fluency by having them reread "You Are There" in the Student Edition.

Text Comprehension

BEFORE READING

Preview the Lesson Guide students in previewing the lesson using Procedure Card 3. Point out the following features of the lesson on Student Edition pages 292–297.

- **Pages 292–293** Read the "What to Know" question. Explain that one immediate effect of the war was freedom from Britain, but becoming a new nation brought about many other changes as well. Preview the time line and the illustrations of antislavery artifacts. Tell students that a stronger antislavery movement was one result of the American Revolution.

- **Pages 294–295** Preview the illustration of settlers moving west and the map of the Northwest Territory. Have students answer the map skill question.

- **Pages 296–297** Have students examine the illustrated time line on these pages. Explain that Native Americans' lives changed greatly after the Revolution. Preview the Review questions on page 297.

Build Comprehension of Expository Text Present the graphic organizer on page 121. Have students preview the organizer by filling in the lesson title and comparing the four main heads in the organizer with the matching subheads in the Student Edition pages 292–297. Tell students that the section subheads provide additional help with identifying important information. Use Procedure Card 4, the Reading Check questions in *Harcourt Social Studies*, and the directed reading suggestions below.

• **Page 292** After students have read "You Are There," have them state in their own words the viewpoints expressed by the speakers. Discuss the reasons that these people give to support their opinions.

• **Page 293** Have students look at the organizer to set a purpose for reading "New Ideas." Either as they read or after reading the section, students can write in the organizer what the states began doing by 1776, what the Declaration of Independence said about people's rights, and what some people believed should happen.

• **Pages 294–295** Have students read "Western Settlements" and fill in the next section of the organizer. Help students see how the section subheads in the text can help them locate information. Then students can read "The Northwest Territory" and fill in that section of the organizer.

• **Pages 296–297** After students have read "Battles for Land" they can complete the graphic organizer by writing the names of the two groups who fought for land in the Northwest Territory and what happened as a result.

AFTER READING

Summarize Have students use their completed graphic organizers to summarize the lesson. Then have them compare their summaries to the lesson summary on page 297.

Review and Respond Work through the Review questions with students. If students need additional help with causes and effects, use Focus Skill Transparency 3.

Write a News Article Remind students that newspaper articles tell Who, When, Where, What, and Why. Suggest that they reread the section of the lesson about Elizabeth Freeman's court case and make notes for each of the five W's. Then students can write articles based on their notes.

Leveled Readers Use the Leveled Readers and Procedure Card 5 to build fluency and comprehension.

Name _____ Date _____

DIRECTIONS Read aloud the words in Part A. Practice reading aloud the phrases and the sentences in Part B.

Part A

Vocabulary Words	Additional Words
abolitionist	press
abolish	antislavery
territory	sued
ordinance	acre

Part B

1. By 1776, / the states had begun to write / their own constitutions, / giving people basic freedoms, / including freedom of the press.

2. In 1775, / Quakers in Philadelphia / had started the country's first abolitionist group.

3. Antislavery feelings grew / after the Declaration was approved.

4. In Massachusetts, / an enslaved woman named Elizabeth Freeman / sued to be free.

5. Massachusetts / abolished slavery in 1783, / and over time, / other northern states / also abolished slavery.

6. After the Revolutionary war ended, / the United States / paid soldiers with land, / and some soldiers / were given hundreds of acres.

7. In 1787, / Congress passed the Northwest Ordinance, / a plan for governing the Northwest Territory / and for forming new states from its lands.

8. Native American forces / soundly defeated United States soldiers / but later gave up most of their land / in the Northwest Territory.

You Are There Turn to Student Edition page 292. Practice reading aloud "You Are There" three times. Try to improve your reading each time. Record your best time on the line below.

Number of words ___61___ My Best Time _____ Words per Minute _____

Name _____ Date _____

Lesson Title: _____

New Ideas

What states did _____

What the Declaration said _____

What some people believed _____

Western Settlements

What the United States had won _____

Who moved west _____

Who lived in the west _____

Fast growing areas _____

The Northwest Territory

Where it was _____

When _____ What happened _____

When _____ What happened _____

Battles for Land

Who fought for land _____

What happened _____

_____

LESSON 1 # The Constitutional Convention

Vocabulary Strategies

Preteach Additional Vocabulary After teaching the Vocabulary words on Student Edition page 316, explain to students that there are several other important words they will see in this lesson. Use Procedure Card 1, along with the suggestions below, to introduce the words.

debt	Explain that a debt is an amount of money that someone owes. We say that someone goes into debt when he or she owes money. Point out that the letter *b* is silent in this word.
convention	Tell students that this word is from the Latin *convenire,* "to come together." One kind of convention is a meeting of delegates to discuss important issues. A related word is *convene.*
supreme	Have students substitute the synonym *highest* for *supreme* in this sentence: "The Constitution of the United States is the supreme law of the land."
house	Explain that a special meaning for the word *house* is "a part of a government." The house can be the group of people who make up that part of the government, or the building where they meet.
approve	Discuss the meaning of *approve* in this context: "Both houses had to approve a bill before it became a law."

WORD CARDS To help teach the lesson vocabulary, use the Word Cards on pages 301–302.

Build Fluency

Use page 124 and the steps on Procedure Card 2 to reinforce vocabulary and build fluency. Read each vocabulary word aloud and have students repeat it. Then have students work in pairs to reread the words. Follow a similar procedure with the phrases and sentences. Continue to help students build fluency by having them reread "You Are There" in the Student Edition.

Text Comprehension

BEFORE READING

Preview the Lesson Guide students in previewing the lesson using Procedure Card 3. Point out the following features of the lesson on Student Edition pages 316–322.

- **Pages 316–317** Read the "What to Know" question. Have students recall what they have learned about the first government of the United States, formed under the Articles of Confederation. Preview the time line and the illustrations. Explain that Shays's Rebellion made some people think that the national government was not strong enough to keep order.

- **Pages 318–319** Have students examine the map on page 318 and use the distance scale to answer the map skill question. Discuss how long it must have taken delegates from various states to get to Philadelphia. Then preview the illustration of the Pennsylvania State House on page 319.

- **Pages 320–321** Preview the illustration of the Constitutional Convention, and have students identify delegates. Discuss the question in the caption. Then preview the illustration of an African American woman on page 321.
- **Pages 322–323** Have students examine the graph and answer the question in the caption. Preview the Review questions on page 322, and the biography of Gouverneur Morris on page 323.

DURING READING

Build Comprehension of Expository Text Present the graphic organizer on page 125. Have students preview the organizer by filling in the lesson title and comparing the five main heads in the organizer with the matching subheads in the Student Edition pages 316–322. Tell students that the section subheads provide additional help with identifying important information. Use Procedure Card 4, the Reading Check questions in *Harcourt Social Studies*, and the directed reading suggestions below.

- **Page 316** After students have read "You Are There," discuss why this meeting in 1787 was so important.
- **Pages 317–318** Have students read "Reasons for Change" and write information in the first box of the organizer. Point out the subhead "Ideas for Change" that matches the section subhead in the text. Next, have students read "The Work Begins" and fill in the second box. Point out that students will need to identify two major decisions that delegates made.
- **Pages 319–320** After students have read "A Major Debate," point out that the subheads "The Virginia Plan" and "The New Jersey Plan" match the section subheads in the text and can help students locate information they need as they fill in the organizer. Then have students read "Working Together" and write information about the Great Compromise in the next box of the organizer.
- **Pages 321–322** Students should read "Compromises on Slavery" and complete the last box of the organizer. Tell them to name the areas of the country that had different points of view on slavery, write a very brief description of the Three-Fifths Compromise, and write the year that was agreed upon for banning states from bringing in slaves from other countries.

AFTER READING

Summarize Have students use their completed graphic organizers to summarize the lesson. Then have them compare their summaries to the lesson summary on page 322.

Review and Respond Work through the Review questions with students. Use Focus Skill Transparency 4, Draw Conclusions, to help students draw conclusions based on information in the lesson.

Write a Persuasive Letter Discuss what students might tell their families about how and why the delegates reached compromises on important issues. Have students identify a point of view that they would want to persuade their family to accept. Remind students to use the correct form for a friendly letter.

Leveled Readers Use the Leveled Readers and Procedure Card 5 to build fluency and comprehension.

Name _____ Date _____

Read aloud the words in Part A. Practice reading aloud the
phrases and the sentences in Part B.

Part A

Vocabulary Words	Additional Words
arsenal	debt
federal system	convention
republic	supreme
compromise	house
bill	approve

Part B

1. During the 1780s, / state courts took away people's farms / or sent people to prison / when the people could not repay / their debts.

2. Because there was no national army, / the governor / had to send the state militia / when farmers tried to take over / a Massachusetts arsenal.

3. The Constitutional Convention / met in Philadelphia / in 1787 / to try to improve the Articles of Confederation.

4. The delegates / finally agreed / to strengthen the existing federal system.

5. The Constitution of the United States / became the supreme law of the land / and helped found / the American republic.

6. After arguing for weeks / about how the states / should be represented in Congress, / the delegates realized that each side / would have to compromise.

7. A committee of delegates / suggested a two-house Congress, / in which either house / could present a bill.

8. On July 16, 1787, / the delegates approved / the Great Compromise.

YOU ARE THERE Turn to Student Edition page 316. Practice reading aloud "You Are There" three times. Try to improve your reading each time. Record your best time on the line below.

Number of words ____72____ My Best Time _____ Words per Minute _____

Name _____ Date _____

Lesson Title _____

Reasons for Change

What people thought _____

_____

_____

Ideas for Change

Date of convention _____

Goal _____

The Work Begins

Creating the Constitution

Major decisions

1. _____

2. _____

Helped found the

_____

A Major Debate

Disagreement about _____

The Virginia Plan Number of representatives based on _____

The New Jersey Plan Each state would be _____.

Working Together

The Great Compromise

One house based on _____

In the other house _____

Compromises on Slavery

Different Points of View Between _____

The Three-Fifths Compromise _____

A Continuing Issue Slave trade with other countries banned after _____

LESSON 2 **Three Branches of Government**

Vocabulary Strategies

Preteach Additional Vocabulary After teaching the Vocabulary words on Student Edition page 328, explain to students that there are several other important words they will see in this lesson. Use Procedure Card 1, along with the suggestions below, to introduce the words.

propose	Tell students that synonyms for *propose* include *suggest* and *recommend*.
majority	Call attention to the root word *major*, which means "greater" in Latin. Divide students into two groups of unequal size. Identify the larger group as the majority because it contains more than half the total number of students.
elector	Point out the root word *elect* and suffix *-or*. Explain that *-or* means "person or thing that does," so electors are people who elect. Other words with this suffix include *actor* and *inventor*.
override	Have students identify the two shorter words, *over* and *ride*, that make up this compound word. Discuss situations in which a teacher might override a decision made by students.

WORD CARDS To help teach the lesson vocabulary, use the Word Cards on pages 301–304.

Build Fluency

Use page 128 and the steps on Procedure Card 2 to reinforce vocabulary and build fluency. Read each vocabulary word aloud and have students repeat it. Then have students work in pairs to reread the words. Follow a similar procedure with the phrases and sentences. Continue to help students build fluency by having them reread "You Are There" in the Student Edition.

Text Comprehension

BEFORE READING

Preview the Lesson Guide students in previewing the lesson using Procedure Card 3. Point out the following features of the lesson on Student Edition pages 328–333.

- **Pages 328–329** Read the "What to Know" question. Have students use the question to set a purpose for reading the lesson. Preview the illustration of delegates at the Constitutional Convention on page 328, and the photograph of the National Archives on page 329.

- **Pages 330–331** Have students examine the illustration of Washington, D.C., and discuss the question about monuments and memorials in the caption.

- **Pages 332–333** Preview the illustration of the Supreme Court building on page 332, and have students locate this building in the illustration on pages 330–331. Preview the photograph and the Review questions on page 333.

Build Comprehension of Expository Text Present the graphic organizer on page 129. Have students preview the organizer by filling in the lesson title and comparing the four main heads in the organizer with the matching subheads in the Student Edition pages 328–333. Tell students that the section subheads provide additional help with identifying important information. Use Procedure Card 4, the Reading Check questions in *Harcourt Social Studies*, and the directed reading suggestions below.

- **Page 328** After students have read "You Are There," have them recall briefly what they learned about Gouverneur Morris from his biography in Lesson 1.

- **Page 329** Have students read "The Preamble" and record in the graphic organizer the opening words of the Preamble, the purpose of the Constitution as stated in the Preamble, and the basic principles on which the new government would be based. Point out that the section subhead in the text, "The Purpose of the Constitution," can help students locate some of this information.

- **Pages 330–333** Point out the subheads ARTICLE I, ARTICLE II, and ARTICLE III in the organizer that show which article of the Constitution describes each branch of government. Have students read "The Legislative Branch," discuss what this branch is and does, and then write the information in the organizer. Follow a similar procedure for "The Executive Branch" and "The Judicial Branch."

Summarize Have students use their completed graphic organizers to summarize the lesson. Then have them compare their summaries to the lesson summary on page 333.

Review and Respond If students need additional help with drawing conclusions, use Focus Skill Transparency 4.

Write a Set of Rules In a group discussion, help students identify some ideas in the Constitution that could apply to the classroom, such as fairness to all and protecting the rights of individuals. Then have students work with partners or in small groups to write their classroom rules. Students can share their rules with other groups and explain how each rule illustrates an idea or ideas in the Constitution.

Leveled Readers Use the Leveled Readers and Procedure Card 5 to build fluency and comprehension.

Name _____ Date _____

DIRECTIONS Read aloud the words in Part A. Practice reading aloud the
phrases and the sentences in Part B.

Part A

Vocabulary Words		Additional Words
separation of powers	impeach	propose
legislative branch	judicial branch	majority
executive branch	justice	elector
electoral college	amendment	override
veto	rule of law	

Part B

1. The delegates to the Constitutional Convention / created a separation of powers / to keep any one branch / from controlling the government.

2. Article I of the Constitution / explains the legislative branch.

3. Either house of Congress / could propose most bills.

4. For a bill to become law, / a majority in each house / must vote for it.

5. Article II / gives the executive branch / the power to enforce laws.

6. Citizens vote / for a group of electors, / called the electoral college, / who vote for the President.

7. The President / can veto bills passed by Congress, / but Congress can then override the President's veto / with a two-thirds vote.

8. Congress / can impeach a President / who does not take care / that the laws are faithfully executed.

9. The Supreme Court justices / and the judicial branch of government / help make sure / we have rule of law.

10. The delegates agreed / on how to / add amendments to the Constitution.

You ARE THERE **Turn to Student Edition page 328. Practice reading aloud "You Are There" three times. Try to improve your reading each time. Record your best time on the line below.**

Number of words ___74___ My Best Time _____ Words per Minute _____

Name _____ Date _____

Lesson Title _____

The Preamble

First words _____ . . .

Purpose of the Constitution _____

Principles _____

ARTICLE I
The Legislative Branch

Reason for three branches _____

Two houses

1. _____

2. _____

ARTICLE II
The Executive Branch

Chief executive _____

Powers

1. _____

2. _____

3. _____

ARTICLE III
The Judicial Branch

Created a _____ Highest court _____

Has the power to _____

_____

Only way to restore a law _____

Citizens could add _____ to the Constitution.

LESSON 3 **The Bill of Rights**

Vocabulary Strategies

Preteach Additional Vocabulary After teaching the Vocabulary words on Student Edition page 334, explain to students that there are several other important words they will see in this lesson. Use Procedure Card 1, along with the suggestions below, to introduce the words.

press	Discuss known meanings. Explain that *press* is often used as a name for the news media, including newspapers, magazines, radio and TV news.
house	Tell students that this word is a verb and a homograph of the familiar word *house*, meaning "home." This word, pronounced *howz*, means "to provide with living quarters or shelter."
minority	Have students recall the meaning of *majority*. Then discuss these sentences: "The Bill of Rights protects the rights of people in the minority. The majority cannot take their rights away."

WORD CARDS To help teach the lesson vocabulary, use the Word Cards on pages 303–304.

Build Fluency

Use page 132 and the steps on Procedure Card 2 to reinforce vocabulary and build fluency. Read each vocabulary word aloud and have students repeat it. Then have students work in pairs to reread the words. Follow a similar procedure with the phrases and sentences. Continue to help students build fluency by having them reread "You Are There" in the Student Edition.

Text Comprehension

BEFORE READING

Preview the Lesson Guide students in previewing the lesson using Procedure Card 3. Point out the following features of the lesson on Student Edition pages 334–339.

• **Pages 334–335** Read the "What to Know" question. Preview the time line and the illustration. Help students identify some of the delegates pictured in the illustration, such as George Washington and Benjamin Franklin. Have students read the Fast Fact.

• **Pages 336–337** Have students examine the table showing votes to ratify the Constitution, and look at the illustration of Alexander Hamilton on page 336. Discuss the question in the caption. Then preview the illustration on page 337.

• **Pages 338–339** Preview the illustrations of the postage stamp honoring Benjamin Banneker and the national capital at Washington, D.C., under construction. On page 339, preview the portrait of John Adams and the Review questions.

Build Comprehension of Expository Text Present the graphic organizer on page 133. Have students preview the organizer by filling in the lesson title and comparing the four main heads in the organizer with the matching subheads in the Student Edition pages 334–339. Tell students that the section subheads provide additional help with identifying important information. Use Procedure Card 4, the Reading Check questions in *Harcourt Social Studies,* and the directed reading suggestions below.

- **Page 334** After students have read "You Are There," have them note the date and place of the conversation with Benjamin Franklin. Be sure they understand that Franklin is talking about the new Constitution.

- **Page 335** Have students read and discuss "The Struggle to Ratify" and identify the issues that created arguments at the state conventions. Then have students write the information in the first box of the organizer.

- **Page 336** After students have read "The Vote of Approval," be sure they understand that only nine states needed to ratify the Constitution but that all thirteen states eventually did approve it. Then have students record information in the organizer.

- **Pages 337–339** Have students read "The Bill of Rights." Discuss how each of the amendments helps protect the rights of the people. Then have students write information in the organizer. After reading "The New Government," students can complete the final box in the organizer.

Summarize Have students use their completed graphic organizers to summarize the lesson. Then have them compare their summaries to the lesson summary on page 339.

Review and Respond If students need additional help with drawing conclusions, use Focus Skill Transparency 4.

Make a Poster Provide or help students locate a copy of the Bill of Rights that lists all ten amendments. Suggest that students design their posters on scrap paper and plan carefully so that everything will fit and look attractive. Provide posterboard and markers or other appropriate art materials.

Leveled Readers Use the Leveled Readers and Procedure Card 5 to build fluency and comprehension.

Name _____ Date _____

DIRECTIONS Read aloud the words in Part A. Practice reading aloud the phrases and the sentences in Part B.

Part A

Vocabulary Words		Additional Words
ratify	Cabinet	press
Federalists	political party	house
Anti-Federalists		minority
due process of law		
reserved powers		

Part B

1. Before the Constitution could become / the law of the land, / 9 of the 13 states / had to ratify it.

2. Those citizens who favored the Constitution / were called Federalists.

3. The Anti-Federalists / feared that the national government / would have too much power.

4. The First Amendment / protects freedom of the press.

5. The government / cannot make people house soldiers / in peacetime.

6. The Fifth through Eighth Amendments / deal with due process of law.

7. The Tenth Amendment / says that the reserved powers / belong to the states / or to the people.

8. The Bill of Rights / protects the rights / of people in the minority.

9. An argument / between two members of George Washington's Cabinet / led to / the rise of political parties.

YOU ARE THERE Turn to Student Edition page 334. Practice reading aloud "You Are There" three times. Try to improve your reading each time. Record your best time on the line below.

Number of words ___72___ My Best Time _____ Words per Minute _____

Name _____ Date _____

Lesson Title _____

The Struggle to Ratify

What some delegates wanted

1. _____

2. _____

What supporters promised

_____

_____

_____

The Vote of Approval

First state to ratify _____

What Federalists wanted _____

_____

What Anti-Federalists feared

_____

_____

When ninth state ratified _____

The Bill of Rights

How many amendments _____

Purpose of the Bill of Rights

_____

_____

Added to Constitution in _____

Reserved powers belong to

_____

The New Government

First President _____

Became President in _____

Federal government moved to

_____

When _____

Second President

_____

LESSON 4 **A Constitutional Democracy**

Vocabulary Strategies

Preteach Additional Vocabulary After teaching the Vocabulary words on Student Edition page 342, explain to students that there are several other important words they will see in this lesson. Use Procedure Card 1, along with the suggestions below, to introduce the words.

empower	Point out the familiar word *power*. Discuss this context sentence: "The Constitution had to empower the federal government, or give it enough power to govern the nation."
misusing	Have students identify the elements of this word: prefix *mis-*, meaning "wrong" or "wrongly," base word *use*, and ending *-ing*. Other words with the same prefix include *misspell* and *misbehave*.
unconstitutional	Identify the word *constitution*, the prefix *un-*, and suffix *-al*. Explain that something that is not allowed by the constitution is unconstitutional.
preserve	Tell students that *preserve* is from the Latin root *servare*, "to keep or guard." To preserve something is to protect it or to keep it safe. Other words with this root include *reserve* and *conserve*.

WORD CARDS To help teach the lesson vocabulary, use the Word Cards on pages 303–306.

Build Fluency

Use page 136 and the steps on Procedure Card 2 to reinforce vocabulary and build fluency. Read each vocabulary word aloud and have students repeat it. Then have students work in pairs to reread the words. Follow a similar procedure with the phrases and sentences. Continue to help students build fluency by having them reread "You Are There" in the Student Edition.

Text Comprehension

BEFORE READING

Preview the Lesson Guide students in previewing the lesson using Procedure Card 3. Point out the following features of the lesson on Student Edition pages 342–349.

• **Pages 342–343** Read the "What to Know" question. Explain that the Constitution empowers the federal government but also limits that power so that the states have power, too. Preview the time line and illustration on page 342 and the photograph of the President and other leaders on page 343.

• **Pages 344–345** Have students examine the diagram of checks and balances on page 344 and answer the question in the caption. Then have students examine the chart on page 345. Explain that the shared powers belong to both the federal and state governments. For instance, the federal government collects taxes, but state governments can collect their own taxes. Discuss the caption question.

- **Pages 346–349** Preview the photographs on pages 346 and 347. On page 348, have students read Children in History and discuss the Make It Relevant question. Then preview the photograph and the Review questions on page 349.

DURING READING

Build Comprehension of Expository Text Present the graphic organizer on page 137. Have students preview the organizer by filling in the lesson title and comparing the six main heads in the organizer with the matching subheads in the Student Edition pages 342–349. Tell students that the section subheads provide additional help with identifying important information. Use Procedure Card 4, the Reading Check questions in *Harcourt Social Studies,* and the directed reading suggestions below.

- **Page 342** After students have read "You Are There," have them tell whether they would like to live in a place with no government and why or why not.

- **Page 343** Have students read and discuss "Sharing Powers." Guide them in writing in the first box of the organizer how the Constitution allows the branches of government to share powers and the reason for doing so.

- **Page 344** After students have read "Checks and Balances," discuss how the system works and have students give examples. Then have students record information in the organizer.

- **Pages 345–347** Have students read "State Powers" and write in the organizer a general statement about the powers that the Constitution gives to the states or the people. Then have students read "State and Local Governments" and record information in the organizer. Follow the same procedure for "Rights and Responsibilities."

- **Pages 348–349** After students have read "Being a Citizen," they can complete the organizer by writing two other responsibilities of citizens, in addition to voting.

AFTER READING

Summarize Have students use their completed graphic organizers to summarize the lesson. Then have them compare their summaries to the lesson summary on page 349.

Review and Respond If students need additional help with drawing conclusions, use Focus Skill Transparency 4.

Write a Persuasive Letter Discuss with students some issues that are important to your community. You may want to provide articles from your local newspaper that address specific issues. You will also want to help students decide what official to write to and how to locate that person's name and address. Remind students of rules for persuasive writing and of proper form for a business letter.

Leveled Readers Use the Leveled Readers and Procedure Card 5 to build fluency and comprehension.

Name _____ Date _____

DIRECTIONS Read aloud the words in Part A. Practice reading aloud the phrases and the sentences in Part B.

Part A

Vocabulary Words		Additional Words
checks and balances	public agenda	empower
union	suffrage	misusing
popular sovereignty	civic virtue	unconstitutional
democracy	naturalization	preserve

Part B

1. The Constitution / had to empower the federal government.

2. The system of checks and balances / keeps any one branch / from becoming too powerful / or misusing its authority.

3. The Supreme Court / can declare new laws / or government actions / unconstitutional.

4. The system of checks and balances / was developed / in the hope that it would allow the nation / to form "a more perfect union."

5. The writers of the Constitution / were careful to preserve / the powers of the states.

6. Our democracy / is based on the principle / of popular sovereignty.

7. Women / were not given suffrage / in national elections / until 1920.

8. One responsibility of citizens / is to act with civic virtue.

9. Immigrants / can become legal citizens / through naturalization.

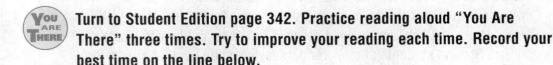 **Turn to Student Edition page 342. Practice reading aloud "You Are There" three times. Try to improve your reading each time. Record your best time on the line below.**

Number of words ____91____ My Best Time _____ Words per Minute _____

Name _____ Date _____

Lesson Title: _____

Sharing Powers

How the federal government's power is shared _____

_____

Why _____

Checks and Balances

What the system does _____

_____

What each branch has _____

_____

State Powers

Powers of the states or the people _____

_____

State and Local Governments

Three levels of government _____

Something they have in common _____

Rights and Responsibilities

How government gets its power

_____

One responsibility _____

Being a Citizen

Two other responsibilities

_____

_____

LESSON 1 **Exploring the West**

Vocabulary Strategies

Preteach Additional Vocabulary After teaching the Vocabulary words on Student Edition page 426, explain to students that there are several other important words they will see in this lesson. Use Procedure Card 1, along with the suggestions below, to introduce the words.

widen	Point out the familiar word *wide* and suffix *-en*, added after dropping final *e*. To widen a road means to make it wider. Other words with the same suffix include *sharpen*, *tighten*, and *shorten*.
wilderness	Tell students that this word comes from an Old English word *wilddeoren*, which means "of wild beasts."
purchase	Tell students that to purchase something is to buy it. A purchase is the thing that has been bought. Discuss examples of purchases such as a carton of milk, a TV, or a piece of land.
corps	Explain that a corps is a team or group of people who are working together or carrying out a duty. Point out that *p* and *s* are silent, so this word is a homophone of *core*.
unknowingly	Have students identify the base word *know*, prefix *-un*, ending *-ing*, and suffix *-ly*. Discuss this context sentence: "Pike and his men unknowingly entered Spanish territory."

WORD CARDS To help teach the lesson vocabulary, use the Word Cards on pages 305–306.

Build Fluency

Use page 140 and the steps on Procedure Card 2 to reinforce vocabulary and build fluency. Read each vocabulary word aloud and have students repeat it. Then have students work in pairs to reread the words. Follow a similar procedure with the phrases and sentences. Continue to help students build fluency by having them reread "You Are There" in the Student Edition.

Text Comprehension

BEFORE READING

Preview the Lesson Guide students in previewing the lesson using Procedure Card 3. Point out the following features of the lesson on Student Edition pages 354–361.

- **Pages 354–355** Read the "What to Know" question. Explain to students that the United States bought a huge amount of land in the Louisiana Purchase. Preview the time line and the illustrations of frontier life and pioneers.

- **Pages 356–357** Have students read the Children in History feature and discuss the Make It Relevant question. Then preview the map of the Louisiana Purchase on page 357 and have students answer the map skill question.

- **Pages 358–359** Tell students that Lewis and Clark explored the lands that the United States gained from the Louisiana Purchase. Have students examine and discuss the illustrated time line of Lewis and Clark's journey.

- **Pages 360–361** Preview the photograph on page 360, and explain that Zebulon Pike explored part of the Louisiana Purchase. Preview the Review questions on page 360 and the biography of Sacagawea on page 361.

DURING READING

Build Comprehension of Expository Text Present the graphic organizer on page 141. Have students preview the organizer by filling in the lesson title and comparing the five main heads in the organizer with the matching subheads in the Student Edition pages 354–360. Tell students that the section subheads provide additional help with identifying important information. Use Procedure Card 4, the Reading Check questions in *Harcourt Social Studies*, and the directed reading suggestions below.

- **Page 354** After students have read "You Are There," have them locate Kentucky on the map on page 357.

- **Pages 355–356** Have students read "Immigrants and Pioneers." Guide them in listing briefly in the first box of the organizer reasons that immigrants came to the United States. Point out the subhead "The Cumberland Gap" that matches the section subhead in the text, and have students write the name of the main route through the gap. Then have students read "Americans Continue West" and list the three new states named in the text under the section subhead "New States."

- **Pages 357–359** After students have read "The Louisiana Purchase," have them write the information in the organizer. Point out that the subhead matches the section subhead in the text and can help students locate information. Follow a similar procedure for the next section, "Lewis and Clark."

- **Page 360** Have students read "Pike in the Southwest" and complete the organizer.

AFTER READING

Summarize Have students use their completed graphic organizers to summarize the lesson. Then have them compare their summaries to the lesson summary on page 360.

Review and Respond If students need additional help with drawing conclusions, use Focus Skill Transparency 4.

Write a Journal Entry Suggest that students reread the section of the lesson that tells about the expedition of the Corps of Discovery. As they read, students can jot down ideas to use in their journal entries. Call attention to the entry that Clark wrote in his journal, quoted on page 359. Remind students that someone writing in a journal may record both observations and feelings.

Leveled Readers Use the Leveled Readers and Procedure Card 5 to build fluency and comprehension.

Name _____ Date _____

DIRECTIONS Read aloud the words in Part A. Practice reading aloud the phrases and the sentences in Part B.

Part A

Vocabulary Words	Additional Words	
gap	widen	corps
pioneer	wilderness	unknowingly
consequence	purchase	

Part B

1. A company / hired Daniel Boone / and about thirty others / to widen an old Native American trail / through the Cumberland Gap.

2. The group / built the Wilderness Road, / which became the main route for pioneers / going to the West.

3. Pioneers / formed the new states / of Kentucky, Tennessee, and Ohio.

4. In 1803, / France sold all of Louisiana / to the United States / in a deal called the Louisiana Purchase.

5. The Corps of Discovery, / led by Lewis and Clark, / set out to learn about the land / in the Louisiana Purchase.

6. Lewis and Clark / had to make many hard decisions / that had important consequences / for the expedition.

7. In 1806, / Captain Zebulon Pike / led an expedition / to explore the southwestern area / of the Louisiana Purchase.

8. After unknowingly entering Spanish territory, / Pike reported / that people there / needed manufactured goods.

YOU ARE THERE Turn to Student Edition page 354. Practice reading aloud "You Are There" three times. Try to improve your reading each time. Record your best time on the line below.

Number of words ___75___ My Best Time _____ Words per Minute _____

Name _____ Date _____

Lesson Title _____

Immigrants and Pioneers	**Americans Continue West**
Why immigrants came _____ _____	**New States**
	1. _____
The Cumberland Gap	2. _____
Main route _____	3. _____

The Louisiana Purchase

President of the United States _____

Problem _____

A Very Big Purchase

Date of final deal _____

Result _____

Lewis and Clark

The Corps of Discovery Set out from _____ in _____

The Expedition Succeeds Reached _____ in _____

What their work did _____
_____

Pike in the Southwest

What he reported _____

Result _____

Expanding Borders

Vocabulary Strategies

Preteach Additional Vocabulary After teaching the Vocabulary words on Student Edition page 364, explain to students that there are several other important words they will see in this lesson. Use Procedure Card 1, along with the suggestions below, to introduce the words.

threatened	Give *endangered* as a synonym for *threatened*. Point out the base words *danger* and *threat*, which are also synonyms.
naval	Explain that this word is from the Latin *navis*, which means "ship." Related words include *navy*, *navigation*, and *navigable*.
doctrine	Tell students that a doctrine is a statement of principles that may be put forth by a government.
colonization	Point out the relationship of this word to *colony* and *colonize*. Explain that colonization is the act of colonizing, or establishing a colony.
removal	Have students identify the familiar word *remove* and suffix *-al*. Removal is the action of removing something.

WORD CARDS To help teach the lesson vocabulary, use the Word Cards on pages 305–308.

Build Fluency

Use page 144 and the steps on Procedure Card 2 to reinforce vocabulary and build fluency. Read each vocabulary word aloud and have students repeat it. Then have students work in pairs to reread the words. Follow a similar procedure with the phrases and sentences. Continue to help students build fluency by having them reread "You Are There" in the Student Edition.

Text Comprehension

BEFORE READING

Preview the Lesson Guide students in previewing the lesson using Procedure Card 3. Point out the following features of the lesson on Student Edition pages 364–369.

- **Pages 364–365** Read the "What to Know" question. Remind students that the United States more than doubled in size with the Louisiana Purchase in 1803. Explain that Native Americans were the only people living on much of that land at that time. Preview the time line, the portrait of Chief Tecumseh and the illustration of trading ships.

- **Pages 366–367** Have students examine the map of major battles of the War of 1812 on page 366 and answer the map skill question. Preview the illustration of Francis Scott Key on page 367, and have students read the words of the "Star-Spangled Banner."

- **Pages 368–369** Preview the painting on page 368. Ask students why they think the walk shown here and described in the caption was called the Trail of Tears. Have students examine the map on page 369 and answer the map skill question. Then preview the Review questions.

DURING READING

Build Comprehension of Expository Text Present the graphic organizer on page 145. Have students preview the organizer by filling in the lesson title and comparing the four main heads in the organizer with the matching subheads in the Student Edition pages 364–369. Tell students that the section subheads provide additional help with identifying important information. Use Procedure Card 4, the Reading Check questions in *Harcourt Social Studies,* and the directed reading suggestions below.

- **Page 364** After students have read "You Are There," tell them that in this lesson they will learn more about Chief Tecumseh and why the Shawnee needed to defend their lands.

- **Page 365** Have students read "Troubles Grow" and write information in the first box of the organizer. Point out the subhead "Conflicts with Britain" that matches the section subhead in the text. Call attention also to the fact that the organizer is a sequence chart or time line with arrows indicating the sequence of events.

- **Pages 366–367** After students have read "The War of 1812," have them fill in the next box of the organizer, using the section subheads to locate information. Then students can read "Extending Democracy" and fill in that box.

- **Pages 368–369** Have students read "The Indian Removal Act" and complete the organizer. Point out that they will need to write a brief summary of the Trail of Tears. After students have completed the organizer, have them look at all the dates shown in it to confirm that the events are in time order.

AFTER READING

Summarize Have students use their completed graphic organizers to summarize the lesson. Then have them compare their summaries to the lesson summary on page 369.

Review and Respond If students need additional help with drawing conclusions, use Focus Skill Transparency 4.

Write an Article Suggest that students reread passages from the lesson that tell about Fort McHenry and Francis Scott Key. Remind them that a newspaper article tells When, Where, Who, What, and Why. Students might like to print their articles in a newspaper column format on the computer.

Leveled Readers Use the Leveled Readers and Procedure Card 5 to build fluency and comprehension.

Name _____ Date _____

DIRECTIONS Read aloud the words in Part A. Practice reading aloud the phrases and the sentences in Part B.

Part A

Vocabulary Words	Additional Words	
impressment	threatened	colonization
national anthem	naval	removal
nationalism	doctrine	
assimilate		

Part B

1. In the early 1800s, / many Americans / believed that British actions / in both the West and the East / threatened the United States.

2. The impressment of American sailors / by the British navy / angered many Americans / and led to the War of 1812.

3. Britain / had the strongest navy / in the world, / but the United States / won several important naval battles.

4. During the British attack / on Fort McHenry, / Francis Scott Key / wrote "The Star-Spangled Banner," / which became the national anthem.

5. After the war ended, / many Americans / felt a sense of nationalism.

6. In 1823, / President James Monroe / announced the Monroe Doctrine.

7. It said / that the American continents / were "not to be considered as subjects / for future colonization / by any European powers."

8. Unlike most other Native American tribes, / the Cherokee / assimilated to the ways of life / of white settlers.

9. In 1830, / President Jackson / signed the Indian Removal Act.

YOU ARE THERE Turn to Student Edition page 364. Practice reading aloud "You Are There" three times. Try to improve your reading each time. Record your best time on the line below.

Number of words ___66___   My Best Time _____   Words per Minute _____

Name _____ Date _____

Lesson Title _____

Troubles Grow

Where pioneers often settled _____

When Britain encouraged Native Americans to do _____

Conflicts with Britain What angered Americans _____

The War of 1812

Important American victories _____

British Attacks on Cities When _____ Events _____

_____

The Growth of Nationalism When _____ Plan _____

Extending Democracy

Who could vote in 1828 _____

New President _____ New Ideas _____

The Indian Removal Act

Purpose _____

The Trail of Tears

When it started _____ What happened _____

_____

_____

From Ocean to Ocean

Vocabulary Strategies

Preteach Additional Vocabulary After teaching the Vocabulary words on Student Edition page 372, explain to students that there are several other important words they will see in this lesson. Use Procedure Card 1, along with the suggestions below, to introduce the words.

mission	Remind students that they learned in Chapter 4 that Spanish missionaries built religious settlements, or missions, in the region of North America called New Spain.
lone	Discuss this sentence: "Texas was called the Lone Star Republic because its flag had one star." Point out that *lone* is a homophone of *loan*. Noticing that *lone* without *l* spells *one* can help students distinguish between the two words.
schooner	Tell students that a schooner is a type of sailing ship. Pioneers went west in covered wagons that they called prairie schooners. Point out the picture of a prairie schooner on page 375.
nugget	Students probably recognize this word as a food term. Explain that a small lump of metal, such as gold, is also called a nugget.

WORD CARDS To help teach the lesson vocabulary, use the Word Cards on pages 307–308.

Build Fluency

Use page 148 and the steps on Procedure Card 2 to reinforce vocabulary and build fluency. Read each vocabulary word aloud and have students repeat it. Then have students work in pairs to reread the words. Follow a similar procedure with the phrases and sentences. Continue to help students build fluency by having them reread "You Are There" in the Student Edition.

Text Comprehension

BEFORE READING

Preview the Lesson Guide students in previewing the lesson using Procedure Card 3. Point out the following features of the lesson on Student Edition pages 372–379.

- **Pages 372–373** Read the "What to Know" question. Remind students that even after the Louisiana Purchase, there were large parts of the present-day United States that were still claimed by other countries. Preview the time line, the illustration showing the battle of the Alamo, and the map of battles in the Texas War of Independence. Have students locate the Alamo on the map and answer the map skill question.

- **Pages 374–375** Have students examine the map showing trails to the West and answer the map skill question. Preview the illustration of a covered wagon on page 375. Have students compare traveling in a wagon like this to traveling in a camper or recreational vehicle today.

- **Pages 376–379** Preview the illustration of the Mexican-American War on page 376 and the map on page 377 showing the growth of the United States. Have students answer the map skill question. Then have students examine the illustration of gold mining on pages 378–379 and discuss the question in the caption. Preview the Review questions on page 379.

DURING READING

Build Comprehension of Expository Text Present the graphic organizer on page 149. Have students preview the organizer by filling in the lesson title and comparing the five main heads in the organizer with the matching subheads in the Student Edition pages 372–379. Tell students that the section subheads provide additional help with identifying important information. Use Procedure Card 4, the Reading Check questions in *Harcourt Social Studies*, and the directed reading suggestions below.

- **Page 372** After students have read "You Are There," tell them that in 1836, Texas was not yet part of the United States. Mexico had won its independence from Spain, so the Southwest region that had once belonged to Spain now belonged to Mexico.

- **Pages 373–374** Have students read "Texas Independence." Then they can write information in the first box of the organizer, after identifying the two subheads that match the section subheads in the text. Next, have students read "The Lone Star Republic" and fill in that box. Point out that students will need to summarize briefly what happened and the result.

- **Pages 374–377** After students have read "Trails West," have them fill in the next box of the organizer, using the section subheads to locate information. Then students can read "Expanding Borders" and fill in that box. Point out that following the subhead "New Borders," there are spaces to list three ways that the United States acquired new borders.

- **Pages 378–379** Have students read "The California Gold Rush" and complete the organizer. Point out that there are spaces after the subhead "Changing California" to write two ways that California changed as a result of the gold rush.

AFTER READING

Summarize Have students use their completed graphic organizers to summarize the lesson. Then have them compare their summaries to the lesson summary on page 379.

Review and Respond If students need additional help with drawing conclusions, use Focus Skill Transparency 4.

Write a Journal Entry Have students recall what they have learned about how to write a journal entry. Point out that forty-niners who traveled to California from other parts of the United States to find gold used the same overland trails as pioneers who went west for other reasons.

Leveled Readers Use the Leveled Readers and Procedure Card 5 to build fluency and comprehension.

Name _____ Date _____

DIRECTIONS Read aloud the words in Part A. Practice reading aloud the phrases and the sentences in Part B.

Part A

Vocabulary Words		Additional Words
dictator	cession	mission
annex	gold rush	lone
ford	forty-niners	schooner
manifest destiny		nugget

Part B

1. Fighting broke out / between American settlers in Mexico / and troops sent by the dictator of Mexico, / General Santa Anna.

2. American defenders / fought Santa Anna's army / at the Alamo, / a mission / they had turned into a fort.

3. Texas gained its independence / and was called the Lone Star Republic / until it was annexed by the United States / in 1845.

4. Pioneers / traveled in covered wagons / called prairie schooners / on the Oregon Trail / to the Pacific Northwest.

5. Wagons faced danger / when they had to ford rivers.

6. Many people in the United States / believed in manifest destiny, / even if it meant / going to war.

7. After the Mexican-American War, / Mexico sold the United States / a large area / known as the Mexican Cession.

8. The news / that workers in California / had found a small nugget / and then more gold / caused a gold rush.

 Turn to Student Edition page 372. Practice reading aloud "You Are There" three times. Try to improve your reading each time. Record your best time on the line below.

Number of words ___59___ My Best Time _____ Words per Minute _____

Name _____ Date _____

Lesson Title _____

Texas Independence

Americans in Texas Angered by

_____

The Alamo Year _____

Who won _____

The Lone Star Republic

Date _____

What happened _____

_____

Result _____

Trails West

The Oregon Trail From _____ to _____

How pioneers traveled _____

The Mormon Trail Mormon leader _____

Route from _____ to _____

Expanding Borders

New Conflicts Solution _____

The Mexican-American War Cause _____

New Borders How I. _____

2. _____ 3. _____

The California Gold Rush

The Forty-Niners Came from _____

Changing California How _____ _____

LESSON 4 · New Ideas and Inventions

Vocabulary Strategies

Preteach Additional Vocabulary After teaching the Vocabulary words on Student Edition page 380, explain to students that there are several other important words they will see in this lesson. Use Procedure Card 1, along with the suggestions below, to introduce the words.

obstacle	Tell students that this word is from the Latin *ob-*, "in the way," and *stare*, "stand." An obstacle is something that blocks the way or prevents progress.
current	Point out that this word has multiple meanings. A current in a river or stream is a swift flow of water in one direction. Have students pantomime what happens to objects in a current.
quantity	Give *amount* and *number* as synonyms for *quantity*. Point out final *y* that changes to *i* before adding *-es* to form the plural.
mass production	Explain that mass production is the manufacture of large numbers of goods at one time by machine instead of making them one at a time by hand.
reaper	Have student use this context sentence to figure out the meaning of *reaper*: "In 1832, Cyrus McCormick invented a mechanical reaper for harvesting grain."

WORD CARDS To help teach the lesson vocabulary, use the Word Cards on pages 307–310.

Build Fluency

Use page 152 and the steps on Procedure Card 2 to reinforce vocabulary and build fluency. Read each vocabulary word aloud and have students repeat it. Then have students work in pairs to reread the words. Follow a similar procedure with the phrases and sentences. Continue to help students build fluency by having them reread "You Are There" in the Student Edition.

Text Comprehension

BEFORE READING

Preview the Lesson Guide students in previewing the lesson using Procedure Card 3. Point out the following features of the lesson on Student Edition pages 380–385.

- **Pages 380–381** Read the "What to Know" question, and invite students to suggest possible answers. Preview the time line and the illustration of how boats use locks to move through different elevations in a canal. Discuss the Illustration question.

- **Pages 382–383** Have students examine the map showing roads and railroads in the United States in 1850 and answer the map skill question. Preview the illustration and the graph on page 383, and have students answer the question in the caption.

- **Pages 384–385** Preview the Primary Sources feature on page 384 and discuss the document-based question. Then preview the photograph of factory workers and the Review questions on page 385.

DURING READING

Build Comprehension of Expository Text Present the graphic organizer on page 153. Have students preview the organizer by filling in the lesson title and comparing the four main heads in the organizer with the matching subheads in the Student Edition pages 380–385. Tell students that the section subheads provide additional help with identifying important information. Use Procedure Card 4, the Reading Check questions in *Harcourt Social Studies,* and the directed reading suggestions below.

- **Page 380** After students have read "You Are There," have them identify the waterway that connected Lake Erie to the Hudson River. Call attention to the illustration of the canal on this page, and discuss how building canals changed transportation by boat.

- **Page 381** Have students read "Transportation" and fill in the information about an important road and an important canal mentioned under the section subhead "Roads and Canals" in the text.

- **Page 382** Then students can read "Steamboats and Railroads" and write information about these two forms of transportation in the next box of the organizer. Point out that the first two boxes are linked because both tell about developments in transportation.

- **Page 383** After students have read "The Industrial Revolution," have them fill in the next box of the organizer. Point out the subhead that matches the section subhead in the lesson and can help students locate information.

- **Pages 384–385** Have students read "More Inventions" and complete the organizer.

AFTER READING

Summarize Have students use their completed graphic organizers to summarize the lesson. Then have them compare their summaries to the lesson summary on page 385.

Review and Respond If students need additional help with drawing conclusions, use Focus Skill Transparency 4.

Make an Advertisement Discuss with the group what makes an advertisement effective. Then have students work individually or with partners to go back through the lesson and list the inventions they read about. Tell students to choose one of these inventions for their advertisement. Suggest that students also look back at the advertisement for the McCormick reaper on page 384 to recall what advertisements were like at the time of the Industrial Revolution.

Leveled Readers Use the Leveled Readers and Procedure Card 5 to build fluency and comprehension.

Name _____ Date _____

Part A

	Vocabulary Words		Additional Words	
canal	cotton gin		obstacle	mass
lock	interchangeable		current	production
locomotive	parts		quantity	reaper
Industrial Revolution				

Part B

1. Canals could avoid obstacles / and extend natural waterways.

2. The Erie Canal, / which was 363 miles long / and had 83 locks, / linked the Great Lakes / to the Atlantic.

3. Steamboats, / which could travel upstream / against the current, / became the main form of travel / on large rivers / across the nation.

4. Peter Cooper / built the first American locomotive in 1830.

5. During the 1800s, / new inventions / allowed people to use machines / instead of hand tools / to make large quantities of goods.

6. This growth of machine use / is called / the Industrial Revolution.

7. Eli Whitney / invented the cotton gin / and also a system of interchangeable parts / for making guns.

8. One result / of Whitney's invention of interchangeable parts / was a system called mass production.

9. With the mechanical reaper / that Cyrus McCormick / invented in 1832, / farmers / could cut wheat much faster / than they had with hand tools.

YOU ARE THERE Turn to Student Edition page 380. Practice reading aloud "You Are There" three times. Try to improve your reading each time. Record your best time on the line below.

Number of words ___66___ My Best Time _____ Words per Minute _____

Name _____ Date _____

Lesson Title: _____

Transportation

Roads and Canals Road _____ Across _____

Canal _____ Linked _____

Effect on New York City _____

Steamboats and Railroads

What steamboats became _____

Effect of railroads _____

The Industrial Revolution

When it began _____ What it was _____

_____

Mills in the North British mill worker _____

What he did _____

What it marked _____

More Inventions

Inventor _____ Invention _____ Result _____

Another invention _____ Result _____

Farm Machinery Inventor _____ Invention _____

Inventor _____ Invention _____

LESSON 1 # The North and the South

Vocabulary Strategies

Preteach Additional Vocabulary After teaching the Vocabulary words on Student Edition page 404, explain to students that there are several other important words they will see in this lesson. Use Procedure Card 1, along with the suggestions below, to introduce the words.

strengthened	Point out the word *strength*, suffix *-en*, and ending *-ed*. Have students use these elements to determine the meaning.
outlawed	Have students identify the parts of this compound word: *out, law*, and ending *-ed*. Explain that to outlaw something is to pass a law against it.
debated	Tell students that *debate* is from the Latin root *battuere,* meaning "to beat." The word *battle* is from the same root. People who debate take part in a "battle of words," a formal argument or discussion.
objection	Have students recall that *object* with the second syllable stressed means "to oppose, or to disagree." To have an objection is to have an opposing, or opposite, opinion.
advantage	Discuss the idea that having an advantage means being in a better position or having a better chance than someone else. Have students offer examples, such as older students having the advantage in some games against younger students.

WORD CARDS To help teach the lesson vocabulary, use the Word Cards on pages 311–312.

Build Fluency

Use page 156 and the steps on Procedure Card 2 to reinforce vocabulary and build fluency. Read each vocabulary word aloud and have students repeat it. Then have students work in pairs to reread the words. Follow a similar procedure with the phrases and sentences. Continue to help students build fluency by having them reread "You Are There" in the Student Edition.

Text Comprehension

BEFORE READING

Preview the Lesson Guide students in previewing the lesson using Procedure Card 3. Point out the following features of the lesson on Student Edition pages 404–409.

- **Pages 404–405** Read the "What to Know" question. Preview the time line and the paintings. Discuss how the information about differences between the Southern economy and the Northern economy might offer clues about what caused conflicts.

- **Pages 406–407** Have students examine the map that shows the Missouri Compromise and answer the question in the caption. Preview the illustration and the portrait of Andrew Jackson on page 407. Have students recall that Andrew Jackson was the President of the United States.

- **Pages 408–409** Preview the map on page 408, and have students answer the map skill question. Preview the painting and flyer, and the Review questions on page 409.

DURING READING

Build Comprehension of Expository Text Present the graphic organizer on page 157. Have students preview the organizer by filling in the lesson title and comparing the four main heads in the organizer with the matching subheads in the Student Edition pages 404–409. Tell students that the section subheads provide additional help with identifying important information. Use Procedure Card 4, the Reading Check questions in *Harcourt Social Studies*, and the directed reading suggestions below.

- **Page 404** After students have read "You Are There," have them compare the observations in the paragraph with the scenes shown in the two paintings on pages 404 and 405.

- **Page 405** Have students read "Different Regions." In the organizer, point out the subhead "Different Ways of Life" that matches the section subhead in the text. In the two boxes below that, have students write briefly about ways of life in the Northern states and in the Southern states.

- **Pages 406–407** After students have read "Division Over Slavery," have them write the information in the organizer. Point out that the subhead matches the section subhead in the text and can help students locate information. Follow a similar procedure for the next section, "Different Ideas."

- **Pages 408–409** Have students read "More Divisions" and complete the organizer, using the section subheads to help them locate information.

AFTER READING

Summarize Have students use their completed graphic organizers to summarize the lesson. Then have them compare their summaries to the lesson summary on page 409.

Review and Respond Work through the Review questions with students. Use Focus Skill Transparency 5, Generalize, to help students make generalizations about information in the lesson.

Make a Chart Discuss how to set up a two-column chart, and what title and headings students might use. Suggest that they reread the lesson and jot down information about the North and the South, either on two separate sheets of paper or by dividing a sheet of paper in half. Then students can use that information to create the chart.

Leveled Readers Use the Leveled Readers and Procedure Card 5 to build fluency and comprehension.

Name _____ Date _____

Part A

Vocabulary Words		Additional Words	
sectionalism	slave state	strengthened	objection
diverse economy	tariff	outlawed	advantage
states' rights	fugitive	debated	
free state			

Part B

1. By the mid-1800s, / national leaders / often decided issues / based on sectionalism.

2. The Northern states / had more industries / than the Southern states.

3. In Southern states, / the money brought in by cash crops / strengthened the system of slavery.

4. By 1804, / all the Northern states / had outlawed slavery.

5. In 1819, / Congress debated admitting Missouri / as a slave state.

6. Henry Clay of Kentucky / suggested the Missouri Compromise, / under which / the number of free states and slave states / remained equal.

7. In 1828, / sectionalism and states' rights / became serious issues / when Congress / passed a high tariff.

8. Despite the objections of Southerners, / Congress passed a new tariff.

9. If California joined the Union / as a free state / that would give the free states / an advantage in the Senate.

You ARE THERE   Turn to Student Edition page 404. Practice reading aloud "You Are There" three times. Try to improve your reading each time. Record your best time on the line below.

Number of words ___66___   My Best Time _____   Words per Minute _____

Name _____ Date _____

Lesson Title _____

Different Regions

Different Ways of Life

Northern States

Southern States

Division Over Slavery

Different Ideas

The Missouri Compromise

When _____ Issue _____

_____

_____

Who suggested a plan _____

Result _____

_____

Arguing Over Trade

Why _____

_____

Ideas About Government

What people disagreed about

_____

_____

More Divisions

Why _____

The Compromise of 1850 Law that was part of it _____

Reaction in the North _____

Bleeding Kansas Why _____

What happened _____

LESSON 2 **Resisting Slavery**

Vocabulary Strategies

Preteach Additional Vocabulary After teaching the Vocabulary words on Student Edition page 410, explain to students that there are several other important words they will see in this lesson. Use Procedure Card 1, along with the suggestions below, to introduce the words.

privilege	Explain that a privilege is a right that is allowed only to certain people or under certain conditions. Have students give examples.
property	Point out items belonging to different students, such as pencils or notebooks, and have students tell whose property each item is. Be sure students understand that anything that someone owns is that person's property.
limb	Discuss known meanings, such as a large tree branch. Tell students that their arms and legs are also sometimes called limbs.
mistreated	Have students identify the word *treat*, prefix *mis-,* and ending *-ed.* Remind them that *mis-* means "wrongly," as in *misuse, misspell,* and *misbehave.*
conductor	Ask students to describe the job of a conductor on a train. Explain that although the Underground Railroad was not an actual railroad, the people who helped runaways along the way were called conductors.

WORD CARDS To help teach the lesson vocabulary, use the Word Cards on pages 311–312.

Build Fluency

Use page 160 and the steps on Procedure Card 2 to reinforce vocabulary and build fluency. Read each vocabulary word aloud and have students repeat it. Then have students work in pairs to reread the words. Follow a similar procedure with the phrases and sentences. Continue to help students build fluency by having them reread "You Are There" in the Student Edition.

Text Comprehension

BEFORE READING

Preview the Lesson Guide students in previewing the lesson using Procedure Card 3. Point out the following features of the lesson on Student Edition pages 410–415.

- **Pages 410–411** Read the "What to Know" question and have students use information they have already learned to predict the answer. Preview the time line and the portrait of Dred Scott. Have students examine the Primary Sources feature and discuss the Document-Based Question.

- **Pages 412–413** Preview the illustrated time line of events in the fight to end slavery. Tell students that they will learn more about these people and events when they read the lesson. Have students study the map of Underground Railroad routes on page 413 and discuss the map skill question.

- **Pages 414–415** Have students read "Follow the Drinking Gourd" and discuss how the secret message in this song might have helped runaways find their way on the Underground Railroad. Preview the Review questions on page 414 and the biography of the famous Underground Railroad conductor Harriet Tubman on page 415.

DURING READING

Build Comprehension of Expository Text Present the graphic organizer on page 161. Have students preview the organizer by filling in the lesson title and comparing the two main heads in the organizer with the matching subheads in the Student Edition pages 410–414. Tell students that the section subheads provide additional help with identifying important information. Use Procedure Card 4, the Reading Check questions in *Harcourt Social Studies*, and the directed reading suggestions below.

- **Page 410** After students have read "You Are There," tell them that the Quakers were one of the groups of people who strongly resisted slavery.

- **Page 411** Have students read "The Dred Scott Decision." Guide them in summarizing important information from this section of the lesson in the organizer. Point out the subhead "Disagreements Over Scott" that matches the section subhead in the text.

- **Pages 412–414** Before students read "Challenging Slavery," have them use the organizer to set a purpose for reading. As students read, they can write in the chart the names of people who challenged slavery and what these people did. Tell students that if two people worked together, their names should be written together on the same line in the chart. Point out the subhead "Women Fight for Change," and tell students they should add to the chart the names of women they read about under this section subhead in the text. Point out the two additional section subheads that are not included in the chart but are also related to the topic of challenging slavery.

AFTER READING

Summarize Have students use their completed graphic organizers to summarize the lesson. Then have them compare their summaries to the lesson summary on page 414.

Review and Respond Work through the Review questions with students. If students need additional help with generalizing, use Focus Skill Transparency 5.

Make a Poster Suggest that students reread the section of the lesson that tells about the Underground Railroad to get information and ideas for their posters. Remind students that a poster may include both art and text. Provide appropriate art materials and a space to display students' work.

Leveled Readers Use the Leveled Readers and Procedure Card 5 to build fluency and comprehension.

Name _____ Date _____

Part A

Vocabulary Words	Additional Words
Underground Railroad	privilege
	property
	limb
	mistreated
	conductor

Part B

1. In 1857, / Supreme Court Chief Justice Roger B. Taney / wrote that Dred Scott, / an enslaved man, / had "none of the rights and privileges / of an American citizen."

2. Taney also wrote / that enslaved people were property, / a ruling / that troubled many people.

3. Frederick Douglass, / who escaped slavery and became famous, / often told audiences / that he had stolen his head, / limbs, / and body / from his master.

4. Harriet Beecher Stowe / wrote a book called *Uncle Tom's Cabin* / that told the story / of how enslaved workers / were mistreated.

5. Some enslaved people who ran away to gain their freedom / found helpers / —the brave men and women / of the Underground Railroad.

6. Harriet Tubman, / an African American / who had escaped from slavery herself, / was one of the best-known conductors / of the Underground Railroad.

YOU ARE THERE Turn to Student Edition page 410. Practice reading aloud "You Are There" three times. Try to improve your reading each time. Record your best time on the line below.

Number of words ___78___ My Best Time _____ Words per Minute _____

Name _____ Date _____

Lesson Title _____

The Dred Scott Decision

Why Scott went to court _____

Disagreements Over Scott

How the Supreme Court ruled _____

What this decision did _____

Challenging Slavery

Who	What they did

Women Fight for Change

The Underground Railroad

What it was _____

One of the best-known conductors _____

Facing Dangers A constant danger _____

LESSON 3 **The Nation Divides**

Vocabulary Strategies

Preteach Additional Vocabulary After teaching the Vocabulary words on Student Edition page 416, explain to students that there are several other important words they will see in this lesson. Use Procedure Card 1, along with the suggestions below, to introduce the words.

opponent	Give *ally* as an antonym of *opponent*. Discuss how the words *opponent, oppose, opposite,* and *opposition* are related.
raid	Tell students that a raid is a surprise attack.
secession	Have students write and compare the words *secede* and *secession*. Explain that secession is the act of seceding.
torn	Ask students to describe what happens when paper or cloth is torn. Then discuss the use of *torn* in this context: "People in the border states—Delaware, Maryland, Kentucky, and Missouri—were torn between the two sides."
resign	Have students role play resigning from a job. Encourage them to use synonyms, such as *quit* and *leave*, in their role play.

WORD CARDS To help teach the lesson vocabulary, use the Word Cards on pages 311–314.

Build Fluency

Use page 164 and the steps on Procedure Card 2 to reinforce vocabulary and build fluency. Read each vocabulary word aloud and have students repeat it. Then have students work in pairs to reread the words. Follow a similar procedure with the phrases and sentences. Continue to help students build fluency by having them reread "You Are There" in the Student Edition.

Text Comprehension

BEFORE READING

Preview the Lesson Guide students in previewing the lesson using Procedure Card 3. Point out the following features of the lesson on Student Edition pages 416–421.

- **Pages 416–417** Read the "What to Know" question and have students discuss events and issues they have read about so far that created tension and disagreement in the nation. Preview the time line and the paintings, along with the meeting notice and poster.

- **Pages 418–419** Preview the photograph and the notice of Lincoln's election on page 418. Explain that John Brown's raid helped to divide the nation, and the election of Abraham Lincoln caused some states to secede. Have students examine the map on page 419, identify Union and Confederate states, and answer the map skill question.

- **Pages 420–421** Preview the painting of Fort Sumter and the South Carolina state flag on page 420. Have students examine the graph on page 421 and answer the question in the caption. Then preview the Review questions.

DURING READING

Build Comprehension of Expository Text Present the graphic organizer on page 165. Have students preview the organizer by filling in the lesson title and comparing the four main heads in the organizer with the matching subheads in the Student Edition pages 416–421. Tell students that the section subheads provide additional help with identifying important information. Use Procedure Card 4, the Reading Check questions in *Harcourt Social Studies*, and the directed reading suggestions below.

- **Page 416** After students have read "You Are There," invite them to share their prior knowledge about Abraham Lincoln.

- **Pages 417–418** Have students read "Abraham Lincoln" and fill in the first box in the organizer. Point out the two subheads that match the section subheads in the text. Then follow the same procedure for the next section of the lesson, "Events Further Divide the Nation."

- **Pages 419–421** After students have read "The Nation Separates," they can write information in the next box in the organizer. Point out the subhead that matches the section subhead in the text. Then have students read "Fort Sumter" and complete the organizer.

AFTER READING

Summarize Have students use their completed graphic organizers to summarize the lesson. Then have them compare their summaries to the lesson summary on page 421.

Review and Respond Work through the Review questions with students. If students need additional help with generalizing, use Focus Skill Transparency 5.

Write Newspaper Headlines Provide examples of newspaper headlines and discuss how headline writers try to give the maximum amount of information in a limited space. Discuss how most people in the North and in the South probably reacted to the election of 1860. Point out that the headlines students write should reflect those viewpoints.

Leveled Readers Use the Leveled Readers and Procedure Card 5 to build fluency and comprehension.

Name _____ Date _____

DIRECTIONS Read aloud the words in Part A. Practice reading aloud the phrases and the sentences in Part B.

Part A

Vocabulary Words	Additional Words
secede	opponent
Confederacy	raid
border state	secession
artillery	torn
civil war	resign

Part B

1. Stephen A. Douglas / was Abraham Lincoln's opponent / in debates about slavery.

2. A raid on a government storehouse, / led by abolitionist John Brown, / divided the nation even more.

3. After Abraham Lincoln was elected President / in 1860, / some states seceded from the Union / and formed their own government, / the Confederacy.

4. President Lincoln / told the Southern states / that he opposed secession / but that he would not use / military force against them.

5. People in the border states / —Delaware, Maryland, Kentucky, and Missouri / —were torn between the two sides.

6. On April 12, 1861, / Confederate troops / fired their artillery / at Fort Sumter, / starting a civil war.

7. When Virginia seceded, / Union officer Robert E. Lee / resigned from the Union army / and later led the Southern army.

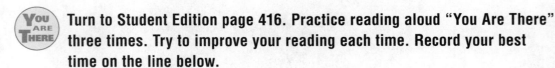 Turn to Student Edition page 416. Practice reading aloud "You Are There" three times. Try to improve your reading each time. Record your best time on the line below.

Number of words ___68___ My Best Time _____ Words per Minute _____

Name _____ Date _____

Lesson Title _____

Abraham Lincoln	Events Further Divide the Nation

Abraham Lincoln

Lincoln's Early Political Life

Elected to _____

and _____

New political party formed to

_____

Called _____

The Lincoln-Douglas Debates

What the debates did _____

_____

Events Further Divide the Nation

John Brown's Raid

Result _____

The Election of 1860

Main issue _____

What some Southerners said

_____

_____

Who won the election

_____

The Nation Separates

What some Southern states did _____

What they formed _____

The Border States How people there felt _____

Fort Sumter

Date _____ What happened _____

The Civil War Begins Effects _____

_____

LESSON 4 # The War Begins

Vocabulary Strategies

Preteach Additional Vocabulary After teaching the Vocabulary words on Student Edition page 424, explain to students that there are several other important words they will see in this lesson. Use Procedure Card 1, along with the suggestions below, to introduce the words.

invade	Discuss what happens when an army invades. Be sure students understand that the invading army comes into an area that belongs to the other side.
prey	Have students use this context sentence to determine the meaning of *prey*: "An anaconda is a snake that squeezes its prey to death." Point out that *prey* is a homophone of *pray*.
battlefield	Have students identify the two shorter words that make up this compound word. Then have them define the compound word.
regiment	Explain that armies are organized into units of different sizes. One such unit, or group of soldiers, is called a regiment. Some students may be interested in researching how armies are organized.
heavy	Discuss familiar usages for *heavy*, such as a heavy load, heavy rain, a heavy coat, a heavy schedule, a heavy line, a heavy heart. Have students use other words to describe heavy fire in a battle.

WORD CARDS To help teach the lesson vocabulary, use the Word Cards on pages 313–314.

Build Fluency

Use page 168 and the steps on Procedure Card 2 to reinforce vocabulary and build fluency. Read each vocabulary word aloud and have students repeat it. Then have students work in pairs to reread the words. Follow a similar procedure with the phrases and sentences. Continue to help students build fluency by having them reread "You Are There" in the Student Edition.

Text Comprehension

BEFORE READING

Preview the Lesson Guide students in previewing the lesson using Procedure Card 3. Point out the following features of the lesson on Student Edition pages 424–429.

- **Pages 424–425** Read the "What to Know" question, and have students identify key events shown on the time line. Preview the photograph on page 424 and the graph and illustrations on page 425. Have students answer the question in the caption.

- **Pages 426–427** Preview the painting of the Battle of Bull Run on page 426 and the painting of Abraham Lincoln and his cabinet on page 427. Have students locate the dates of the Battle of Bull Run and the Emancipation Proclamation on the time line on page 424.

- **Pages 428–429** Preview the portraits of three women on page 428, and tell students that they will read in the lesson about each woman's contribution to the war effort. On page 429, preview the painting and poster. Tell students that the 54th regiment, which led the attack on Fort Wagner, was one of the best-known African American regiments. Preview the Review questions.

DURING READING

Build Comprehension of Expository Text Present the graphic organizer on page 169. Have students preview the organizer by filling in the lesson title and comparing the four main heads in the organizer with the matching subheads in the Student Edition pages 424–429. Tell students that the section subheads provide additional help with identifying important information. Use Procedure Card 4, the Reading Check questions in *Harcourt Social Studies*, and the directed reading suggestions below.

- **Page 424** After students have read "You Are There," discuss the feelings that people in both the North and South may have had about the war at that point.

- **Pages 425–426** Have students read "War Plans." Point out the two boxes with subheads that match the section subheads in the text. Guide students in writing key ideas of the Union plans and Confederate plans. Follow a similar procedure for the next section of the lesson, "Early Battles."

- **Pages 427–429** After students have read "The Emancipation Proclamation," have them write a brief summary of this section of the lesson in the organizer. Then have students read "Americans at War" and complete the organizer by writing important information under the two subheads that match the section subheads in the text.

AFTER READING

Summarize Have students use their completed graphic organizers to summarize the lesson. Then have them compare their summaries to the lesson summary on page 429.

Review and Respond Work through the Review questions with students. If students need additional help with generalizing, use Focus Skill Transparency 5.

Write a Letter Discuss with students the kind of information they might include in their letters, such as who is running the farm while the father is away in the army and how the family feels about events such as major battles and the Emancipation Proclamation. Remind students to use the correct form for a friendly letter.

Leveled Readers Use the Leveled Readers and Procedure Card 5 to build fluency and comprehension.

Name _____ Date _____

Read aloud the words in Part A. Practice reading aloud the phrases and the sentences in Part B.

Part A

Vocabulary Words	Additional Words
strategy	invade
emancipate	prey
prejudice	battlefield
	regiment
	heavy

Part B

1. The Union strategy for winning the war / was first to weaken the South / and then to invade it.

2. Lincoln's plan to blockade Southern ports / was called the Anaconda Plan / because an anaconda / squeezes its prey to death.

3. The Confederates / won the first major battle, / which was fought on a battlefield near Manassas Junction, Virginia, / on July 21, 1861.

4. On January 1, 1863, / President Lincoln / issued a proclamation / to emancipate enslaved people / in areas still fighting against the Union.

5. African American soldiers who served in the Union army / faced prejudice / from people in the North / and the South.

6. One of the best-known African American regiments / was the Fifty-fourth Massachusetts, / led by Robert Gould Shaw.

7. In 1863, / the Fifty-fourth / led an attack on Fort Wagner, / in South Carolina, / fighting their way into the fort, / despite heavy fire.

YOU ARE THERE Turn to Student Edition page 424. Practice reading aloud "You Are There" three times. Try to improve your reading each time. Record your best time on the line below.

Number of words ___59___ My Best Time _____ Words per Minute _____

Name _____ Date _____

Lesson Title: _____

War Plans

Union Plans	Confederate Plans

Early Battles

The Battle of Bull Run	The Battle of Antietam

The Emancipation Proclamation

Americans At War

Women Help the War Effort	African American Soldiers

LESSON 5 **Toward a Union Victory**

Vocabulary Strategies

Preteach Additional Vocabulary After teaching the Vocabulary words on Student Edition page 432, explain to students that there are several other important words they will see in this lesson. Use Procedure Card 1, along with the suggestions below, to introduce the words.

effective	Explain that *effective* is often used to describe a person or action that brings about the results that were wanted or hoped for.
siege	Tell students that this word is from the Latin word *sedere*, "to sit." During a siege, an army blockades a city or fort so that no supplies can reach it, and then waits for it to surrender.
deadliest	Help students see that this word is formed by adding the suffix *-ly* and ending *-est* to the word *dead*. Discuss the difference between a deadly battle or accident, in which many die, and the deadliest battle or accident.
evacuate	Tell students that *evacuate* is from the Latin word *vacuus,* meaning "empty." Other words from this root include *vacant* and *vacuum*.
short-lived	Have students use the shorter words that make up this hyphenated word to determine its meaning. Explain that some people pronounce the second syllable with the short *i* sound and others with the long *i* sound.

WORD CARDS To help teach the lesson vocabulary, use the Word Cards on pages 313–314.

Build Fluency

Use page 173 and the steps on Procedure Card 2 to reinforce vocabulary and build fluency. Read each vocabulary word aloud and have students repeat it. Then have students work in pairs to reread the words. Follow a similar procedure with the phrases and sentences. Continue to help students build fluency by having them reread "You Are There" in the Student Edition.

Text Comprehension

BEFORE READING

Preview the Lesson Guide students in previewing the lesson using Procedure Card 3. Point out the following features of the lesson on Student Edition pages 432–437.

- **Pages 432–433** Read the "What to Know" question, and have students locate the end of the Civil War on the time line. Preview the painting of Vicksburg on page 432, and have students locate Vicksburg in the state of Mississippi on the map on page 433. Then have them answer the map skill question.

- **Pages 434–435** Have students examine and discuss the illustration of the Battle of Gettysburg.

- **Pages 436–437** Preview the painting on page 436 that shows the surrender of General Lee. Explain that this surrender marked the end of the Civil War. Preview the photograph of the city of Richmond, Virginia, left in ruins when the war ended. Then preview the Review questions.

DURING READING

Build Comprehension of Expository Text Present the graphic organizer on page 173. Have students preview the organizer by filling in the lesson title and comparing the three main heads in the organizer with the matching subheads in the Student Edition pages 432–437. Tell students that the section subheads provide additional help with identifying important information. Use Procedure Card 4, the Reading Check questions in *Harcourt Social Studies,* and the directed reading suggestions below.

- **Page 432** After students have read "You Are There," discuss what it must have felt like to know that a great battle would take place so close to home.

- **Page 433** Have students read "Two Major Battles" and fill in the first box in the organizer. Point out the subhead in the organizer that is the same as the section subhead in the text.

- **Pages 434–435** After students have read "Union Victories," have them write information in the next box in the organizer. Point out that the section subheads can help students locate information in the text.

- **Pages 436–437** Have students read "The War Ends" and complete the organizer.

AFTER READING

Summarize Have students use their completed graphic organizers to summarize the lesson. Then have them compare their summaries to the lesson summary on page 437.

Review and Respond Work through the Review questions with students. If students need additional help with generalizing, use Focus Skill Transparency 5.

Write a Poem Review with students what they have learned about writing poetry, including the use of rhythm, imagery, and figurative language. Possible extensions of this activity include having students combine their individual poems to create an anthology or researching famous Civil War poems.

Leveled Readers Use the Leveled Readers and Procedure Card 5 to build fluency and comprehension.

Name _____ Date _____

DIRECTIONS Read aloud the words in Part A. Practice reading aloud the phrases and the sentences in Part B.

Part A

Vocabulary Words	Additional Words
address	effective
assassinate	siege
	deadliest
	evacuate
	short-lived

Part B

1. By May 1863, / the Union army / finally had a general as effective / as Confederate General Robert E. Lee.

2. This general, / Ulysses S. Grant, / laid siege to the city of Vicksburg, Mississippi / and won a major victory for the Union.

3. The Union victory at the Battle of Gettysburg, / one of the deadliest battles of the war, / marked a turning point.

4. On November 19, 1863, / President Lincoln went to Gettysburg / and gave an address / that is one of the most famous speeches / in American history.

5. In April 1865, / Confederate troops / evacuated Richmond, Virginia.

6. The Civil War / was soon over, / but in the North / the joy at the victory / was short-lived.

7. On April 14, 1865, / just five days after the war ended, / President Lincoln was assassinated.

YOU ARE THERE Turn to Student Edition page 432. Practice reading aloud "You Are There" three times. Try to improve your reading each time. Record your best time on the line below.

Number of words ___69___ My Best Time _____ Words per Minute _____

Name _____ Date _____

Lesson Title: _____

Two Major Battles

Effective Union general _____

Vicksburg and Chancellorsville

Outcome at Vicksburg _____

Union Victories

The Battle of Gettysburg When _____ How long _____

Outcome _____

The Gettysburg Address When _____ Who _____

What it is _____

Sherman's March When _____ Who _____

What happened _____

The War Ends

Appomattox Courthouse When _____

What happened _____

Bitter Victory Why _____

_____

LESSON 1 # Reconstruction

Vocabulary Strategies

Preteach Additional Vocabulary After teaching the Vocabulary words on Student Edition page 446, explain to students that there are several other important words they will see in this lesson. Use Procedure Card 1, along with the suggestions below, to introduce the words.

rejoin	Have students identify the word *join* and prefix *re-*, which means "again." Other words with this prefix include *rebuild*, *reconstruct*, and *regain*.
corrupt	Give *dishonest* as a synonym for *corrupt*. Related words include *corruption* and *corruptible*.
society	Tell students that one meaning of *society* is "an organized group with common interests or beliefs."
trade school	Explain that skilled occupations are sometimes called trades. A trade school teaches skills that prepare students for work in these occupations.

WORD CARDS To help teach the lesson vocabulary, use the Word Cards on pages 313–316.

Build Fluency

Use page 176 and the steps on Procedure Card 2 to reinforce vocabulary and build fluency. Read each vocabulary word aloud and have students repeat it. Then have students work in pairs to reread the words. Follow a similar procedure with the phrases and sentences. Continue to help students build fluency by having them reread "You Are There" in the Student Edition.

Text Comprehension

BEFORE READING

Preview the Lesson Guide students in previewing the lesson using Procedure Card 3. Point out the following features of the lesson on Student Edition pages 446–453.

- **Pages 446–447** Read the "What to Know" question, and have students recall conditions in much of the South when the Civil War ended. Preview the time line, the photograph of Lincoln's funeral procession, and the portrait of the new President, Andrew Johnson.

- **Pages 448–449** Preview the painting and the chart comparing Johnson's and Congress's plans for Reconstruction. Have students identify points on which Johnson and Congress agreed and disagreed. Then have students examine the Primary Sources feature and discuss the document-based question.

- **Pages 450–451** Preview the photographs, and discuss what they show about the lives of African Americans in the South during Reconstruction.

- **Pages 452–453** Preview the painting of African Americans leaving the South. On page 453, preview the photograph of the school, the portrait of Booker T. Washington, and the Review questions.

DURING READING

Build Comprehension of Expository Text Present the graphic organizer on page 177. Have students preview the organizer by filling in the lesson title and comparing the four main heads in the organizer with the matching subheads in the Student Edition pages 446–453. Tell students that the section subheads provide additional help with identifying important information. Use Procedure Card 4, the Reading Check questions in *Harcourt Social Studies*, and the directed reading suggestions below.

- **Page 466** After students have read "You Are There," point out that the death of President Lincoln not only made people very sad but also brought about a change in government.

- **Pages 447–449** Have students read "Plans for Rebuilding" and fill in the first box in the organizer. Point out the subheads in the organizer that match the section subheads in the text. Follow the same procedure for the next section of the lesson, "Reconstruction Politics."

- **Pages 450–451** After students have read "Hard Times," have them write information in the next box in the organizer. Point out that the section subheads can help students locate information in the text.

- **Pages 452–453** Have students read "Reconstruction Ends" and complete the organizer.

AFTER READING

Summarize Have students use their completed graphic organizers to summarize the lesson. Then have them compare their summaries to the lesson summary on page 453.

Review and Respond Work through the Review questions with students. If students need additional help with generalizing, use Focus Skill Transparency 5.

Write a Summary In a discussion, have students identify and list on the board the main points of each plan. Encourage students to look back at the text to recall or confirm information. Remind students to include only the most important ideas in their summary paragraphs.

Leveled Readers Use the Leveled Readers and Procedure Card 5 to build fluency and comprehension.

Name _____ Date _____

Read aloud the words in Part A. Practice reading aloud the phrases and the sentences in Part B.

Part A

Vocabulary Words		Additional Words
Reconstruction	acquit	rejoin
sharecropping	freedmen	corrupt
black codes	segretation	society
secret ballot		trade school

Part B

1. President Andrew Johnson's plan for Reconstruction / allowed the Confederate states / to rejoin the Union / after they abolished slavery.

2. After the Southern state legislatures / went back to work, / they passed laws called black codes / to limit the rights of former enslaved people.

3. The House of Representatives / impeached President Johnson / because of disagreements over Reconstruction, / but he was acquitted.

4. Many freedmen / worked at sharecropping, / but most workers' shares / were very small.

5. Many Southerners / believed that their state governments / were corrupt / because of Reconstruction.

6. Not all states / had secret ballots, / so secret societies formed / to keep African Americans from voting / or to make sure / they only voted in certain ways.

7. Over time, / state governments passed laws / that established segregation.

8. In 1881, / Booker T. Washington / helped found the Tuskegee Institute, / a trade school / for African Americans in Alabama.

You ARE THERE Turn to Student Edition page 446. Practice reading aloud "You Are There" three times. Try to improve your reading each time. Record your best time on the line below.

Number of words ___46___ My Best Time _____ Words per Minute _____

Name _____ Date _____

Lesson Title _____

<table>
<tr><td>

Plans for Rebuilding

Lincoln's Plan

What he believed

_____

Johnson's Plan

What the Thirteenth Amedment did

_____

_____

</td><td>

Reconstruction Politics

Congress's Plan

What they wanted

_____

Impeachment   Result

_____

New Elections   Result

_____

</td></tr>
<tr><td>

Hard Times

The Freedmen's Bureau

What it did _____

_____

_____

Sharecropping

What workers did _____

_____

What they got _____

_____

Economic Troubles

Why _____

_____

_____

</td><td>

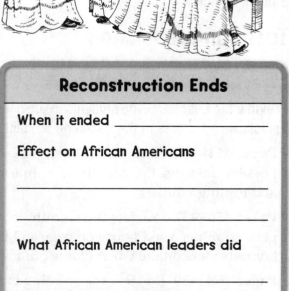

Reconstruction Ends

When it ended _____

Effect on African Americans

_____

_____

What African American leaders did

_____

_____

</td></tr>
</table>

LESSON 2 **The Last Frontier**

Vocabulary Strategies

Preteach Additional Vocabulary After teaching the Vocabulary words on Student Edition page 454, explain to students that there are several other important words they will see in this lesson. Use Procedure Card 1, along with the suggestions below, to introduce the words.

sheriff	Tell students that a sheriff today is a county official who enforces laws. In frontier times in the West, it was often the job of the sheriff to keep order in a community.
decline	Give *decrease* and *weakening* as synonyms for *decline* in the phrase *economic decline*. Have students give antonyms, such as *increase*, *growth*, and *strengthening*.
cowhand	Discuss the various meanings students know for *hand*, including "worker," as in the compound words *farmhand* and *dockhand*. Then have students give the meaning of *cowhand*.
plot	Students are probably most familiar with the meaning of *plot* in literature. Explain that another meaning for plot is "a piece of land."
range	Ask whether students know the song "Home on the Range." Talk about the meaning of *range* as a large area of open land where cattle and other livestock can roam and graze.

WORD CARDS To help teach the lesson vocabulary, use the Word Cards on pages 315–316.

Build Fluency

Use page 180 and the steps on Procedure Card 2 to reinforce vocabulary and build fluency. Read each vocabulary word aloud and have students repeat it. Then have students work in pairs to reread the words. Follow a similar procedure with the phrases and sentences. Continue to help students build fluency by having them reread "You Are There" in the Student Edition.

Text Comprehension

BEFORE READING

Preview the Lesson Guide students in previewing the lesson using Procedure Card 3. Point out the following features of the lesson on Student Edition pages 454–459.

- **Pages 454–455** Read the "What to Know" question, and have students predict possible answers. Preview the time line and the photographs of a mining town and mining families.

- **Pages 456–457** Preview the painting of a cattle drive on page 456 and the photograph of a sod house on page 457. Discuss the reason that many homesteaders on the Great Plains built sod houses rather than houses of wood.

- **Pages 458–459** Preview the painting of the Battle of the Little Bighorn on page 458, and the photograph of Chief Joseph on page 459. Then preview the Review questions.

Build Comprehension of Expository Text Present the graphic organizer on page 181. Have students preview the organizer by filling in the lesson title and comparing the three main heads in the organizer with the matching subheads in the Student Edition pages 454–459. Tell students that the section subheads provide additional help with identifying important information. Use Procedure Card 4, the Reading Check questions in *Harcourt Social Studies*, and the directed reading suggestions below.

- **Page 454** After students have read "You Are There," have them recall what they have learned about the California gold rush. Ask them to predict what may happen if people learn about the discovery of a gold nugget in South Dakota.

- **Page 455** Have students read "Western Mining" and fill in the first box in the organizer. Point out the subhead, and explain that the dates and places students will write in the organizer are found after this section subhead in the text. Point out that the cause and effect relationships refer specifically to effects on the economy.

- **Pages 456–457** After students have read "Life on the Frontier," have them write information in the next box in the organizer. Point out that the section subheads can help students locate information in the text.

- **Pages 458–459** Have students read "Western Conflict" and complete the organizer.

AFTER READING

Summarize Have students use their completed graphic organizers to summarize the lesson. Then have them compare their summaries to the lesson summary on page 459.

Review and Respond Work through the Review questions with students. If students need additional help with generalizing, use Focus Skill Transparency 5.

Prepare a Question List Have students brainstorm and categorize the kinds of information a person planning to become a homesteader in the 1860s might need. For example, information might be grouped under headings such as food, shelter, dangers, and so on. Students can refer to these categories as they write their lists of questions.

Leveled Readers Use the Leveled Readers and Procedure Card 5 to build fluency and comprehension.

Name _____ Date _____

DIRECTIONS Read aloud the words in Part A. Practice reading aloud the phrases and the sentences in Part B.

Part A

Vocabulary Words		Additional Words	
prospector	boom	sheriff	plot
homesteader	bust	decline	range
reservation		cowhand	

Part B

1. When gold or silver / was discovered in a place, / prospectors / moved into the area / and set up mining camps.

2. At first, / the mining towns / had no sheriffs, / so law and order / did not exist.

3. Business owners / set up stores / to meet the needs of miners, / causing a boom.

4. When the gold and silver deposits / ran out, / a bust, / or time of fast economic decline, / often followed.

5. Cattle ranchers / on the vast grasslands in Texas / needed skilled cowhands to deliver their herds safely to the railroads.

6. After the Homestead Act of 1862 / opened the Great Plains to settlement, / homesteaders / rushed to claim these plots of land.

7. Disagreements between ranchers and farmers / over land use / sometimes led to fights / called range wars.

8. By 1880, / almost all Native Americans in the United States / lived on reservations.

YOU ARE THERE Turn to Student Edition page 454. Practice reading aloud "You Are There" three times. Try to improve your reading each time. Record your best time on the line below.

Number of words ___52___ My Best Time _____ Words per Minute _____

Name _____ Date _____

Lesson Title _____

Western Mining

More Discoveries

When _____ Where _____

When _____ Where _____

CAUSE ━━━━━━━━━━▶ **EFFECT ON ECONOMY**

Gold or silver discovered _____

Gold or silver deposits ran out _____

Life on the Frontier

Cattle Trails Where to _____

How cattle got there

_____

Where meat was taken

_____

Challenges on the Great Plains

When _____ Law _____

Challenges _____

_____

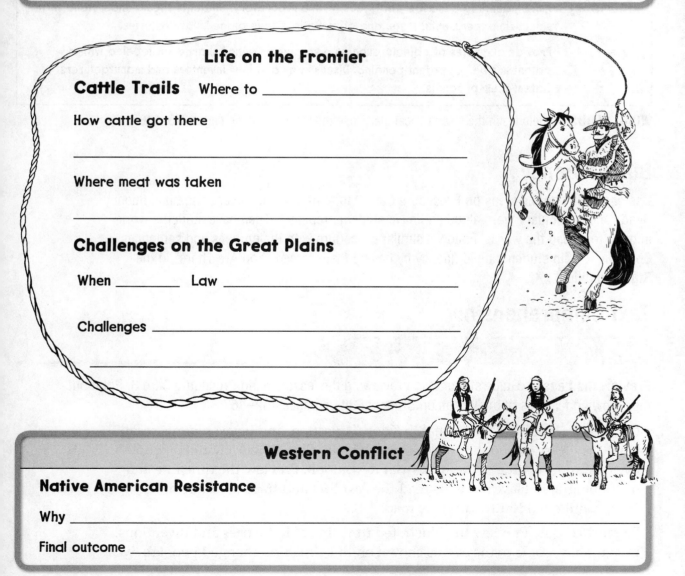

Western Conflict

Native American Resistance

Why _____

Final outcome _____

LESSON 3 # New Industries

Vocabulary Strategies

Preteach Additional Vocabulary After teaching the Vocabulary words on Student Edition page 462, explain to students that there are several other important words they will see in this lesson. Use Procedure Card 1, along with the suggestions below, to introduce the words.

blast	Discuss how tunnels are constructed. Explain that machines may be used to dig through soil and that workers also may use explosives, such as dynamite, to blast through rock.
ledge	Tell students that a rock ledge is a narrow flat surface on a rock wall that resembles a shelf. Have a volunteer draw a sketch on the board to show what a ledge looks like.
investor	Explain that an investor is someone who invests, or puts money into a company in the hope of making a profit. Point out the suffix -*or*. Other words with this suffix include *inventor*, *actor*, and *sailor*.
laboratory	Ask students to describe what goes on in a laboratory. Students should understand that scientific experiments, tests, and observations take place in laboratories.
patent	Provide examples of objects, such as a stapler or pencil sharpener, labeled with a patent number or patent pending. Discuss why and how inventors and manufacturers patent their products.

WORD CARDS To help teach the lesson vocabulary, use the Word Cards on pages 315–316.

Build Fluency

Use page 184 and the steps on Procedure Card 2 to reinforce vocabulary and build fluency. Read each vocabulary word aloud and have students repeat it. Then have students work in pairs to reread the words. Follow a similar procedure with the phrases and sentences. Continue to help students build fluency by having them reread "You Are There" in the Student Edition.

Text Comprehension

BEFORE READING

Preview the Lesson Guide students in previewing the lesson using Procedure Card 3. Point out the following features of the lesson on Student Edition pages 462–467.

- **Pages 462–463** Read the "What to Know" question, and have students recall what they learned about how new industries and inventions changed people's lives around the time of the Industrial Revolution. Preview the time line and the photograph. Have students read the Fast Fact and trace the route of the Transcontinental Railroad on the map.

- **Pages 464–465** Preview the illustrated time line of industries and inventions. Discuss how some of the events shown on this time line changed people's lives.

• **Pages 466–467** Have students read Children in History and discuss the Make It Relevant question. Preview the photograph of labor union members and the Review questions on page 467.

DURING READING

Build Comprehension of Expository Text Present the graphic organizer on page 185. Have students preview the organizer by filling in the lesson title and comparing the three main heads in the organizer with the matching subheads in the Student Edition pages 462–467. Tell students that the section subheads provide additional help with identifying important information. Use Procedure Card 4, the Reading Check questions in *Harcourt Social Studies,* and the directed reading suggestions below.

• **Page 462** After students have read "You Are There," discuss why the joining of the two sets of railroad tracks was such an exciting event.

• **Page 463** Have students read "The Transcontinental Railroad" and fill in the first box in the organizer by writing an effect for each cause.

• **Pages 464–465** Before students read "Industries and Inventions," have them set a purpose for reading by looking at the organizer. Point out that they will need to write an effect for the cause that is stated before the first section subhead. Have students match the three subheads in the chart with the section subheads in the text. Explain that students will add names to the chart under each subhead and write a very brief summary of what each person did.

• **Pages 466–467** Have students read "Workers Struggle " and complete the organizer.

AFTER READING

Summarize Have students use their completed graphic organizers to summarize the lesson. Then have them compare their summaries to the lesson summary on page 467.

Review and Respond Work through the Review questions with students. If students need additional help with generalizing, use Focus Skill Transparency 5.

Create a Chart Discuss how the charts that students create may be similar to and different from the chart they completed in the graphic organizer. Emphasize that starting a new business or industry is not the same as inventing a new technology. Point out that the time line on pages 464–465 may also be helpful to students in deciding what to include in their charts of inventors and inventions.

Leveled Readers Use the Leveled Readers and Procedure Card 5 to build fluency and comprehension.

Name _____ Date _____

Part A

Vocabulary Words		Additional Words	
collective	labor union	blast	laboratory
bargaining	skyscraper	ledge	patent
transcontinental	petroleum	investor	
railroad	strike		

Part B

1. In 1862, / Congress gave two railroad companies / —the Union Pacific / and the Central Pacific / —the right to build a transcontinental railroad.

2. Workers blasted tunnels / and cut ledges / into the Sierra Nevada / and the Rocky Mountains.

3. After Andrew Carnegie / saw a new method / for making steel, / he found investors / to help him build a steel mill.

4. In the 1880s, / William Jenney / used steel frames / to build skyscrapers.

5. When kerosene, / a fuel made from petroleum, / became widely used for lighting lamps, / the demand for petroleum / increased sharply.

6. The team / that worked in Thomas Alva Edison's laboratory / patented about one invention / every five days.

7. In the late 1800s, / workers began to join labor unions / to fight for better working conditions / and pay.

8. Sometimes / unions organized strikes.

9. Samuel Gompers encouraged / the use of collective bargaining.

YOU ARE THERE **Turn to Student Edition page 462. Practice reading aloud "You Are There" three times. Try to improve your reading each time. Record your best time on the line below.**

Number of words ____59____ My Best Time _____ Words per Minute _____

Name _____ Date _____

Lesson Title _____

The Transcontinental Railroad

Building the Railroad

CAUSE Two railroads met. ⟶ **EFFECT** _____

CAUSE More railroads built. ⟶ **EFFECT** _____

Industries and Inventions

CAUSE New inventions ⟶ **EFFECT** _____

The Steel Industry

WHO	WHAT HE DID

The Oil Industry

Inventions Change Lives

Workers Struggle

Labor Unions Fight for _____

How _____ and _____

LESSON 4 **Cities and Immigration**

Vocabulary Strategies

Preteach Additional Vocabulary After teaching the Vocabulary words on Student Edition page 468, explain to students that there are several other important words they will see in this lesson. Use Procedure Card 1, along with the suggestions below, to introduce the words.

poverty	Tell students that this word is from the Latin *pauper*, meaning "poor."
qualified	Discuss who is qualified to drive a car and how to become qualified as a teacher. Be sure students understand that being qualified means having the necessary training and experience.
exclusion	Have students use this context clue to first define *excluded* and then the related word *exclusion*: "In 1882, Congress passed the Chinese Exclusion Act. This law excluded, or kept out, all Chinese immigrants."
migration	Students may be familiar with this term from science. Explain that when people migrate, they move from one area to another. Point out the similarity to *immigration*. Explain that *im*- means "in," so immigration is moving into a new country.
ideal	Tell students that this word, often used as an adjective, can also be a noun, meaning "principle, belief, or value."

WORD CARDS To help teach the lesson vocabulary, use the Word Cards on pages 317–318.

Build Fluency

Use page 188 and the steps on Procedure Card 2 to reinforce vocabulary and build fluency. Read each vocabulary word aloud and have students repeat it. Then have students work in pairs to reread the words. Follow a similar procedure with the phrases and sentences. Continue to help students build fluency by having them reread "You Are There" in the Student Edition.

Text Comprehension

BEFORE READING

Preview the Lesson Guide students in previewing the lesson using Procedure Card 3. Point out the following features of the lesson on Student Edition pages 468–473.

- **Pages 468–469** Read the "What to Know" question, and have students predict some challenges they may read about. Preview the time line and the photographs. Ask students what the photograph of Mulberry Street in New York City shows about challenges that some immigrants faced.

- **Pages 470–471** Preview the photograph of Asian immigrants and the boycott sign on page 470, and discuss challenges these immigrants faced. Preview the photograph on page 471. Explain that great numbers of African Americans moved to northern cities to take jobs in factories.

- **Pages 472–473** Preview the photograph and the graph on page 472. Have students identify the bar on the graph that shows the number of immigrants from Asia between 1991 and 2000. Preview the Review questions. On page 473, call attention to the biography of Jane Addams, who helped immigrant families.

DURING READING

Build Comprehension of Expository Text Present the graphic organizer on page 189. Have students preview the organizer by filling in the lesson title and comparing the three main heads in the organizer with the matching subheads in the Student Edition pages 468–472. Tell students that the section subheads provide additional help with identifying important information. Use Procedure Card 4, the Reading Check questions in *Harcourt Social Studies,* and the directed reading suggestions below.

- **Page 468** After students have read "You Are There," discuss why the day an immigrant family arrived in America might be a great day in their lives.

- **Page 469** Have students read "Many Immigrants Arrive" and fill in the first box in the organizer. Point out the subhead "New Immigrants" that matches the section subhead in the text.

- **Page 470** After students have read "Reactions to Immigration," have them write information in the next section of the organizer. Point out the subheads that can help students locate information.

- **Pages 471–472** Have students read "Migration and Immigration " and complete the organizer.

AFTER READING

Summarize Have students use their completed graphic organizers to summarize the lesson. Then have them compare their summaries to the lesson summary on page 472.

Review and Respond Work through the Review questions with students. If students need additional help with generalizing, use Focus Skill Transparency 5.

Write a Diary Entry Have students recall the reasons that immigrants came to America and what they hoped to find here. Encourage students to look back at the text to help them remember this information. Discuss the feelings that a child might have coming to a new life in a new land, and remind students to write their diary entries from the child's point of view.

Leveled Readers Use the Leveled Readers and Procedure Card 5 to build fluency and comprehension.

DIRECTIONS Read aloud the words in Part A. Practice reading aloud the phrases and the sentences in Part B.

Part A

Vocabulary Words	Additional Words
tenement	poverty
reformer	qualified
settlement house	exclusion
	migration
	ideal

Part B

1. People / often came to the United States / to escape violence / and poverty.

2. Many lived in tenements / and struggled to find jobs / and learn English.

3. Some Americans / felt that because some immigrants / had little education, / they were not qualified/ to take part in a democracy.

4. In 1882, / Congress passed / the Chinese Exclusion Act, / which prevented any Chinese immigrants / from coming to the United States / for ten years.

5. Jane Addams and Lillian Wald / were reformers / who started settlement houses / to help immigrants.

6. Between 1910 and 1930, / so many African Americans / moved to northern cities / that this movement became known as / the Great Migration.

7. Although Americans / are different from one another, / they are united / by basic American ideals / —freedom, / opportunity, / and a belief in individual rights.

YOU ARE THERE Turn to Student Edition page 468. Practice reading aloud "You Are There" three times. Try to improve your reading each time. Record your best time on the line below.

Number of words ___68___ My Best Time _____ Words per Minute _____

Name _____ Date _____

Lesson Title: _____

Many Immigrants Arrive

When _____ How many _____

What they hoped for _____

New Immigrants

Where European immigrants arrived _____

Challenges _____

_____

Where Asian immigrants arrived _____

Reactions to Immigration

Unfair Treatment Year _____ Law _____

Help for Immigrants Problems _____

Who helped _____

What they did _____

_____

Migration and Immigration

African Americans Migrate When _____

To where _____ Name of movement _____

What many found _____

Immigration Today Where most are from _____

What unites Americans _____

LESSON 1 A New Role in the World

Vocabulary Strategies

Preteach Additional Vocabulary After teaching the Vocabulary words on Student Edition page 494, explain to students that there are several other important words they will see in this lesson. Use Procedure Card 1, along with the suggestions below, to introduce the words.

revolted	Write *revolt* and *revolution*. Tell students that to revolt is to rebel against a government or other authority. Adding the *-ed* ending shows that the action took place in the past.
exaggerated	Ask students to recall tall tales they have read or heard. Point out that tellers of tall tales often exaggerated to make their stories more interesting. Have students give specific examples.
fleet	Tell students that a fleet of ships is a group of ships under one command.
program	Have students give meanings they know for this word. Then discuss the meaning in this context: "President Roosevelt set up a program called the Square Deal."
standard	Explain that *standard* has multiple meanings. Discuss the idea that the government may set standards, or rules, for products, such as safety standards for cars or toys.

WORD CARDS To help teach the lesson vocabulary, use the Word Cards on pages 319–320.

Build Fluency

Use page 192 and the steps on Procedure Card 2 to reinforce vocabulary and build fluency. Read each vocabulary word aloud and have students repeat it. Then have students work in pairs to reread the words. Follow a similar procedure with the phrases and sentences. Continue to help students build fluency by having them reread "You Are There" in the Student Edition.

Text Comprehension

BEFORE READING

Preview the Lesson Guide students in previewing the lesson using Procedure Card 3. Point out the following features of the lesson on Student Edition pages 494–499.

- **Pages 494–495** Read the "What to Know" question. Preview the time line and the photographs. Tell students that Alaska and Hawaii are the newest states of the United States.

- **Pages 496–497** Preview the picture of the Battle of Manila Bay. Have students examine the map of United States Possessions in 1900 and answer the map skill question.

- **Pages 498–499** Preview the portrait of President Theodore Roosevelt and the photograph of the Panama Canal. Tell students that building the canal was one of Roosevelt's main goals. Preview and discuss the photograph of a NAACP march. Then preview the Review questions.

DURING READING

Build Comprehension of Expository Text Present the graphic organizer on page 193. Have students preview the organizer by filling in the lesson title and comparing the three main heads in the organizer with the matching subheads in the Student Edition pages 494–499. Tell students that the section subheads provide additional help with identifying important information. Use Procedure Card 4, the Reading Check questions in *Harcourt Social Studies,* and the directed reading suggestions below.

- **Page 494** After students have read "You Are There," ask them to predict what may happen as a result of the Alaska gold rush.

- **Page 495** Have students read "The United States Grows." In the organizer, point out the subheads "Alaska" and "Hawaii" that match the section subheads in the text. Have students fill in the information.

- **Pages 496–497** After students have read "The Spanish-American War," have them fill in the next part of the organizer, using the section subheads as a guide.

- **Pages 498–499** Have students read "Changes at Home and Abroad" and complete the organizer, using the section subheads to help them locate information.

AFTER READING

Summarize Have students use their completed graphic organizers to summarize the lesson. Then have them compare their summaries to the lesson summary on page 499.

Review and Respond Work through the Review questions with students. Use Focus Skill Transparency 6, Summarize, to help students summarize information in the lesson.

Make a Time Line Suggest that students begin by going back through the lesson to write down dates and events. You may want to have students work in pairs to gather this information and then to create a time line.

Leveled Readers Use the Leveled Readers and Procedure Card 5 to build fluency and comprehension.

Name _____   Date _____

Read aloud the words in Part A. Practice reading aloud the phrases and the sentences in Part B.

Part A

Vocabulary Words	Additional Words	
armistice	revolted	program
progressive	exaggerated	standard
conservation	fleet	

Part B

1. Americans took over / the government of Hawaii / after farmers revolted / and imprisoned the queen / who had ruled the islands.

2. American newspapers / published exaggerated stories / to persuade people / to support a war with Spain.

3. In the first battle / of the Spanish-American War, / an American fleet / destroyed the Spanish fleet.

4. On August 12, 1898, / after many defeats, / Spain signed an armistice.

5. After Theodore Roosevelt became President, / he set up a program / called the Square Deal.

6. Roosevelt's supporters / were called progressives.

7. In 1906, / Congress passed / the Pure Food and Drug Act / that set safe standards / for food and medicines.

8. In addition, / Roosevelt supported / conservation.

9. African American leaders / also used progressive ideas / to fight prejudice.

You ARE There **Turn to Student Edition page 494. Practice reading aloud "You Are There" three times. Try to improve your reading each time. Record your best time on the line below.**

Number of words ___76___   My Best Time _____   Words per Minute _____

Name _____ Date _____

Lesson Title: _____

The United States Grows

Alaska When added _____

How _____

Hawaii When added _____

How _____

The Spanish-American War

Reasons for War 1. _____

2. _____

The Fighting Begins

Where _____

Date of armistice _____

The Effects of the War United States became _____

Changes at Home and Abroad

The Panama Canal

Connected _____

_____

How long to build

_____

Government Action

Progressives believed

_____

_____

_____ .

Expanding Rights

To fight _____

Leader _____

Group _____

_____ Rights

LESSON 2 **World War I**

Vocabulary Strategies

Preteach Additional Vocabulary After teaching the Vocabulary words on Student Edition page 500, explain to students that there are several other important words they will see in this lesson. Use Procedure Card 1, along with the suggestions below, to introduce the words.

pledged	Tell students that a synonym for *pledged* is *promised*. Point out that this word is the past tense of *pledge*, as in "I pledge allegiance to the flag..."
rebel	Explain that this word, with the stress on the first syllable, means "a person who takes action against a government or authority." The word *rebel*, with the stress on the second syllable, means "to take action against a government or authority."
advance	Ask a volunteer to stand and then advance, or move forward.
conference	Tell students that synonyms for this word include *meeting* and *discussion*.
league	Students are probably familiar with this word in connection with sports. Remind students that they learned about the Iroquois League in Chapter 2. Explain that a league is a group that shares common interests or goals.

WORD CARDS To help teach the lesson vocabulary, use the Word Cards on pages 319–320.

Build Fluency

Use page 196 and the steps on Procedure Card 2 to reinforce vocabulary and build fluency. Read each vocabulary word aloud and have students repeat it. Then have students work in pairs to reread the words. Follow a similar procedure with the phrases and sentences. Continue to help students build fluency by having them reread "You Are There" in the Student Edition.

Text Comprehension

BEFORE READING

Preview the Lesson Guide students in previewing the lesson using Procedure Card 3. Point out the following features of the lesson on Student Edition pages 500–505.

- **Pages 500–501** Read the "What to Know" question. Preview the time line and the photograph. Have students point out differences between the soldiers in the photograph and soldiers of today. Then have students examine the map and discuss the map skill question.

- **Pages 502–503** Preview and discuss the photographs showing trench warfare and how Americans at home helped the war effort.

- **Pages 504–505** Preview the photograph of the ruins after World War I and of women marching for suffrage. Explain that women won the right to vote after the war, partly because women's work during the war led more people to support women's suffrage.

DURING READING

Build Comprehension of Expository Text Present the graphic organizer on page 197. Have students preview the organizer by filling in the lesson title and comparing the four main heads in the organizer with the matching subheads in the Student Edition pages 500–505. Tell students that the section subheads provide additional help with identifying important information. Use Procedure Card 4, the Reading Check questions in *Harcourt Social Studies*, and the directed reading suggestions below.

- **Page 500** After students have read "You Are There," remind them that in 1914, people did not have TV or the Internet as sources of information about what was happening in the world.

- **Page 501** Have students read "Causes of World War I." In the organizer, point out the subheads "Two Sides" and "Ocean Attacks" that match the section subheads in the text. Tell students to write the names of the two sides, or alliances, in the first box. In the second box, students should tell briefly what caused the United States to declare war.

- **Pages 502–503** After students have read "Fighting the War," have them list new types of warfare and weapons in the organizer. Then students can read "The War at Home" and describe briefly important changes in the nation.

- **Pages 504–505** Have students read "The Effects of War" and complete the organizer by writing important information under each subhead. Tell them to use the matching section subheads in the text to locate information.

AFTER READING

Summarize Have students use their completed graphic organizers to summarize the lesson. Then have them compare their summaries to the lesson summary on page 505.

Review and Respond Work through the Review questions with students. If students need additional help with summarizing, use Focus Skill Transparency 6.

Write a Letter Suggest that students reread the section of the lesson that tells about life at home in the United States while the war was going on in Europe. Tell them to imagine what they and other family members might be doing if they were living at that time. Then they can use these ideas in their letters.

Leveled Readers Use the Leveled Readers and Procedure Card 5 to build fluency and comprehension.

DIRECTIONS Read aloud the words in Part A. Practice reading aloud the phrases and the sentences in Part B.

Part A

Vocabulary Words	Additional Words	
military draft	pledged	conference
trench warfare	rebel	league
no-man's land	advance	

Part B

1. In 1914, / Europe was divided / into two alliances, / with nations pledged to help each other / if they were attacked.

2. World War I began / after a Serbian rebel / shot and killed Archduke Francis Ferdinand / of Austria-Hungary.

3. After Germany sank American ships, / the United States / joined the war / on the side of the Allies / and set up a military draft.

4. The fighting in the war / was trench warfare.

5. Both armies / dug deep trenches, / and then each side / tried to advance into "no man's land" / between the trenches.

6. After the war ended, / the Allies met / at the Paris Peace Conference.

7. President Wilson / presented his idea / for a League of Nations / to help nations find / peaceful ways to solve problems.

8. The League of Nations / was set up, / but the United States / did not join.

YOU ARE THERE Turn to Student Edition page 500. Practice reading aloud "You Are There" three times. Try to improve your reading each time. Record your best time on the line below.

Number of words ___80___   My Best Time _____   Words per Minute _____

Name _____ Date _____

Lesson Title: _____

Causes of World War I

Two Sides

Ocean Attacks

Fighting the War

New Types of Warfare

The War at Home

Changes in the Nation

The Effects of the War

The League of Nations

The Nineteenth Amendment

LESSON 3 **Good Times and Hard Times**

Vocabulary Strategies

Preteach Additional Vocabulary After teaching the Vocabulary words on Student Edition page 506, explain to students that there are several other important words they will see in this lesson. Use Procedure Card 1, along with the suggestions below, to introduce the words.

affordable	Point out the base word *afford* and suffix *-able*. Explain that something is affordable if you have enough money to pay for it.
stockholder	Have students identify the parts of this word, *stock, hold,* and suffix *-er*. Guide them to define a stockholder as someone who holds, or owns, stock in a company.
reserve	Tell students that something held in reserve is set aside for a certain purpose. Explain how this word is related to *reservoir*. Water in a reservoir is in reserve for later use.
prosperity	Write *prosper, prosperous,* and *prosperity*. Have students recall the meanings of the first two words. Explain that prosperity is the state of being wealthy or successful.
agency	Tell students that governments set up agencies to do certain tasks. For example, the Environmental Protection Agency was created to work for a cleaner, healthier environment.

WORD CARDS To help teach the lesson vocabulary, use the Word Cards on pages 319–320.

Build Fluency

Use page 200 and the steps on Procedure Card 2 to reinforce vocabulary and build fluency. Read each vocabulary word aloud and have students repeat it. Then have students work in pairs to reread the words. Follow a similar procedure with the phrases and sentences. Continue to help students build fluency by having them reread "You Are There" in the Student Edition.

Text Comprehension

BEFORE READING

Preview the Lesson Guide students in previewing the lesson using Procedure Card 3. Point out the following features of the lesson on Student Edition pages 506–513.

- **Pages 506–507** Read the "What to Know" question. Discuss the meaning of a stock market crash, and have students locate that event on the time line. Preview and discuss the photographs that show new consumer goods that became available after World War I.

- **Pages 508–509** Preview the photograph and poster. Tell students that in addition to new consumer goods, new art forms developed in the good times after World War I. Then preview the photograph and unemployment graph on page 509, and have students answer the question in the caption. Explain that the good times immediately after the war were followed by hard times.

- **Pages 510–511** Preview the photograph and map of the Dust Bowl region. Explain how the Dust Bowl came about. Then preview the photograph and poster on page 511. Tell students what CCC and WPA stand for.

- **Pages 512–513** Preview the photograph of President Franklin D. Roosevelt. Preview the Review questions. Call attention to the biography of Eleanor Roosevelt. Tell students that they will read about her many accomplishments.

DURING READING

Build Comprehension of Expository Text Present the graphic organizer on page 201. Have students preview the organizer by filling in the lesson title and comparing the five main heads in the organizer with the matching subheads in the Student Edition pages 506–512. Tell students that the section subheads provide additional help with identifying important information. Use Procedure Card 4, the Reading Check questions in *Harcourt Social Studies,* and the directed reading suggestions below.

- **Page 506** After students have read "You Are There," ask what new products they know about that have come out in their own lifetimes.

- **Pages 507–508** Have students read "The Good Times." Point out the subhead "Changes in Industry" in the organizer, and have students list major changes that took place after World War I. Then have students read "New Art Forms" and list new types of arts and entertainment in that box in the organizer.

- **Pages 509–510** After students have read "The End of Good Times," have them write in the organizer a brief explanation of what happened. Then students can read "Hard Times" and list the reasons that Americans were suffering.

- **Pages 511–512** Have students read "The New Deal" and complete the organizer by writing information under each subhead. Tell them to use the matching section subheads in the text to locate information.

AFTER READING

Summarize Have students use their completed graphic organizers to summarize the lesson. Then have them compare their summaries to the lesson summary on page 512.

Review and Respond Work through the Review questions with students. If students need additional help with summarizing, use Focus Skill Transparency 6.

Write a Letter Have students suggest some ideas about how owning a car might have changed a family's life in the 1920s. Write students' responses in a list or a web. Students can refer to this list or web as they write their letters.

Leveled Readers Use the Leveled Readers and Procedure Card 5 to build fluency and comprehension.

Name _____   Date _____

DIRECTIONS   Read aloud the words in Part A. Practice reading aloud the
phrases and the sentences in Part B.

Part A

Vocabulary Words		Additional Words	
consumer good	depression	affordable	prosperity
assembly line	bureaucracy	stockholder	agency
stock market		reserve	

Part B

1. When World War I ended, / factories started to make / new consumer goods.

2. Henry Ford / developed a system of mass production / that relied on an assembly line / and made automobiles more affordable.

3. In 1929, / the stock market crashed / after stock prices fell / and stockholders tried to sell / all their stocks.

4. People raced to banks / to get their savings, / but banks had loaned more money / than they had in reserve.

5. President Herbert Hoover, / who was elected in 1928, / tried to give people hope by saying, / "Prosperity / is just around the corner."

6. Instead, / the 1930s / were a decade of hard times / called the Great Depression.

7. When Franklin D. Roosevelt / was elected President / in 1932, / he created federal agencies / to help combat the effects / of the Great Depression.

8. The growing number of government workers / created a bureaucracy.

YOU ARE THERE Turn to Student Edition page 506. Practice reading aloud "You Are There" three times. Try to improve your reading each time. Record your best time on the line below.

Number of words ___71___   My Best Time _____   Words per Minute _____

Name _____ Date _____

Lesson Title: _____

The Good Times

Changes in Industry

New Art Forms

Arts and Entertainment

The End of Good Times

The Big Crash   What happened

Hard Times

Americans Suffer   Causes

The New Deal

Putting People to Work   How

Effects of the New Deal

World War II

Vocabulary Strategies

Preteach Additional Vocabulary After teaching the Vocabulary words on Student Edition page 514, explain to students that there are several other important words they will see in this lesson. Use Procedure Card 1, along with the suggestions below, to introduce the words.

seized	Tell students that synonyms include *took* and *grabbed*. Discuss the difference between a leader who seizes power and one who is elected or chosen.
infamy	Write *fame, famous, infamy,* and *infamous*. Explain that people may be famous, or have fame, for good reasons. People or events that are infamous are well-known because they are bad or evil. Infamy is the state of being infamous.
enlisted	Tell students that to enlist means to sign up for something. Discuss the difference between someone who was drafted into the army and someone who enlisted.
front	Have students offer familiar meanings for this multiple-meaning word. Explain that a line of battle in a war is called a front.
atomic	Point out the word *atom* and suffix *-ic. Atomic* means "of or relating to atoms." Tell students that an atomic bomb gets its power by releasing energy from atoms of substances such as uranium or plutonium.

WORD CARDS To help teach the lesson vocabulary, use the Word Cards on pages 319–322.

Build Fluency

Use page 204 and the steps on Procedure Card 2 to reinforce vocabulary and build fluency. Read each vocabulary word aloud and have students repeat it. Then have students work in pairs to reread the words. Follow a similar procedure with the phrases and sentences. Continue to help students build fluency by having them reread "You Are There" in the Student Edition.

Text Comprehension

BEFORE READING

Preview the Lesson Guide students in previewing the lesson using Procedure Card 3. Point out the following features of the lesson on Student Edition pages 514–521.

- **Pages 514–515** Read the "What to Know" question. Preview the time line and the photographs that show what was taking place in Germany before World War II.
- **Pages 516–517** Preview the illustration of the Japanese attack on Pearl Harbor and have students answer the question in the caption.
- **Pages 518–519** Preview the poster and the photograph of Japanese-Americans. Have students read and discuss the Fast Fact. Preview the photograph on page 519, and ask whether students have heard of D-Day. Explain that this invasion helped bring about the end of the war in Europe.

• **Pages 520–521** Preview the World War II map, and have students discuss the map skill question. Then preview the Review questions.

DURING READING

Build Comprehension of Expository Text Present the graphic organizer on page 205. Have students preview the organizer by filling in the lesson title and comparing the six main heads in the organizer with the matching subheads in the Student Edition pages 514–521. Tell students that the section subheads provide additional help with identifying important information. Use Procedure Card 4, the Reading Check questions in *Harcourt Social Studies*, and the directed reading suggestions below.

• **Page 514** After students have read "You Are There," discuss how it might feel to have your country invaded and taken over by soldiers of another country. Tell students that Germany's invasion of Poland was the beginning of World War II.

• **Pages 515–516** Have students read "Before the War" and fill in the first box in the organizer. Then have them read "A Global Conflict" and add information to that section of the organizer. Point out that students can use the section subhead "The War Begins" in the text to help them locate information.

• **Pages 517–518** After students have read "The United States Enters the War," have them write the reason and the date of the Pearl Harbor attack in the organizer. Then students can read "Americans and the War." Point out that the subheads in this box of the organizer match the section subheads in the text. Tell students to state briefly what Americans did on the home front and what happened to Japanese Americans.

• **Pages 519–521** Have students read "The War in Europe and Africa" and then make a chart of dates and events according to the directions in the organizer. Then students will read "The War in the Pacific" and make another chart. You may have students write on the back of the organizer page, or you may provide additional paper and then attach those pages to the completed organizer.

AFTER READING

Summarize Have students use their completed graphic organizers to summarize the lesson. Then have them compare their summaries to the lesson summary on page 521.

Review and Respond Work through the Review questions with students. If students need additional help with summarizing, use Focus Skill Transparency 6.

Make a Time Line Have students look at the time line on page 514 for some important dates that they may want to include on their time lines. Have students suggest and discuss other important dates from the lesson that they may want to include as well.

Leveled Readers Use the Leveled Readers and Procedure Card 5 to build fluency and comprehension.

Name _____ Date _____

DIRECTIONS Read aloud the words in Part A. Practice reading aloud the
phrases and the sentences in Part B.

Part A

Vocabulary Words	Additional Words	
rationing	seized	front
internment camps	infamy	atomic
	enlisted	

Part B

1. After World War I, / dictators seized power / in several countries.

2. Japanese planes / attacked American ships and planes /
   on December 7, 1941, / a date which President Roosevelt said /
   "will live in infamy."

3. Tens of thousands of American men and women, / eager to defend
   their country, / enlisted in the armed forces.

4. The government / began rationing some items / to make sure there
   were enough goods / to supply all the soldiers.

5. In February 1942, / President Roosevelt ordered soldiers / to put most
   Japanese Americans / in internment camps.

6. World War II / was fought on two major fronts, / one in the Pacific, /
   and the other in Europe and Africa.

7. Japan finally surrendered / after American bombers dropped
   atomic bombs / on two Japanese cities.

You ARE THERE **Turn to Student Edition page 514. Practice reading aloud "You Are There"
three times. Try to improve your reading each time. Record your best
time on the line below.**

Number of words ___60___ My Best Time _____ Words per Minute _____

Lesson Title: _____

Before the War

What much of the world faced _____

What some leaders promised _____

A Global Conflict

When war began _____ Why _____

By the end of 1941 _____

The United States Enters the War

Why _____

"A date which will live in infamy" _____

Americans and the War

The Home Front _____

Japanese Americans _____

The War in Europe and Africa

On the back of this page, or on another sheet of paper, make a chart with two columns. In one column, list all the dates from this section of the lesson. In the other column, write the events that took place.

The War in the Pacific

Make a chart of dates and events. Look at the map on page 520 for dates of some events, such as the battle on Iwo Jima.

LESSON 5 The Effects of the War

Vocabulary Strategies

Preteach Additional Vocabulary After teaching the Vocabulary words on Student Edition page 524, explain to students that there are several other important words they will see in this lesson. Use Procedure Card 1, along with the suggestions below, to introduce the words.

civilian	Tell students that anyone who is not on active duty as a soldier, police officer, or firefighter is called a civilian. Ask students to name someone they know who is not a civilian and explain.
convicted	Discuss the idea that a trial jury decides whether someone who has been accused of a crime is guilty or innocent. If the jury decides that the person is guilty, the person has been convicted.
sentenced	Explain that after someone is convicted of a crime, the person is sentenced, or given the terms of the punishment. Often, a person is sentenced to spend a certain amount of time in jail.
promote	Tell students that *encourage* and *support* are synonyms for *promote*. Have them substitute each synonym for *promote* in this sentence: "The purpose of the UN is to promote cooperation among nations."
airlift	Have students identify the two shorter words that make up this compound word. Explain that an airlift is moving goods or passengers by air, usually to or from a hard to reach area.

WORD CARDS To help teach the lesson vocabulary, use the Word Cards on pages 321–322.

Build Fluency

Use page 208 and the steps on Procedure Card 2 to reinforce vocabulary and build fluency. Read each vocabulary word aloud and have students repeat it. Then have students work in pairs to reread the words. Follow a similar procedure with the phrases and sentences. Continue to help students build fluency by having them reread "You Are There" in the Student Edition.

Text Comprehension

BEFORE READING

Preview the Lesson Guide students in previewing the lesson using Procedure Card 3. Point out the following features of the lesson on Student Edition pages 524–527.

• **Pages 524–525** Read the "What to Know" question. Preview the time line and the photograph of Anne Frank. Explain that Anne Frank's family was Jewish and hid to try to avoid being sent to concentration camps. Preview the photograph of concentration camp inmates on page 525.

- **Pages 526–527** Have students examine the map of Europe, identify communist and noncommunist countries, and answer the map skill question. Preview the photograph of a plane taking part in the Berlin Airlift.

DURING READING

Build Comprehension of Expository Text Present the graphic organizer on page 209. Have students preview the organizer by filling in the lesson title and comparing the two main heads in the organizer with the matching subheads in the Student Edition pages 524–527. Tell students that the section subheads provide additional help with identifying important information. Use Procedure Card 4, the Reading Check questions in *Harcourt Social Studies*, and the directed reading suggestions below.

- **Page 524** After students have read "You Are There," tell them that the Frank family's hiding place was discovered by the Nazis. Anne Frank died in a concentration camp.

- **Page 525** Have students read "The Holocaust." Guide them in discussing and writing information in the first box of the organizer.

- **Pages 526–527** After students have read "A Hard Peace," have them complete the organizer. Point out that the three subheads in the organizer match the section subheads in the text.

AFTER READING

Summarize Have students use their completed graphic organizers to summarize the lesson. Then have them compare their summaries to the lesson summary on page 527.

Review and Respond Work through the Review questions with students. If students need additional help with summarizing, use Focus Skill Transparency 6.

Write an Essay Help students relate the topic to their own experiences by asking why it is better for people to discuss their differences and try to work them out in a friendly way than to get into fights and become enemies. Point out that the same is true for nations. Suggest that students use some of the ideas from their discussion in their essays.

Leveled Readers Use the Leveled Readers and Procedure Card 5 to build fluency and comprehension.

Name _____ Date _____

Part A

Vocabulary Words		Additional Words	
concentration	Holocaust	civilian	promote
camps	communism	convicted	airlift
genocide	free world	sentenced	

Part B

1. About 20 million soldiers / and nearly 30 million civilians / died in World War II.

2. After the war was over, / people discovered / that the Nazis had put millions of innocent people / in concentration camps.

3. The murder of more than 6 million Jewish people / was genocide, / an attempt / to kill an entire people.

4. This terrible mass murder / of more than two-thirds / of all European Jews / became known as the Holocaust.

5. Many Nazi leaders / were brought to trial, / convicted, / and sentenced to death / for their crimes.

6. The United Nations / was formed in 1945 / to promote cooperation / among nations.

7. After the war, / the Soviet Union / set up communist governments / in eastern European countries.

8. The free world / saw this as a threat.

9. The Allies / started an airlift / after the Soviets blocked all travel / between Germany's capital, Berlin, / and West Germany.

YOU ARE THERE Turn to Student Edition page 524. Practice reading aloud "You Are There" three times. Try to improve your reading each time. Record your best time on the line below.

Number of words ___76___   My Best Time _____   Words per Minute _____

Name _____ Date _____

Lesson Title: _____

The Holocaust

A Deadly Plan

Where Nazis put millions of people _____

Hitler's plan _____

Result _____

What happened to Nazi leaders _____

_____

A Hard Peace

The United Nations

When formed _____

Location today _____

Purpose _____

_____

_____

New Trouble in Europe

Why _____

_____

_____

The Berlin Airlift

What Soviets did _____

_____

What Allies did _____

_____

_____

_____

The 1950s

Vocabulary Strategies

Preteach Additional Vocabulary After teaching the Vocabulary words on Student Edition page 532, explain to students that there are several other important words they will see in this lesson. Use Procedure Card 1, along with the suggestions below, to introduce the words.

parallel	Draw a set of horizontal parallel lines and define *parallel*. Explain that *parallel* also refers to a line of latitude. On a world map or globe, have students locate the 38th parallel north of the equator. Point out that it runs roughly along the border between North Korea and South Korea.
interstate	Tell students that the prefix *inter-* means "between." Have students define *interstate*.
impact	Tell students that one meaning for *impact* is "crash or collision." We also use *impact* to mean "effect," especially when the effect is a strong one.
hearing	Explain that this familiar word sometimes has a special meaning. For example, a committee of the House or Senate may hold hearings to investigate an issue. People go before the committee and answer questions about the matter being investigated.
reckless	Give *irresponsible* and *careless* as synonyms for *reckless*.

WORD CARDS To help teach the lesson vocabulary, use the Word Cards on pages 321–322.

Build Fluency

Use page 212 and the steps on Procedure Card 2 to reinforce vocabulary and build fluency. Read each vocabulary word aloud and have students repeat it. Then have students work in pairs to reread the words. Follow a similar procedure with the phrases and sentences. Continue to help students build fluency by having them reread "You Are There" in the Student Edition.

Text Comprehension

BEFORE READING

Preview the Lesson Guide students in previewing the lesson using Procedure Card 3. Point out the following features of the lesson on Student Edition pages 532–537.

- **Pages 532–533** Read the "What to Know" question. Preview the photograph of the Korean War Memorial, and have students find on the time line the dates for the beginning and end of the Korean War. Preview the photograph and map on page 533, and have students answer the map skill question.

- **Pages 534–535** Preview the photographs, and discuss the changes they show in American life during the 1950s.

- **Pages 536–537** Preview the photograph of a fallout shelter. Explain that the Cold War and the arms race between the United States and the Soviet Union caused people to fear a possible nuclear attack by the Soviet Union. On page 537, preview the photograph of the Jupiter rocket. Ask students what NASA stands for.

DURING READING

Build Comprehension of Expository Text Present the graphic organizer on page 213. Have students preview the organizer by filling in the lesson title and comparing the four main heads in the organizer with the matching subheads in the Student Edition pages 532–537. Tell students that the section subheads provide additional help with identifying important information. Use Procedure Card 4, the Reading Check questions in *Harcourt Social Studies*, and the directed reading suggestions below.

- **Page 532** After students have read "You Are There," call attention to the photograph of the Korean War Memorial on this page. Ask students why they think the artist may have decided on this design to honor the soldiers.

- **Page 533** Have students read "The Korean War" and fill in the first box in the organizer.

- **Page 534** Before students read "A Growing Economy," have them examine the Cause and Effect chart in the organizer. Tell them to think about causes and effects as they read and then to fill in the blanks in the chart.

- **Pages 535–537** Have students read "Television Brings Changes" and fill in that box in the organizer. Discuss how television has made it easier for citizens to see their government in action. Then students can read "The Cold War" and complete the organizer. Point out the two subheads that match the section subheads in the text.

AFTER READING

Summarize Have students use their completed graphic organizers to summarize the lesson. Then have them compare their summaries to the lesson summary on page 537.

Review and Respond Work through the Review questions with students. If students need additional help with summarizing, use Focus Skill Transparency 6.

Write a Letter Suggest that students reread the section of the lesson that tells about television in the 1950s for ideas about what to include in their letters. Remind them also to look again at the illustration that shows what a television set in the 1950s looked like. Explain that screens were smaller than they are today and that early television shows were in black and white, not color.

Leveled Readers Use the Leveled Readers and Procedure Card 5 to build fluency and comprehension.

Name _____ Date _____

DIRECTIONS Read aloud the words in Part A. Practice reading aloud the phrases and the sentences in Part B.

Part A

Vocabulary Words		**Additional Words**	
cease-fire	arms race	parallel	hearing
suburb	satellite	interstate	reckless
cold war		impact	

Part B

1. In June 1950, / North Korean soldiers / crossed the 38th parallel, / which was the boundary / between North and South Korea.

2. The Korean War / lasted until 1953, / when both sides / agreed to a cease-fire.

3. In the 1950s, / builders / started building huge suburbs / outside of cities.

4. The United States / started building interstate highways / that made it easier to travel by car / and to ship goods by truck.

5. Television / first became popular in the 1950s / and made a great impact / on Americans.

6. A Senate investigation, / the Army-McCarthy hearings, / was shown live on television / in 1954.

7. Millions of Americans / saw that McCarthy was reckless / and had no proof / to back up charges / that he had made.

8. The Cold War / started an arms race / between the United States / and the Soviet Union.

9. In October 1957, / the Soviet Union / launched the world's first space satellite.

YOU ARE THERE Turn to Student Edition page 532. Practice reading aloud "You Are There" three times. Try to improve your reading each time. Record your best time on the line below.

Number of words ___72___ My Best Time _____ Words per Minute _____

Name _____ Date _____

Lesson Title: _____

The Korean War

North Korea Invades   When _____   What country _____

Who voted to send soldiers _____

Outcome _____

A Growing Economy

Economic Boom

Cause		Effect
demand for housing	→	
	→	easier to travel and to ship goods
bought more goods	→	

Television Brings Changes

What changed _____

Television and Politics   What changed _____

The Cold War

Was about _____

The Arms Race   Between _____

_____

The Space Race   First space satellite _____

Congress set up _____.   When _____

LESSON 2 **The 1960s**

Vocabulary Strategies

Preteach Additional Vocabulary After teaching the Vocabulary words on Student Edition page 538, explain to students that there are several other important words they will see in this lesson. Use Procedure Card 1, along with the suggestions below, to introduce the words.

inauguration	Tell students that the official ceremony in which a newly elected President takes office is called an inauguration.
spaceship	Have students identify the two smaller words that make up this compound word. Then ask them to define *spaceship*.
insurance	Explain that people buy insurance to help them financially in case something bad happens. Automobile insurance pays for damage to a person's car. Health insurance pays medical bills when someone is ill.
opposition	Write *oppose* and *opposition*. Tell students that to oppose something is to disagree with it or to be against it. Then ask students to define *opposition* in this sentence: "Opposition to the war began to grow."
reelection	Point out the base word *elect*, to which the prefix *re-* and suffix *-tion* have been added. Remind students that *re-* means "again," and *-tion* means "act of." Ask what *reelection* means.

WORD CARDS To help teach the lesson vocabulary, use the Word Cards on pages 321–324.

Build Fluency

Use page 216 and the steps on Procedure Card 2 to reinforce vocabulary and build fluency. Read each vocabulary word aloud and have students repeat it. Then have students work in pairs to reread the words. Follow a similar procedure with the phrases and sentences. Continue to help students build fluency by having them reread "You Are There" in the Student Edition.

Text Comprehension

BEFORE READING

Preview the Lesson Guide students in previewing the lesson using Procedure Card 3. Point out the following features of the lesson on Student Edition pages 538–543.

• **Pages 538–539** Read the "What to Know" question. Preview the time line, the photograph of President Kennedy, and the photograph of a Peace Corps worker speaking to villagers in a developing country. Explain that President Kennedy started the Peace Corps.

- **Pages 540–541** Have students examine the Cuban missile crisis map and answer the map skill question. Explain that Americans were upset to have these missiles so close to the United States. Preview the illustration of the Apollo 11 moon landing. Have students answer the question in the caption.

- **Pages 542–543** Preview the map of Vietnam and the photographs of American soldiers in Vietnam and of people in the United States protesting the war. Then preview the Review questions.

DURING READING

Build Comprehension of Expository Text Present the graphic organizer on page 217. Have students preview the organizer by filling in the lesson title and comparing the four main heads in the organizer with the matching subheads in the Student Edition pages 538–543. Tell students that the section subheads provide additional help with identifying important information. Use Procedure Card 4, the Reading Check questions in *Harcourt Social Studies*, and the directed reading suggestions below.

- **Page 538** After students have read "You Are There," call attention to the photograph of President Kennedy on this page.

- **Pages 539–540** Have students read "A New Decade" and fill in the first box in the organizer. Then have them read "Trouble in Cuba." Point out that they can find some information in the text before the section subhead "The Cuban Missile Crisis." The rest of the information for this box is found under that section subhead in the text.

- **Page 541** Before students read "Changes at Home," have them notice the structure of the organizer. Point out the two subheads that match the section subheads in the text. Tell students that they can write information in each of the three boxes either as they read or after reading this section of the lesson.

- **Pages 542–543** Have students read "The Vietnam War" and complete the organizer. Students can match the subheads to the section subheads in the text to help them locate information.

AFTER READING

Summarize Have students use their completed graphic organizers to summarize the lesson. Then have them compare their summaries to the lesson summary on page 543.

Review and Respond Work through the Review questions with students. If students need additional help with summarizing, use Focus Skill Transparency 6.

Write a Journal Entry Discuss how television viewers in 1969 must have felt watching the first moon landing. Suggest that students reread the section of the lesson that tells about the voyage to the moon and look again at the illustration on page 541. Tell them to include information from the lesson in their journal entries and also to imagine and describe the feelings they would have had.

Leveled Readers Use the Leveled Readers and Procedure Card 5 to build fluency and comprehension.

Name _____ Date _____

DIRECTIONS Read aloud the words in Part A. Practice reading aloud the phrases and the sentences in Part B.

Part A

Vocabulary Words	Additional Words	
developing country	inauguration	opposition
crisis	spaceship	reelection
	insurance	

Part B

1. At his inauguration, / President John F. Kennedy / encouraged Americans / to work to help their country.

2. He started the Peace Corps, / which sends Americans / to developing countries / to work as teachers, / health educators, / and engineers.

3. The first step / in President Kennedy's plan to land an astronaut on the moon / was to build a spaceship / that could orbit Earth.

4. In October 1962, / a crisis developed / between the United States / and the Soviet Union / over nuclear missiles in Cuba.

5. President Lyndon Johnson / started new programs, / including Medicare, / which provides health insurance / to older Americans.

6. American soldiers / were sent to fight in Vietnam, / but opposition to the war / began to grow.

7. President Johnson / decided not to run for reelection, / and Richard Nixon / was elected President / in 1968.

YOU ARE THERE Turn to Student Edition page 538. Practice reading aloud "You Are There" three times. Try to improve your reading each time. Record your best time on the line below.

Number of words ___50___ My Best Time _____ Words per Minute _____

Name _____ Date _____

Lesson Title: _____

A New Decade

John F. Kennedy   Program he started _____

Goal for the space program _____

Trouble in Cuba

When _____   Cause _____

The Cuban Missile Crisis   How long it lasted _____

How it ended _____

Changes at Home

New President _____

The Great Society
Programs that continue today

_____

Voyage to the Moon

When _____

The Vietnam War

The United States Goes to War   Why _____

What President Johnson did _____

The War Divides Americans   What broke out _____

The War Ends   When _____   How _____

LESSON 3 **Equal Rights for All**

Vocabulary Strategies

Preteach Additional Vocabulary After teaching the Vocabulary words on Student Edition page 546, explain to students that there are several other important words they will see in this lesson. Use Procedure Card 1, along with the suggestions below, to introduce the words.

public	Explain that this word is related to the Latin *populus*, which means "people." Something that is public, such as a public school or public transportation, is shared by all the people in a community.
lawful	Tell students that this word is a synonym for *legal*. Point out the base word *law* and suffix *-ful*.
riot	Point out that we may call something that is very funny a *riot*. However, the word *riot* also names a violent situation that occurs when a group of people is angry.
content	Tell students that this word, with the stress on the first syllable, means "what is contained." It is a homograph of *content*, with the stress on the second syllable, which means "satisfied."
employer	Point out the base word *employ* and suffix *-er*. An employer is a person who provides others with jobs and pays them for the work they do.

WORD CARDS To help teach the lesson vocabulary, use the Word Cards on pages 323–324.

Build Fluency

Use page 220 and the steps on Procedure Card 2 to reinforce vocabulary and build fluency. Read each vocabulary word aloud and have students repeat it. Then have students work in pairs to reread the words. Follow a similar procedure with the phrases and sentences. Continue to help students build fluency by having them reread "You Are There" in the Student Edition.

Text Comprehension

BEFORE READING

Preview the Lesson Guide students in previewing the lesson using Procedure Card 3. Point out the following features of the lesson on Student Edition pages 546–551.

- **Pages 546–547** Read the "What to Know" question. Preview the time line, the New York Times headline, and the photograph of children in school. Explain that African American children and white children did not always attend school together. Have students read Children in History and discuss the Make It Relevant question.

- **Pages 548–549** Preview and discuss the illustrated time line of the Civil Rights movement.

- **Pages 550–551** Preview the photograph of Cesar Chavez and the Review questions on page 550. Call attention to the biography of Martin Luther King, Jr., on page 551. Ask what students already know about this leader.

DURING READING

Build Comprehension of Expository Text Present the graphic organizer on page 221. Have students preview the organizer by filling in the lesson title and comparing the three main heads in the organizer with the matching subheads in the Student Edition pages 546–550. Tell students that the section subheads provide additional help with identifying important information. Use Procedure Card 4, the Reading Check questions in *Harcourt Social Studies,* and the directed reading suggestions below.

- **Page 546** After students have read "You Are There," discuss the decision in *Brown v. Board of Education* and why it was so important.

- **Page 547** Have students read "A Supreme Court Ruling" and fill in the first box in the organizer.

- **Pages 548–549** After students have read "A National Movement," discuss the structure of the organizer. Point out that students will write information under the head that matches the section head and under the two subheads that match the section subheads in the text.

- **Pages 549–550** Have students read "Civil Rights for All" and complete the organizer. Remind them to use the section subhead to help locate information.

AFTER READING

Summarize Have students use their completed graphic organizers to summarize the lesson. Then have them compare their summaries to the lesson summary on page 550.

Review and Respond Work through the Review questions with students. If students need additional help with summarizing, use Focus Skill Transparency 6.

Deliver a Speech Provide a copy or copies of Dr. King's "I Have a Dream" speech. You may want to go through the speech with students to help with any unfamiliar pronunciations and meanings before students take turns reading parts of the speech aloud.

Leveled Readers Use the Leveled Readers and Procedure Card 5 to build fluency and comprehension.

Name _____ Date _____

DIRECTIONS **Read aloud the words in Part A. Practice reading aloud the phrases and the sentences in Part B.**

Part A

Vocabulary Words	Additional Words	
integration	public	content
civil rights	lawful	employer
nonviolence	riot	

Part B

1. In 1896, / the Supreme Court / said that separate public places / for white people and African Americans / were lawful / as long as the places were equal.

2. In 1951, / Thurgood Marshall / called for integration / in public schools.

3. After the Supreme Court / ordered an end to segregation in public schools, / there were riots / in Little Rock, Arkansas.

4. In the 1950s, / more and more African Americans / demanded their full civil rights.

5. Martin Luther King, Jr., / was an African American leader / who believed in using nonviolence / to bring about change.

6. He hoped that his children / would one day / "not be judged by the color of their skin, / but by the content of their character."

7. Malcolm X / was an African American leader / who did not agree with King's ideas / about nonviolence.

8. Migrant farm workers / and women / also worked for equal rights / and to be treated equally by employers.

YOU ARE THERE Turn to Student Edition page 546. Practice reading aloud "You Are There" three times. Try to improve your reading each time. Record your best time on the line below.

Number of words ___53___ My Best Time _____ Words per Minute _____

Name _____ Date _____

Lesson Title: _____

A Supreme Court Ruling

Brown v. Board of Education   What Linda Brown wanted

_____

What the Supreme Court ordered _____

_____

A National Movement

Who _____   What they demanded _____

The Montgomery Bus Boycott   What led up to it

_____

Outcome _____

_____

The Struggle for Civil Rights

Leader _____   Believed in _____

Leader _____   Wanted _____

Civil Rights for All

What Congress passed _____   When _____

Rights for Everyone   Other groups _____

LESSON 4 # The 1970s and 1980s

Vocabulary Strategies

Preteach Additional Vocabulary After teaching the Vocabulary words on Student Edition page 556, explain to students that there are several other important words they will see in this lesson. Use Procedure Card 1, along with the suggestions below, to introduce the words.

foreign policy	Tell students that a nation's foreign policy is its plan for dealing with other nations.
unemployment	Have students identify the base word *employ*, prefix *un-*, and suffix *-ment*. Remind them that *un-* means "not." Unemployment is the state of not having a job.
accord	Tell students that synonyms for *accord* include *agreement* and *treaty*.
hostage	Discuss the concept of holding someone hostage. Be sure students understand that hostage-takers usually hope to get something in return for the safe return of a hostage.
marked	Remind students that one meaning for *marked* is "graded." It can also mean "signaled," as in this sentence: "The meeting between the two leaders marked a change in the Cold War."
reunited	Have students use the base word *unite*, prefix *re-*, and ending *-ed* to define *reunited*. ("joined, or put together, again")

WORD CARDS To help teach the lesson vocabulary, use the Word Cards on pages 323–324.

Build Fluency

Use page 224 and the steps on Procedure Card 2 to reinforce vocabulary and build fluency. Read each vocabulary word aloud and have students repeat it. Then have students work in pairs to reread the words. Follow a similar procedure with the phrases and sentences. Continue to help students build fluency by having them reread "You Are There" in the Student Edition.

Text Comprehension

BEFORE READING

Preview the Lesson Guide students in previewing the lesson using Procedure Card 3. Point out the following features of the lesson on Student Edition pages 556–561.

- **Pages 556–557** Read the "What to Know" question. Preview the time line and the photographs. Explain that information that came out in the Watergate hearings caused President Nixon to resign.

- **Pages 558–559** Have students examine the unemployment graph and answer the question in the caption. Preview the photographs showing gas shortages in the 1970s and President Reagan in the 1980s.

- **Pages 560–561** Preview the photographs of the Berlin Wall. Have students examine the map on page 561 and answer the map skill question. Then preview the Review questions.

Build Comprehension of Expository Text Present the graphic organizer on page 225. Have students preview the organizer by filling in the lesson title and comparing the four main heads in the organizer with the matching subheads in the Student Edition pages 556–561. Tell students that the section subheads provide additional help with identifying important information. Use Procedure Card 4, the Reading Check questions in *Harcourt Social Studies,* and the directed reading suggestions below.

- **Page 556** After students have read "You Are There," tell them that many families in the United States watched the Watergate hearings on TV and so were able to make up their own minds about what they saw and heard.

- **Page 557** Have students read "President Richard M. Nixon" and fill in the first box in the organizer.

- **Pages 558–559** After students have read "Global Challenges," discuss the structure of the organizer. Point out that students will write information under the head that matches the section head and under the two subheads that match the section subheads in the text. Then have students read "President Ronald Reagan" and fill in that box in the organizer.

- **Pages 560–561** Have students read "Ending the Cold War" and complete the organizer. Remind them to use the section subheads to locate information.

Summarize Have students use their completed graphic organizers to summarize the lesson. Then have them compare their summaries to the lesson summary on page 561.

Review and Respond Work through the Review questions with students. If students need additional help with summarizing, use Focus Skill Transparency 6.

Write a Diary Entry Discuss with students the worries and uncertainty that the Cold War caused for people in the United States and how people may have felt when it ended. Suggest that students reread the section of the lesson that tells how and why the Cold War ended. Tell them to use information from the lesson when they write their diary entries.

Leveled Readers Use the Leveled Readers and Procedure Card 5 to build fluency and comprehension.

Name _____ Date _____

Part A

Vocabulary Words	Additional Words	
arms control	foreign policy	hostage
scandal	unemployment	marked
deficit	accord	reunited

Part B

1. President Richard M. Nixon / accomplished important things / in foreign policy.

2. In 1972, / he and Soviet leader Leonid Brezhnev / agreed on a plan / for arms control.

3. A scandal / called the Watergate scandal / ended Nixon's presidency.

4. During the 1970s, / the nation's economy slowed/ and unemployment rose.

5. President Jimmy Carter / helped bring about a peace agreement, / called the Camp David Accords, / between Israel and Egypt.

6. In 1979, / a group of armed students in Iran / seized workers at the American Embassy / and held them hostage.

7. President Ronald Reagan's tax cuts / helped the economy / but created budget deficits.

8. The 1986 meeting / between Mikhail Gorbachev, the leader of the Soviet Union, / and President Reagan / marked a change in the Cold War.

9. In 1989, / the government leaders of East Germany / opened the gates of the Berlin Wall, / and Germany was reunited / the following year.

YOU ARE THERE Turn to Student Edition page 556. Practice reading aloud "You Are There" three times. Try to improve your reading each time. Record your best time on the line below.

Number of words ___64___ My Best Time _____ Words per Minute _____

Name _____ Date _____

Lesson Title: _____

President Richard M. Nixon

Nixon in Office Worked to lessen _____

Resigned because of _____

Global Challenges

Challenges during the 1970s _____

_____

Uncertain Times	President Jimmy Carter

Uncertain Times

Cause	Effect
high gas prices	_____

President Jimmy Carter

Camp David Accords between

_____

President Ronald Reagan

A Different Approach What he believed_____

_____

A Wall Comes Down
New Soviet leader

_____

What came down _____

When

_____

Ending the Cold War

A New Eastern Europe

What ended _____

When _____

What broke out _____

LESSON 5 **The 1990s**

Vocabulary Strategies

Preteach Additional Vocabulary After teaching the Vocabulary words on Student Edition page 562, explain to students that there are several other important words they will see in this lesson. Use Procedure Card 1, along with the suggestions below, to introduce the words.

failing	Tell students that an antonym for *failing* is *succeeding*. Have them tell what happens when a business is failing.
dealt	Point out the word *deal* and ending *-t*. Explain that the past tense of *deal*, as in "deal with problems" is *dealt*, which rhymes with *belt*.
prospect	Tell students that this word is formed from the Latin root *pro-*, which means "forward," and *specere*, which means "to look." A prospect is something you look forward to in the future.
swept	Point out that *swept* is the past tense of *sweep*. Discuss its meaning in this context: "The ground troops swept into Kuwait and drove out the Iraqi forces."
controversy	Explain that controversy is a dispute or disagreement that often involves strong feelings on both sides.

WORD CARDS To help teach the lesson vocabulary, use the Word Cards on pages 323–324.

Build Fluency

Use page 228 and the steps on Procedure Card 2 to reinforce vocabulary and build fluency. Read each vocabulary word aloud and have students repeat it. Then have students work in pairs to reread the words. Follow a similar procedure with the phrases and sentences. Continue to help students build fluency by having them reread "You Are There" in the Student Edition.

Text Comprehension

BEFORE READING

Preview the Lesson Guide students in previewing the lesson using Procedure Card 3. Point out the following features of the lesson on Student Edition pages 562–567.

- **Pages 562–563** Read the "What to Know" question. Preview the time line and the photographs of the space shuttle Discovery and of President George H. W. Bush.

- **Pages 564–565** Preview the photograph of soldiers in the Gulf War and the portrait of their commander, General Colin Powell. On page 565, preview the photograph of President Bill Clinton and members of Congress who worked together to balance the national budget.

• **Pages 566–567** Preview the photograph of the Oklahoma City National Memorial, and discuss the significance of the empty chairs. Point out the small inset photograph showing the USS *Cole*. Then preview the Review questions.

DURING READING

Build Comprehension of Expository Text Present the graphic organizer on page 229. Have students preview the organizer by filling in the lesson title and comparing the four main heads in the organizer with the matching subheads in the Student Edition pages 562–567. Tell students that the section subheads provide additional help with identifying important information. Use Procedure Card 4, the Reading Check questions in *Harcourt Social Studies*, and the directed reading suggestions below.

• **Page 562** After students have read "You Are There," have them look at the photograph of the launch on this page and reread the caption. Students may be interested in researching the space shuttle or the Hubble Space Telescope.

• **Page 563** Have students read "Challenges for a New President" and fill in the first box in the organizer.

• **Pages 564–565** After students have read "The Persian Gulf War," point out the structure of the organizer. Students will write information under the head that matches the section head and under the two subheads that match the section subheads in the text. Then have students read "Changes at Home" and fill in that box in the organizer.

• **Pages 566–567** Have students read "Facing New Dangers" and complete the organizer.

AFTER READING

Summarize Have students use their completed graphic organizers to summarize the lesson. Then have them compare their summaries to the lesson summary on page 567.

Review and Respond Work through the Review questions with students. If students need additional help with summarizing, use Focus Skill Transparency 6.

Write an Editorial Remind students that an editorial expresses an opinion. Have them identify the opinion they will express in the editorials they are going to write. Discuss how students might use facts and examples from the lesson to support this opinion.

Leveled Readers Use the Leveled Readers and Procedure Card 5 to build fluency and comprehension.

Name _____ Date _____

DIRECTIONS Read aloud the words in Part A. Practice reading aloud the
phrases and the sentences in Part B.

Part A

Vocabulary Words	Additional Words	
recession	failing	swept
coalition	dealt	controversy
terrorism	prospect	

Part B

1. The new decade / brought challenges, / including a recession / that lasted for more than two years.

2. President George H. W. Bush / tried to boost the nation's economy / by passing laws / to help failing industries.

3. Although President Bush / was busy with problems at home, / he also / dealt with world events.

4. He talked about / the prospect of a world / without the conflicts of the past, / but new conflicts / soon developed.

5. After the nation of Iraq / invaded the small country of Kuwait, / thirty-three nations / joined the American coalition / against Iraq.

6. Allied ground troops / swept into Kuwait / and drove out / the Iraqi forces.

7. President Bill Clinton / oversaw a period / of great economic growth, / but he also experienced / controversy.

8. At the end of the twentieth century, / the United States / faced new dangers / in the form of terrorism.

You ARE THERE Turn to Student Edition page 562. Practice reading aloud "You Are There" three times. Try to improve your reading each time. Record your best time on the line below.

Number of words ___63___ My Best Time _____ Words per Minute _____

Name _____ Date _____

Lesson Title: _____

Challenges for a New President

New President _____ When elected _____

The Economy and Politics Problem at home _____

The Persian Gulf War

When _____ What happened _____

_____

Building a Coalition

How many nations _____

Led by _____

Operation Desert Storm

Outcome _____

_____

Changes at Home

New President _____ When elected _____

New Leadership Period of _____

Balanced _____ Also experienced _____

Facing New Dangers

Terrorism

When _____ Where _____

When _____ Where _____

When _____ Where _____

_____

LESSON 1 # New Challenges

Vocabulary Strategies

Preteach Additional Vocabulary After teaching the Vocabulary words on Student Edition page 572, explain to students that there are several other important words they will see in this lesson. Use Procedure Card 1, along with the suggestions below, to introduce the words.

recount	Ask students to count several items. Then ask them to recount the items. Remind them that the prefix *re-* means "again."
vehicle	Have students quickly name as many different kinds of vehicles as they can. Point out that a vehicle may carry people on land, on or under the water, in the air, or in space.
Pentagon	Draw a five-sided shape. Explain that it is called a pentagon from the Greek word *penta,* meaning "five." The headquarters of the Department of Defense in Washington, D.C., is this shape and is called the Pentagon.
security	Give *safety* and *protection* as synonyms for *security.*
prescription	Explain that a prescription medicine is one for which a doctor writes an order, or prescription, to be filled at a pharmacy.
landfall	Have students identify the two shorter words that make up this compound word. Explain that hurricanes form over water. Ask what students think it means for a hurricane to make landfall.

WORD CARDS To help teach the lesson vocabulary, use the Word Cards on pages 325–326.

Build Fluency

Use page 232 and the steps on Procedure Card 2 to reinforce vocabulary and build fluency. Read each vocabulary word aloud and have students repeat it. Then have students work in pairs to reread the words. Follow a similar procedure with the phrases and sentences. Continue to help students build fluency by having them reread "You Are There" in the Student Edition.

Text Comprehension

BEFORE READING

Preview the Lesson Guide students in previewing the lesson using Procedure Card 3. Point out the following features of the lesson on Student Edition pages 572–575.

• **Page 572** Read the "What to Know" question. Preview the time line, and explain that George W. Bush, who became President in 2001, is the son of former President George H. W. Bush. Preview the photograph of workers recounting ballots in the 2000 election.

- **Page 573** Preview the photograph showing the twin towers of the World Trade Center. Explain that this picture was taken shortly after the planes hit, before the towers collapsed and fell. Call attention to the inset photograph of President Bush speaking with rescue workers after the attacks.

- **Pages 574–575** Preview the photograph of soldiers in Iraq on page 574, and the photograph of New Orleans on page 575. Tell students that Hurricane Katrina was one of the worst natural disasters ever in the United States.

DURING READING

Build Comprehension of Expository Text Present the graphic organizer on page 233. Have students preview the organizer by filling in the lesson title and comparing the two main heads in the organizer with the matching subheads in the Student Edition pages 572–575. Tell students that the section subheads provide additional help with identifying important information. Use Procedure Card 4, the Reading Check questions in *Harcourt Social Studies*, and the directed reading suggestions below.

- **Page 572** After students have read "You Are There," tell them that it did take several weeks before the final results of the election were known.

- **Page 573** Have students read "Events Shape the Nation." Point out the structure of the organizer, with a separate box for each of the section subheads in the text. Guide students in writing brief summaries of the events.

- **Pages 574–575** After students have read "Modern Challenges," point out the structure of the organizer. Students can then write information under the subhead in each box to complete the organizer.

AFTER READING

Summarize Have students use their completed graphic organizers to summarize the lesson. Then have them compare their summaries to the lesson summary on page 575.

Review and Respond Work through the Review questions with students. If students need additional help with summarizing, use Focus Skill Transparency 6.

Write Newspaper Headlines You may want to provide examples of some recent headlines. Discuss how headline writers express the main idea about an event in a limited number of words. Remind students to pick three important events from the lesson and write a headline to give readers important information about each event.

Leveled Readers Use the Leveled Readers and Procedure Card 5 to build fluency and comprehension.

Name _____ Date _____

DIRECTIONS Read aloud the words in Part A. Practice reading aloud the phrases and the sentences in Part B.

Part A

Vocabulary Words	Additional Words	
hijack	recount	security
	vehicle	prescription
	Pentagon	landfall

Part B

1. The vote / in the presidential election of 2000 / was too close to call, / so Florida state officials / began to recount the votes.

2. On September 11, 2001, / terrorists / hijacked four American airplanes / and used the vehicles / as weapons.

3. The terrorists / flew airplanes / into the twin towers of the World Trade Center / in New York City / and into the Pentagon / in Washington, D.C.

4. The United States sent troops / to Afghanistan and Iraq, / and set up / the Department of Homeland Security.

5. President George W. Bush / led efforts / to help pay for prescription medicines / for older Americans.

6. Four hurricanes / made landfall in Florida / in 2004, / and Hurricane Katrina / hit the Gulf Coast / in 2005.

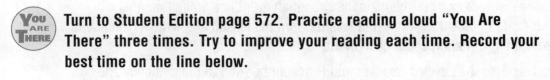 Turn to Student Edition page 572. Practice reading aloud "You Are There" three times. Try to improve your reading each time. Record your best time on the line below.

Number of words ___61___ My Best Time _____ Words per Minute _____

Name _____ Date _____

Lesson Title: _____

Events Shape the Nation

The 2000 Election

Problem _____

_____

Outcome _____

_____

Terrorists Strike

Date _____

What happened _____

_____

_____

Modern Challenges

Fighting Terrorism

When _____

Where _____

Outcome _____

_____

_____

When _____

Where _____

Outcome _____

_____

Changes at Home

Set up _____

_____

Other Problems _____

_____

_____

_____

UNIT 6

Chapter 14

LESSON 2 **Our Nation's Economy**

Vocabulary Strategies

Preteach Additional Vocabulary After teaching the Vocabulary words on Student Edition page 576, explain to students that there are several other important words they will see in this lesson. Use Procedure Card 1, along with the suggestions below, to introduce the words.

consumer	Have students use this context clue: "They produce the goods and services that consumers, or buyers, want." Point out that we are all consumers when we buy things that we want or need.
factor	Explain that a factor is something that helps bring about a certain result. Factors of production include the different things that are needed to produce goods.
allocation	Discuss this sentence from the lesson: "Different societies have different allocation methods, or ways of distributing scarce goods and services." Tell students that *allocation* and *allocate* are from the Latin word *locus*, meaning "place." Other words from *locus* include *locate*, *location*, and *local*.
quality	Tell students that this word has several meanings. One meaning is "level of excellence." Ask which product is more likely to break or wear out, a product of higher quality or one of lower quality.

WORD CARDS To help teach the lesson vocabulary, use the Word Cards on pages 325–326.

Build Fluency

Use page 236 and the steps on Procedure Card 2 to reinforce vocabulary and build fluency. Read each vocabulary word aloud and have students repeat it. Then have students work in pairs to reread the words. Follow a similar procedure with the phrases and sentences. Continue to help students build fluency by having them reread "You Are There" in the Student Edition.

Text Comprehension

BEFORE READING

Preview the Lesson Guide students in previewing the lesson using Procedure Card 3. Point out the following features of the lesson on Student Edition pages 576–581.

- **Pages 576–577** Read the "What to Know" question. Preview the photograph of people at a shopping mall and discuss the term "economic decisions." Then preview the photograph of people working in a factory. Tell students that they will be able to answer the question about factors of production after they read this section of the lesson.

- **Pages 578–579** Preview the photograph showing a boy making a purchase. Then preview the photograph on page 579, and have students examine the graph. Discuss the question in the caption.

234 ■ Reading Support and Intervention

Unit 6, Chapter 14, Lesson 2

• **Pages 580–581** Preview and discuss the photograph of skilled workers. Then preview the Review questions.

DURING READING

Build Comprehension of Expository Text Present the graphic organizer on page 237. Have students preview the organizer by filling in the lesson title and comparing the four main heads in the organizer with the matching subheads in the Student Edition pages 576–581. Tell students that the section subheads provide additional help with identifying important information. Use Procedure Card 4, the Reading Check questions in *Harcourt Social Studies,* and the directed reading suggestions below.

• **Page 576** After students have read "You Are There," ask what they think about when they have to make economic decisions like the one described in this passage.

• **Page 577** Before students read "Free Enterprise," have them examine the first part of the organizer. Explain that students will write three fundamental economic questions in the first set of three boxes. In the second set of boxes, students will write three factors of production, which will be discussed in the text under the section subhead "Providing Goods and Services."

• **Pages 578–579** After students have read "Using Scarce Resources," have them write the names of two different economic systems in the organizer. Then students can read "Prices in a Market Economy" and write three factors that affect prices.

• **Pages 580–581** Have students read "Productivity" and complete the organizer by listing factors that affect productivity under the subhead in the first box. Tell them to list three general terms rather than specific items under the subhead in the second box.

AFTER READING

Summarize Have students use their completed graphic organizers to summarize the lesson. Then have them compare their summaries to the lesson summary on page 581.

Review and Respond Work through the Review questions with students. If students need additional help with summarizing, use Focus Skill Transparency 6.

Make a Poster Discuss the three economic questions named in this lesson and concepts students have learned about how producers make decisions on what to produce. Then discuss how students might explain and illustrate these ideas in a poster. You may want to have students work in pairs to plan and create their posters.

Leveled Readers Use the Leveled Readers and Procedure Card 5 to build fluency and comprehension.

DIRECTIONS   Read aloud the words in Part A. Practice reading aloud the phrases and the sentences in Part B.

Part A

Vocabulary Words		Additional Words
free enterprise	command	consumer
productivity	economy	factor
interdependent	competition	allocation
market economy	human	quality
capital goods	resources	
specialization	scarcity	

Part B

1. In a free enterprise economy, / people are free to produce the goods and services / that consumers want.

2. Together, / human resources, natural resources, and capitals goods / are called / the factors of production.

3. Different societies / have different allocation methods / to deal with a scarcity / of goods and services.

4. In a command economy, / the government controls / the factors of production.

5. In a market economy, / goods and services / are allocated largely by prices.

6. Without competition, / prices often rise / and quality suffers.

7. Important factors in productivity / include an educated workforce, / capital goods, / and specialization.

8. People in different places / are interdependent / —they depend on one another / for natural resources, / finished products, / and services.

You ARE There Turn to Student Edition page 576. Practice reading aloud "You Are There" three times. Try to improve your reading each time. Record your best time on the line below.

Number of words ___81___   My Best Time _____   Words per Minute _____

Name _____ Date _____

Lesson Title: _____

Free Enterprise
Three fundamental economic questions

[ ]   [ ]   [ ]

Providing Goods and Services   Factors of production

[ ]   [ ]   [ ]

Using Scarce Resources

Allocating Resources   Different economic systems

[ ]   [ ]

Prices in a Market Economy

Prices and Competition   What affects prices

[ ]   [ ]   [ ]

Productivity

Productivity Levels   Factors

Interdependence   Depend on one another for

LESSON 3 **A Global Economy**

Vocabulary Strategies

Preteach Additional Vocabulary After teaching the Vocabulary words on Student Edition page 584, explain to students that there are several other important words they will see in this lesson. Use Procedure Card 1, along with the suggestions below, to introduce the words.

defined	Have students give familiar meanings for *define* or *defined*. Explain that a time in history is defined by something that makes that period of time different or special.
restrict	Give *limit* and *control* as synonyms for *restrict*.
tariff	Have students recall what they learned about tariffs in Chapter 10. Explain that nations today still set tariffs on imported or exported goods.
illegally	Remind students that they have learned the meaning of *illegal*. Tell them that the suffix *-ly* means "in a way," so *illegally* means "in a way that is illegal, or against the law."
interact	Tell students that they interact when they work together on a project or play a game with others. Ask students to give other examples of how people, groups, or nations interact.

WORD CARDS To help teach the lesson vocabulary, use the Word Cards on pages 325–328.

Build Fluency

Use page 240 and the steps on Procedure Card 2 to reinforce vocabulary and build fluency. Read each vocabulary word aloud and have students repeat it. Then have students work in pairs to reread the words. Follow a similar procedure with the phrases and sentences. Continue to help students build fluency by having them reread "You Are There" in the Student Edition.

Text Comprehension

BEFORE READING

Preview the Lesson Guide students in previewing the lesson using Procedure Card 3. Point out the following features of the lesson on Student Edition pages 584–587.

- **Pages 584–585** Read the "What to Know" question and have students predict possible answers. Preview the photograph of the New York Stock Exchange and discuss what happens there. Preview the photograph of a veterinarian and have students name other examples of service industries.

- **Pages 586–587** Preview the photograph. Have students examine the graph of exports and answer the question in the caption. Then preview the Review questions.

Build Comprehension of Expository Text Present the graphic organizer on page 241. Have students preview the organizer by filling in the lesson title and comparing the two main heads in the organizer with the matching subheads in the Student Edition pages 584–587. Tell students that the section subheads provide additional help with identifying important information. Use Procedure Card 4, the Reading Check questions in *Harcourt Social Studies*, and the directed reading suggestions below.

- **Page 584** After students have read "You Are There," have students recall what they have learned previously about stocks and about the stock market, or stock exchange.

- **Page 585** Before students read, have them examine the first part of the organizer. Point out the box with the section head and two boxes below it with subheads that match section subheads in the text. Students can fill in these three boxes after reading "A Changing Economy."

- **Pages 586–587** After students have read "Free Trade," have them complete the organizer by filling in the boxes. Point out that the subheads match the section subheads in the text.

Summarize Have students use their completed graphic organizers to summarize the lesson. Then have them compare their summaries to the lesson summary on page 587.

Review and Respond Work through the Review questions with students. If students need additional help with summarizing, use Focus Skill Transparency 6.

Write a Letter to the Editor Discuss students' opinions about globalization, listing ideas on the board under the headings Advantages and Disadvantages. Encourage students to use information from the lesson to support their opinions, both in your discussion and when they write their letters.

Leveled Readers Use the Leveled Readers and Procedure Card 5 to build fluency and comprehension.

Name _____ Date _____

DIRECTIONS Read aloud the words in Part A. Practice reading aloud the phrases and the sentences in Part B.

Part A

Vocabulary Words	Additional Words	
service industry	defined	illegally
high-tech	restrict	interact
globalization	tariff	

Part B

1. Service industries / now make up the largest part / of the United States economy.

2. The Information Age / is a period in history / that has been defined by the growing amount of information / available to people.

3. In recent years, / high-tech industries / have become increasingly important / to the American economy.

4. A free-trade agreement / is a treaty / in which countries agree / not to restrict trade by charging tariffs on goods / they buy from and sell to each other.

5. Workers from other countries, / especially Mexico, / have tried to enter the United States / illegally.

6. The United States / interacts with other countries / through international trade / and in other ways.

7. The nations of the world / have experienced globalization.

YOU ARE THERE Turn to Student Edition page 584. Practice reading aloud "You Are There" three times. Try to improve your reading each time. Record your best time on the line below.

Number of words ___57___ My Best Time _____ Words per Minute _____

Lesson Title: _____

A Changing Economy

Early in history _____

By 1900s _____

Service Industries

Now make up the largest part of

_____

What they provide _____

_____

The Information Age

Began in _____

Important part of economy

_____

Free Trade

Cooperation and Conflict

What makes it easier for countries to be interdependent

_____

_____

Many countries have signed

_____

NAFTA countries _____

_____

Globalization

What the global economy is

_____

_____

_____

LESSON 4 # Growth and the Environment

Vocabulary Strategies

Preteach Additional Vocabulary After teaching the Vocabulary words on Student Edition page 590, explain to students that there are several other important words they will see in this lesson. Use Procedure Card 1, along with the suggestions below, to introduce the words.

densely	Draw two squares of equal size to represent areas of land. Make many dots close together in one square to represent people who live there, and only a few scattered dots in the other square. Ask which square represents an area that is densely settled.
clear	Discuss known meanings for *clear*. Then ask what it means to clear land. Explain that before buildings can be built on a piece of land, trees and other plants must be removed.
species	Give *kind* and *type* as synonyms for *species*. Different species of animals, birds, fish, and insects may live in different places.
zebra mussel	Explain that a mussel is a kind of animal that lives in a shell, as a clam does. The zebra mussel is a kind of mussel that was brought to the United States from other parts of the world.
conserve	Write *conservation* and have students recall its meaning. Then write *conserve* and have students name some ways to conserve resources.

WORD CARDS To help teach the lesson vocabulary, use the Word Cards on pages 327–328.

Build Fluency

Use page 244 and the steps on Procedure Card 2 to reinforce vocabulary and build fluency. Read each vocabulary word aloud and have students repeat it. Then have students work in pairs to reread the words. Follow a similar procedure with the phrases and sentences. Continue to help students build fluency by having them reread "You Are There" in the Student Edition.

Text Comprehension

BEFORE READING

Preview the Lesson Guide students in previewing the lesson using Procedure Card 3. Point out the following features of the lesson on Student Edition pages 590–593.

- **Pages 590–591** Read the "What to Know" question and have students predict possible answers. Preview the photographs of a city council meeting and of new suburbs. Point out that this photograph shows an aerial view. Have students point out roads, homes, and open areas.

- **Pages 592–593** Preview the photograph of a highway. Explain that it shows a traffic pattern called a cloverleaf. Preview the photograph of the Rio Grande. Tell students that the United States and Mexico have had conflicts because people in both countries use the water of the Rio Grande for irrigation. Then preview the Review questions.

DURING READING

Build Comprehension of Expository Text Present the graphic organizer on page 245. Have students preview the organizer by filling in the lesson title and comparing the two main heads in the organizer with the matching subheads in the Student Edition pages 590–593. Tell students that the section subheads provide additional help with identifying important information. Use Procedure Card 4, the Reading Check questions in *Harcourt Social Studies,* and the directed reading suggestions below.

- **Page 590** After students have read "You Are There," ask their opinions on the question of whether to build a mall or a park. Remind them to give reasons to support their opinions.

- **Page 591** Have students read "The Effects of Growth." Tell them to fill in the blanks in the top box and then to write a cause and an effect.

- **Pages 592–593** After students have read "Changing the Environment," have them complete the organizer by writing brief summaries in the boxes. Point out that the subheads match the section subheads in the text.

AFTER READING

Summarize Have students use their completed graphic organizers to summarize the lesson. Then have them compare their summaries to the lesson summary on page 593.

Review and Respond Work through the Review questions with students. If students need additional help with summarizing, use Focus Skill Transparency 6.

Create a Poster Have students brainstorm ways that people can help the environment. List their responses. Tell students that they may want to choose ideas from the list to use for their posters.

Leveled Readers Use the Leveled Readers and Procedure Card 5 to build fluency and comprehension.

Name _____ Date _____

DIRECTIONS Read aloud the words in Part A. Practice reading aloud the phrases and the sentences in Part B.

Part A

Vocabulary Words	Additional Words	
urban sprawl	densely	zebra mussel
	clear	conserve
	species	

Part B

1. The metropolitan areas / in some parts of the United States / are among the most densely settled areas / in the world.

2. The spread of urban areas / is sometimes called / urban sprawl.

3. Growth creates jobs, / but it also affects the environment / as people clear land / for building.

4. People sometimes bring / different species of plants and animals / to an area.

5. These new species / can harm the plants and animals / already in the area.

6. For example, / ships sailing the Great Lakes / have brought zebra mussels / to places / where they did not exist before.

7. The zebra mussel/ can damage local fish / and plants.

8. The United States and other countries / cooperate to use resources / and work together / to conserve nonrenewable resources.

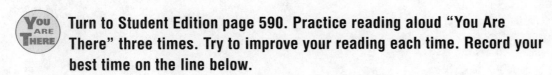 **Turn to Student Edition page 590. Practice reading aloud "You Are There" three times. Try to improve your reading each time. Record your best time on the line below.**

Number of words ___72___ My Best Time _____ Words per Minute _____

Name _____ Date _____

Lesson Title: _____

The Effects of Growth

United States population in 1990 _____

United States population today _____

Crowded and Open Places

CAUSE

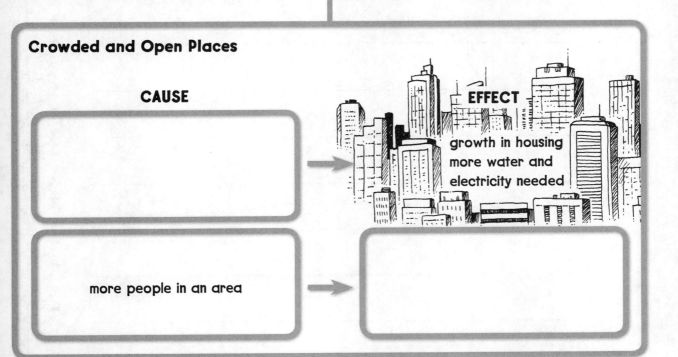

EFFECT

growth in housing
more water and
electricity needed

more people in an area

Changing the Environment

Consequences of Change
Interstate highway system

Ships from Great Lakes ports

Conflict and Cooperation
Cause of conflict

What United States has agreed

Teacher Notes

Use the following steps to introduce the Additional Words in each lesson.

1. Write the word on the board or on chart paper.

2. Say the word aloud.

3. Track the word and have students repeat it.

4. Give the meaning of the word or context that makes the meaning clear. For example, you might

- demonstrate or dramatize the meaning

- point out meanings of roots, root words, prefixes, and suffixes

- point out endings such as *-ed* and *-ing*

- give examples

- give synonyms or antonyms

- relate to familiar concepts

- draw a sketch or display a picture

Suggested Vocabulary Activities Use or adapt the following activities to give students further practice using Vocabulary Words and Additional Words.

FRAYER MODEL

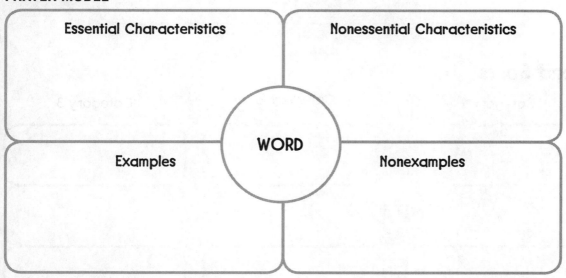

(continued)

Semantic Mapping

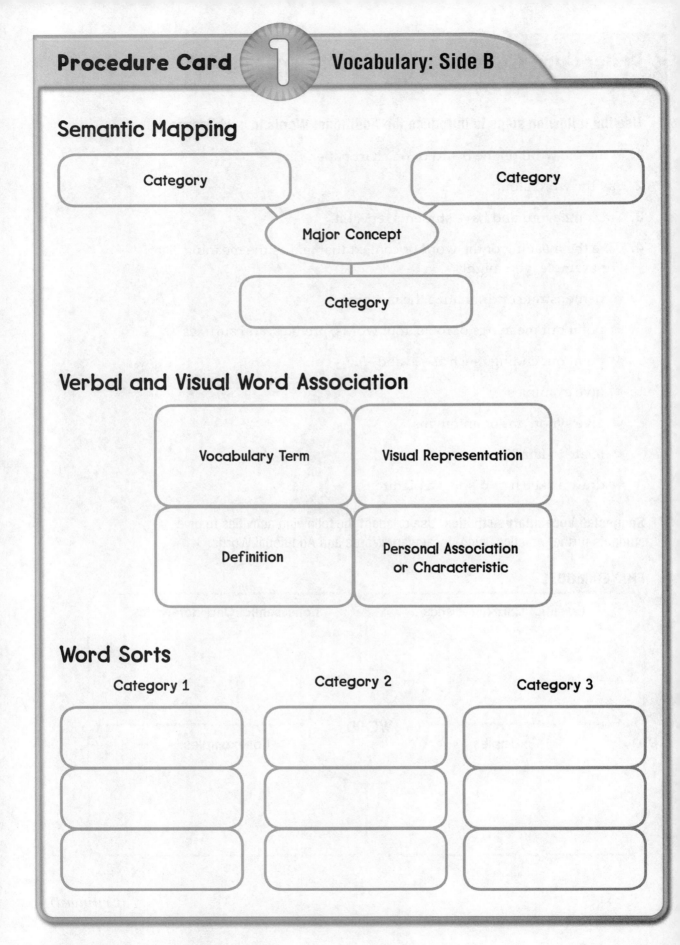

| Category | | Category |

Major Concept

Category

Verbal and Visual Word Association

| Vocabulary Term | Visual Representation |
| Definition | Personal Association or Characteristic |

Word Sorts

| Category 1 | Category 2 | Category 3 |

Procedure Card 2   Build Fluency: Side A

Use the following steps to help students build fluency.

Vocabulary Words

1. Read each vocabulary word aloud and have students repeat it.

2. Then have students work in pairs to read the vocabulary words aloud to each other.

3. Follow the same procedure with the additional words.

4. After partners have practiced reading aloud the words in each list by themselves, have them listen to each other as they practice the entire list.

Sentences

1. Read each sentence aloud and have students repeat it. As you read, model natural phrasing (intonation and rhythm), pacing, and tone.

2. Then read the sentences aloud as a coherent text. Point out that the sentences read together give a preview of the content of the lesson.

3. Have students practice reading the phrases and sentences with a partner. When the partners are satisfied with their progress, have them practice reading the sentences as a text several times.

(continued)

Help students continue to build fluency by having them do oral rereadings of "You Are There" in the Student Edition. Provide them with a stopwatch to time themselves on each reading.

Choose from the following options for the repeated readings.

- Students read the passage aloud to their partners three times. The reader rates his or her own reading on a scale of 1–4. The partner offers positive comments on the reader's improvement.

- Students read the passage aloud to themselves three times and rate their own reading on a scale of 1–4. Encourage students to note ways in which they have improved from one reading to the next.

- Students read the passage aloud into a tape recorder three times. After they listen to each reading, they rate the reading on a scale of 1–4. Then they listen to previous readings and compare to note improvements.

Use the following steps to preview the lesson with students.

1. Read aloud the title of the lesson.

2. Have students look over each page. Call attention to text features such as the following:

   - the "What to Know" question

   - time lines

   - subheads

   - illustrations and captions

   - maps, charts, graphs, and other visual aids

   - features such as Primary Sources and Children in History

   - words that are highlighted in the text

   - Review questions

3. Discuss each text feature as needed to help students understand how it relates to the topic of the lesson.

4. Work with students to set a purpose for reading the first section of the lesson by turning the first subhead into a question. Remind them to use this strategy as they read each section of the lesson.

Choose from the following options to have students read the text and complete the graphic organizer.

Reading the Text

- Have students read the lesson silently to themselves.

- Have students read together in pairs. Where possible, pair a struggling reader with a more proficient reader. Partners may take turns reading sections of the lesson aloud to each other.

- Have students read in pairs. Partners read together silently, pausing often to discuss and summarize what they have read so far.

- Have students take turns reading sections of the lesson aloud to the group.

Completing the Graphic Organizer

- If students are reading in pairs, they may work with their partners to complete the graphic organizer.

- If students are not reading in pairs, you may want to assign partners for the purpose of completing the graphic organizer.

Leveled Readers

Before Reading

1. Build background by talking about the topic of the book.

2. Discuss the cover illustration. Have children track the print as you read the title and the name of the author.

3. Preview the book by discussing the first few illustrations. Ask children what they think the book is about.

4. Help children set a purpose for reading.

During Reading

1. Have children read one or two pages at a time. If necessary, read the pages aloud as children follow along.

2. Ask questions about each page or set of pages to check children's comprehension.

3. Define any unfamiliar words, using illustrations, gestures, or context sentences.

4. Occasionally ask children to summarize or retell what they have read so far.

After Reading

1. Discuss what children liked about the book. Then guide them to summarize or retell the selection.

2. Have children respond to the book through discussion, drama, art, writing, or another appropriate activity.

You can use a KWL chart to guide your reading. Follow the steps.

Step 1. Before you read the lesson, make a KWL chart like this one.

K What we know	W What we want to find out	L What we learned

Step 2. Read the title of the lesson. Discuss with your partner or group what you already know about the topic of this lesson. For instance, you may have information from previous social studies chapters or from other sources.

Step 3. Record the information you already know in the K column of the chart. Keep in mind that sometimes information that we think we know may turn out to be incorrect. As you read the lesson, look back at the K column to check whether each fact you listed is correct.

Step 4. Preview the lesson by reading the subheads and looking at time lines, maps, illustrations, and other special features. Discuss what you want to find out when you read the lesson. One way to do this is by asking questions about the subheads. Record your questions in the W column of the chart.

Step 5. Read the lesson. As you find information to answer your questions, record the answers in the L column of the chart.

Step 6. Use your completed KWL chart to review and summarize the lesson.

You can use the SQ3R strategy to guide your reading. The letters SQRRR stand for the steps in the process—Survey, Question, Read, Recite, and Review.

Step 1. SURVEY

- Read the title of the lesson. Ask yourself what you know about the topic and what you want to find out about it.
- Read the lesson subheads and skim the first sentences of sections or paragraphs.
- Look over illustrations, maps, graphic aids, and special features.
- Read the first paragraph of the lesson.
- Read the lesson summary.

Step 2. QUESTION

- Set your main purpose for reading by turning the title of the lesson into a question.
- Write down questions you thought of during your survey.
- Set a purpose for reading each section of the lesson by turning each subhead into a question.
- Ask yourself questions about illustrations, graphic aids, and special features.
- Write down unfamiliar words and find out what they mean.

Step 3. READ

- Read to find answers to your questions.
- Use the answers to your questions to be sure you understand each section of the lesson.
- If there are ideas or words that you don't understand, ask yourself more questions.

(continued)

Step 4. RECITE

- Look away from the book and your questions to recall what you have read.
- Recite the answers to your questions aloud or write them down.
- Reread the lesson to find answers to questions that you have not already answered.

Step 5. REVIEW

- Answer the main purpose question that you formed from the lesson title.
- Look over the answers to the questions formed from the subheads and any other questions you had.
- Summarize the lesson by creating a graphic organizer, discussing the lesson with your partner or group, or writing a summary.

Student Card 3

QAR Strategy

What is QAR? The letters QAR stand for Question-Answer Relationship. You can use the QAR strategy to help you answer questions as you read and the Review questions at the end of each lesson.

Step 1. Read the information in the chart to learn about the four types of questions.

Question-Answer Relationships (QAR)

in the text		based on what you already know	
"Right There" The answer is stated in a single sentence in the text.	**"Think and Search"** The answer is not stated directly but can be found in several sentences or parts of the text.	**"Author and You"** You need to read the text to understand the question, but the answer is not found in the text.	**"On My Own"** You can answer the question based on what you already know without reading the text.

Step 2. Before you answer a question, identify which type of question it is. Decide what you will need to do in order to answer the question.

Step 3. Use the text, what you already know, or both to answer the question.

Build Fluency Words per Minute Formula

Use the following formula to calculate words per minute:

1. Count the words in the passage.

2. Record the student's reading time in seconds.

3. Divide the number of words by the number of seconds.

4. Multiply (number of words per second) by 60 to convert to words per minute.

Here is an example:

1. 90 words (in the passage)

2. 75 seconds (student's reading time)

3. 90 ÷ 75 = 1.2 (words per second)

4. 1.2 x 60 = 72 words per minute

Answer Key

 Chapter 1

Lesson 1 **States and Regions,** p. 5
A Nation of 50 States 48; Alaska; Hawaii; West, Southwest, Midwest, Southeast, Northeast; kinds of land, how people earn their living, history, culture
A Country in North America both explored by the French and the British, were once under British rule; settlers came from Spain to Mexico and southwestern United States

Lesson 2 **The Land,** p. 9
Landform Regions because of the shape of its landforms; the United States
The Coastal Plain flat, low land; wider; south
The Appalachians the Piedmont; valleys and hills; from southern Canada to central Alabama; peaks worn down, highest about 7,000 feet
The Interior Plains Central Plains; tall-grass prairie; flat, few rivers, almost no trees
The Rocky Mountains and Beyond western; sharp, jagged peaks; the Great Basin
More Mountains and Valleys Sierra Nevada, Cascade Range, Coast Ranges; San Francisco

Lesson 3 **Bodies of Water,** p. 13
Inlets and Lakes Gulf of Mexico, Gulf of Alaska; harbors where ships can safely dock; the Great Lakes; five; the Midwest and the Atlantic Ocean
Rivers the Mississippi River and its tributaries
Rivers in the East where rivers flow into oceans; inland along the Fall Line; to make electricity
Rivers in the West the Atlantic Ocean; into the Pacific Ocean

Lesson 4 **Climate and Vegetation,** p. 17
Climate distance from the equator; distance from oceans and other large bodies of water; elevation; changes in seasons; different amounts of sunlight and heat at different times of the year
Vegetation soil; temperature; precipitation; forest; trees; grassland; grasses; desert; short grasses, low bushes, cactuses; tundra; mosses, herbs, low shrubs

Lesson 5 **People and the Environment,** p. 21
Patterns of Settlement physical features, such as climate, water, and landforms; desert, tundra, or mountainous regions; People use tools and inventions to live in those areas.
Patterns of Land Use farming; mining; cities with human features; renewable resources; nonrenewable resources; limited
Changing the Environment wells, dams, irrigation systems, modifying waterways; cut down trees, dig oil wells, build mines, plow land; by using natural resources carefully

 Chapter 2

Lesson 1 **Early People,** p. 25
The Land Bridge Story Early people crossed a bridge of land from Asia to North America.
Other Theories recent discoveries; their people have always lived in the Americas
Early Ways of Life from hunting animals to farming and settling in one place; because climate became warmer and drier, and giant animals died out
The Olmec and the Maya strong trade system, systems of writing and counting, calendar; influenced by Olmec traditions, writing and counting system, social classes, built stone cities
Other Civilizations Mound Builders; large earth mounds; Ancient Puebloans; had many levels, often built against canyon walls or in caves

Lesson 2 **The Eastern Woodlands,** p. 29
Life in the Eastern Woodlands canoes, shelters, tools, weapons, food
The Iroquois near the Great Lakes; Iroquoian; on top of steep hills; longhouses; corn, beans, and squash; Iroquois League, Council to settle disputes
The Algonquians Coastal Plain or near Great Lakes; Algonquian; most groups had 1 to 20; longhouses or wigwams; crops, fish; leaders governed more than one village, some groups had two chiefs

Lesson 3 **The Plains,** p. 33
Life on the Plains (meat) raw, cooked, pemmican; (skins) clothing, moccasins, shelter, shields, drums; (hair) cord; (bones) tools, arrowheads, pipes; (stomach) bags to carry water; (hooves) glue; (horns) cups, spoons, tools
Farmers and Hunters beans, corn, sunflowers; deer, elk, buffalo
A Nomadic Society tepee; travois
Plains Cultures Cheyenne sent leaders to council of chiefs, every person equal; many groups shared traditions and beliefs, ceremonies to celebrate and give thanks

Lesson 4 **The Southwest and the West,** p. 37
The Southwest mesas, canyons, cliffs, mountains; corn, beans, squash; cotton; blankets and clothing
Pueblo Culture the desert environment; trade; medicine people; religion
Groups to the West Shoshone; hunted in Great Basin and mountains; Nez Perce; fished for salmon; Chumash; lived near Pacific Ocean; trade networks; to get goods from faraway places

Lesson 5 The Northwest and the Arctic, p. 41
A Region of Plenty forests and rivers; Kwakiutl, Makah, Chinook; coastal waters, salmon, whales

Resource and Trade giant trees; longhouses, all members of a clan; center of trade network, the Chinook; a celebration to show wealth

Lands of the North the Aleut; the Inuit; foxes, caribou, polar bears, seals, walruses, whales; beams of whalebone and walls of sod, igloos, tents of animal skin, sod houses; south of the Arctic; Cree; hunting, trees; long winters

 Chapter 3

Lesson 1 Exploration and Technology, p. 45
A Rush of New Ideas 1400s; the Renaissance; to buy and resell Asian goods; did not have correct maps or technology

The World Awaits Prince Henry of Portugal; opened a school of navigation; better ships, maps, and navigational tools, made ocean exploration possible

The Business of Exploring Christopher Columbus; sail west to Asia; money for a ship, crew, and supplies; king and queen of Spain agreed to help him

Two Worlds Meet an island in the Caribbean Sea; Asia; treated like heroes

Lesson 2 A Changing World, p. 49
England Explores John Cabot (Giovanni Caboto); 1497; Asia; the coast of present-day Newfoundland and Labrador

A New Map of the World Amerigo Vespucci; coast of South America; had found lands not yet known to Europeans; South America and North America

Reaching the Pacific Vasco Núñez de Balboa; 1513; crossed the Isthmus of Panama and reached the Pacific Ocean

A New View of the World Ferdinand Magellan; Pacific Ocean; the first Europeans to travel around the world; Spain and Portugal

Lesson 3 Spanish Explorations, p. 53
The Spanish Explore Florida Ponce de León; Bimini, Fountain of Youth; landed in what is now Florida, claimed it for Spain

Early Conquistadors to find gold in the land of the Aztecs; conquered the Aztecs and built Mexico City; to find golden cities; explored lands in what is now the south-western United States, claimed lands for Spain

Expeditions Continue took control of the Inca Empire in Peru; explored the southeastern United States, claimed land for Spain

Missionaries to America the Reformation and Counter-Reformation; to gain new followers, to share in the wealth of the lands claimed by European countries, to convert Native Americans to the Catholic Church

Lesson 4 Other Nations Explore, p. 57
The Northwest Passage a shortcut to Asia; to gain wealth and power

Verrazano and Cartier met Native Americans, searched the coastlines of North America and South America; a passage; claimed land around St. Lawrence River for France, went as far as what is now Montreal; the Northwest Passage

Hudson's Voyages Henry Hudson; four; sailed through the Arctic Ocean, claimed Hudson River valley for the Dutch; claimed land around Hudson Bay for England; the Northwest Passage

 Chapter 4

Lesson 1 The Spanish Colonies, p. 61
New Spain Spain formed colonies.

Slavery in the Americas They forced Native Americans into slavery. Many Native Americans died from hunger, work, and diseases.

Settling the Borderlands Spanish soldiers built presidios. Missionaries built missions. Settlers built haciendas.

Lesson 2 The Virginia Colony, p. 65
England Attempts a Colony 1584; Roanoke Island; ran low on food and returned to England; 1587; still a mystery, known as the Lost Colony; early 1600s; group of English merchants; to try again to start a colony in Virginia

Jamestown Captain John Smith; colonists had no interest in farming, but Smith made them plant crops; trouble between the Powhatan and colonists

Growth and Government John Rolfe; tobacco; indentured servants, Africans; 1619; Virginia's legislature; fighting between colonists and Powhatan, Virginia made a royal colony

Lesson 3 The Plymouth Colony, p. 69
The Pilgrims' Journey Pilgrims; North America; 1620, the *Mayflower*

The Mayflower Compact that fair laws would be made for the good of the colony; self-government and majority rule

Building a Colony Tisquantum; showed them where to fish and how to plant squash, corn, and pumpkins; helped them trade with neighboring tribes

Plymouth Grows from farming, fishing, and fur trading; after 1630; new colonists not friendly to Native Americans, settled on more of their lands

Lesson 4 The French and the Dutch, p. 73
New France wealth from the fur trade; start colonies in North America; Quebec; Champlain; 1608; slowly

New Netherland along Hudson River, parts of what are now New York and New Jersey; to profit from the fur trade; Manhattan Island; New Amsterdam; trade; many colonists and Native Americans killed, Algonquian almost wiped out

Exploring New France Marquette; Joliet; Mississippi River; La Salle; Mississippi River valley; France; Louisiana; settlement failed

Louisiana proprietary colony; 1712; New Orleans; failed to attract many people

 Chapter 5

Lesson 1 The New England Colonies, p. 77
The Puritans Arrive Masssachusetts Bay Colony

Change and Conflict Roger Williams, Anne Hutchinson; started settlements; formed Rhode Island Colony; colonists and Native Americans

Life In New England strict rules; schools; small towns; at a town meeting

New England's Economy shipbuilding, fishing; shipping and trading; English colonies, England, the West Indies, west coast of Africa

The Middle Passage the cruel slave-trade business; some New England colonists

Lesson 2 The Middle Colonies, p. 81
Settling the Middle Colonies England; Quakers; a refuge

Pennsylvania William Penn; people of different religions to live together peacefully, to treat Native Americans fairly

Life in the Middle Colonies number of church members grew, religious toleration grew; religion

The Breadbasket Colonies wheat, corn, rye; New York City; Philadelphia; skilled trades

Lesson 3 The Southern Colonies, p. 85
Life in Maryland and Virginia location, climate, growing tobacco, governor, elected assemblies

The Carolinas and Georgia North Carolina; South Carolina; plantations and slavery

Heading West mid-1700s; settlers spreading onto Native American lands

Slavery in the Colonies all 13 colonies

Life in the South plantations; small farms; imported and exported goods

The Southern Economy tobacco, rice, indigo; forest goods, sawmills, naval stores, shipbuilding

 Chapter 6

Lesson 1 Fighting for Control, p. 89
Conflicting Claims the Ohio Valley; both Britain and France; sent soldiers and built forts; to fight back

The French and Indian War Begins France and Britain with Native American tribes in the Ohio Valley; 1754; Albany, New York; colonial leaders; how to deal with the French forces; 1754; Fort Necessity

The War Expands 1763; most of Canada, all French lands east of the Mississippi River, and Spanish Florida

More Troubles colonists did not like British telling them to stay out of frontier lands; colonists angry about new taxes

Lesson 2 Colonists Speak Out, p. 93
The Stamp Act 1765; tax on paper documents in the colonies; no taxation without representation

Colonists Work Together to force Britain to take back the Stamp Act; the Sons and Daughters of Liberty; Parliament voted to repeal the Stamp Act; Committees of Correspondence; to spread information more quickly; to protest British policies

The Townshend Acts 1767; taxes on imports to the colonies; boycotted British goods; repealed all except tax on tea, sent more soldiers to the colonies

The Boston Massacre March 5, 1770; Some colonists were killed in a fight with British soldiers.

Lesson 3 Disagreements Grow, p. 97
The Boston Tea Party December 16, 1773; to protest the Tea Act; Sons of Liberty; boarded British ships in Boston Harbor and threw tea overboard

The Coercive Acts March 1774; new laws passed by Parliament; to punish Massachusetts colonists; against Britain

The First Continental Congress September 1774; Philadelphia; colonial leaders; sent a petition to the king; voted to stop most trade with Britain; asked the colonies to form militias

Lexington and Concord April 1775; fighting between Minutemen and British soldiers, beginning of the American Revolution

Lesson 4 The Road to War, p. 101
The Second Continental Congress May 10, 1775; Pennsylvania State House in Philadelphia; formed the Continental Army; chose George Washington as commander in chief; asked each colony to give money; printed its own paper money

The Battle of Bunker Hill June 17, 1775; Breed's Hill; Israel Putnam and William Prescott; The British won the battle but suffered heavy losses.

Trying for Peace July 15, 1775; Congress sent Olive Branch Petition to King George, but he promised to crush the rebellion.

Lesson 5 Declaring Independence, p. 105
Moving Toward Independence Common Sense;
Thomas Paine; independence; a resolution of
independence
The Declaration of Independence rights; grievances;
free and independent
Congress Approves the Declaration July 4, 1776;
members of the Second Continental Congress;
freedom; equal rights
Forming a New Government John Dickinson;
Articles of Confederation; the Confederation
Congress; left most power with the states, limited
power of national government

 Chapter 7

Lesson 1 Americans and the Revolution, p. 109
Personal Hardships People faced hardships from
taking sides and from British soldiers robbing and
destroying towns.
Economic Hardships Problems included a shortage of
imported goods, inflation, and profiteering.
Women and the War Women took on new roles in
battle and at home.
African Americans, Free and Enslaved Many
African Americans fought for the Continental Army,
while others fought for the British to win their
freedom.
People in the West Native Americans were divided,
while many settlers wanted to help drive the British
out.

Lesson 2 Fighting for Independence, p. 113
Comparing Armies no uniforms; many had no
guns; most had no military training; needed a lot of
supplies; experienced soldiers; 50,000 soldiers in the
colonies; used mercenaries; long wait for supplies
Early Battles in the North Long Island; British won;
Trenton; American victory
An Important Victory Saratoga; a turning point in
the war
Winter at Valley Forge soldiers a ragged group, food
running low; Lafayette; von Steuben
Contributions from Other Nations The French
agreed to help the Americans. Bernardo de Gálvez
gave guns, food, money, and helped fight. The
Netherlands gave a loan to Congress. Russian
leaders tried to keep the British from blocking trade.

Lesson 3 Winning Independence, p. 117
Revolutionary Heroes Nathan Hale; served as an
American spy; John Paul Jones; battled larger British
ships; Mary Ludwig Hays McCauley; carried water
to soldiers and loaded cannons; Tadeusz Kosciuszko;
helped design fort at West Point
The War Moves Savannah, Georgia; British victory;
Charles Town, South Carolina; British victory;
Cowpens, South Carolina; major American victory;
Guilford Courthouse, North Carolina; British won
but weakened
The War Ends October 19, 1781; General Cornwallis
surrendered at Yorktown, Virginia, after being
surrounded for weeks. September 3, 1783; named
the United States of America as a new nation, set
borders; George Washington retired.

Lesson 4 Effects of the War, p. 121
New Ideas began to write their own constitutions;
that each person had the right to life and liberty; that
slavery should be ended
Western Settlements more land; former soldiers and
other settlers; Native Americans; south of the Ohio
River
The Northwest Territory north of the Ohio River;
1785; ordinance about dividing land; 1787; Northwest
Ordinance passed
Battles for Land Native Americans and new settlers;
Native Americans gave up or sold most of their lands

Chapter 8

Lesson 1 The Constitutional Convention, p. 125
Reasons for Change that the national government could not keep order or protect them; May 1787; to fix the Articles

The Work Begins needed a new Constitution; strengthen the existing federal system; American republic

A Major Debate how each state would be represented in the new Congress; state's population; equally represented

Working Together the population of each state; each state equally represented

Compromises on Slavery southern states and northern states; agreed to count three-fifths of the total number of slaves; 1808

Lesson 2 Three Branches of Government, p. 129
The Preamble We the People of the United States; to create a fairer form of government; individual liberty, other personal freedoms, justice, peace

The Legislative Branch to keep any one branch from controlling the government; House of Representatives; Senate

The Executive Branch President; veto bills passed by Congress; commander in chief of the military; "take care that the laws be faithfully executed"

The Judicial Branch federal court system; the Supreme Court; strike down any law that goes against the Constitution; amendments

Lesson 3 The Bill of Rights, p. 133
The Struggle to Ratify to limit the power of the federal government; to protect people's individual rights; to propose a bill of rights after the Constitution was ratified

The Vote of Approval Delaware; a strong federal government; that the national government would have too much power; June 21, 1788

The Bill of Rights ten; to protect the rights of the people; 1791; the states or the people

The New Government George Washington; 1789; Washington, D.C.; 1800; John Adams

Lesson 4 A Constitutional Government, p. 137
Sharing Powers among the legislative, executive, and judicial branches; to keep the federal government from becoming too powerful

Checks and Balances keeps any one branch from becoming too powerful or misusing its authority; ways to check the powers of the others

State Powers any powers not clearly given to the federal government or denied to the states

State and Local Governments federal, state, and local; collect taxes to pay for government services

Rights and Responsibilities from the people; voting
Being a Citizen to act with civic virtue, to help control the government

Chapter 9

Lesson 1 Exploring the West, p. 141
Immigrants and Pioneers to escape hard times, earn money, own land; the Wilderness Road

Americans Continue West Kentucky; Tennessee; Ohio

The Louisiana Purchase Thomas Jefferson; no ports on Gulf of Mexico; April 30, 1803; more than doubled the size of the United States

Lewis and Clark St. Louis, Missouri; May 1804; the Pacific Ocean; November 1805; added to the knowledge about the lands that became the West

Pike in the Southwest that people in Spanish territories needed manufactured goods; American traders traveled there to sell goods.

Lesson 2 Expanding Borders, p. 145
Troubles Grow on lands that belonged to Native Americans; fight the Americans; impressment of American sailors

The War of 1812 Battle of Lake Erie, Battle of the Thames; 1823; the Monroe Doctrine

Extending Democracy all white American men; Andrew Jackson; Jacksonian Democracy

The Indian Removal Act to take Cherokee lands; 1838; Cherokee and others had to walk about 800 miles to Indian Territory

Lesson 3 From Ocean to Ocean, p. 149
Texas Independence Mexican government raising taxes; 1836; the Mexicans

The Lone Star Republic April 21, 1836; Texans attacked, captured Santa Anna; Texas granted independence

Trails West Missouri; the Oregon Country; covered wagons, wagon trains; Brigham Young; Illinois; Great Salt Lake valley

Expanding Borders treaty that set Oregon Country border; dispute over border; Treaty of Guadalupe Hidalgo with Mexico; Mexican Cession; Gadsden Purchase

The California Gold Rush other parts of United States and the world; population growth, became a state

Lesson 4 New Ideas and Inventions, p. 153

Transportation National Road; the Appalachians; Erie Canal; Great Lakes and Atlantic; made it a center of trade

Steamboats and Railroads the main form of travel on large rivers; made it easier for people to travel and ship goods

The Industrial Revolution 1800s; a change to using machines for manufacturing large quantities of goods; Samuel Slater; built the first American textile mill; the beginning of large-scale manufacturing in the United States

More Inventions Eli Whitney; cotton gin; changed plantation farming; interchangeable parts for guns; mass production; Cyrus McCormick; mechanical reaper; John Deere; strong steel plow

 Chapter 10

Lesson 1 The North and the South, p. 157

Different Regions small farms, slavery abolished, diverse economy, new industries; plantations, system of slavery

Division Over Slavery 1819; Missouri wanted to join the Union as a slave state; Henry Clay; number of free states and slave states remained equal

Different Ideas tariff helped North but hurt South; whether states or national government should have final say

More Divisions new lands not covered by Missouri Compromise; Fugitive Slave Act; law was very unpopular; fighting between groups for and against slavery; Kansas joined Union as a free state

Lesson 2 Resisting Slavery, p. 161

The Dred Scott Decision to try to win his freedom; that enslaved people were property; made disagreements over slavery worse

Challenging Slavery Samuel Cornish and John Russwurm; started a newspaper called *Freedom's Journal*; William Lloyd Garrison; founded the American Antislavery Society; Frederick Douglass; writings and speeches against slavery; Sojourner Truth; traveled the country speaking out against slavery; Elizabeth Cady Stanton and Lucretia Mott; called for equality for all Americans; Harriet Beecher Stowe; wrote a book about slavery; a system of secret escape routes to free lands; Harriet Tubman; slave catchers

Lesson 3 The Nation Divides, p. 165

Abraham Lincoln Illinois legislature; United States Congress; fight the spread of slavery; the Republican Party; made Lincoln well known

Events Further Divide the Nation divided the nation even more; slavery; they would secede if Lincoln was elected; Lincoln

The Nation Separates seceded from the Union; the Confederate States of America; torn between the two sides

Fort Sumter April 12, 1861; Confederate troops fired at the fort; divided the country, divided states, sometimes divided families

Lesson 4 The War Begins, p. 169

War Plans Anaconda Plan, blockade to weaken South, then invade; defend its lands, make the war last a long time

Early Battles first major battle, a confusing battle, Confederates won; many killed, neither side won a clear victory

The Emancipation Proclamation issued by President Lincoln, said that all enslaved people in areas still fighting against the Union were free

Americans At War took over factory, business, and farm jobs, also worked as nurses and even served as spies; about 180,000 served in Union army, led raids, served as spies and scouts, fought in major battles

Lesson 5 Toward a Union Victory, p. 173

Two Major Battles Ulysses S. Grant; major victory for the Union; victory for Confederacy

Union Victories July 1863; three days; Union victory, turning point in the war; November 19, 1863; President Lincoln; one of the most famous speeches in American history; September 1864; General William Tecumseh Sherman; Sherman's army cut a path of destruction through Georgia

The War Ends April 9, 1865; Lee surrendered to Grant, ending the war; many soldiers died, South in ruins, Lincoln assassinated five days after war ended

 Chapter 11

Lesson 1 Reconstruction, p. 177

Plans for Rebuilding the South should not be punished; ended slavery everywhere in the nation

Reconstruction Politics to punish the South; Johnson was acquitted; African Americans elected

Hard Times gave food and supplies, built schools; farmed land owned by someone else; a cabin, mules, tools, seed; bridges, buildings, and railroads had been destroyed

Reconstruction Ends 1877; lost many of the rights they had gained; continued to work to help

Lesson 2 The Last Frontier, p. 181

Western Mining 1859; Comstock Lode in Nevada; 1860 to 1896; Idaho, Montana, Alaska; boom, fast growth; bust, fast decline

Life on the Frontier railroad stations; herded over trails by cowhands; to cities in the East; 1862; the Homestead Act; few streams or trees, bad weather, insects, range wars

Western Conflict did not want to be forced onto reservations; by 1880, almost all lived on reservations

Lesson 3 New Industries, p. 185

The Transcontinental Railroad trains could travel across country; helped the economy grow

Industries and Inventions helped economy grow rapidly; Andrew Carnegie; built steel mills; William Jenney; used steel frames to build skyscrapers; John D. Rockefeller; started Standard Oil Company, controlled industry; Thomas Alva Edison; set up first central electrical power station; Lewis Lattimer; directed the building of the power station; Alexander Graham Bell; started first telephone company

Workers Struggle better working conditions and pay; strikes; collective bargaining

Lesson 4 Cities and Immigration, p. 189

Many Immigrants Arrive between 1860 and 1910; about 23 million; freedom, safety, a better life; Ellis Island; were poor, lived in tenements, struggled to find jobs and learn English; Angel Island

Reactions to Immigration 1882; Chinese Exclusion Act; no clean water, garbage in streets; reformers Jane Addams and Lillian Wald; started settlement houses to provide food, health care, and classes for immigrants

Migration and Immigration between 1910 and 1930; northern cities; the Great Migration; jobs in factories; Asia and Latin America; basic American ideals

 Chapter 12

Lesson 1 A New Role in the World, p. 193

The United States Grows 1867; bought from Russia; 1898; annexed

The Spanish-American War support for Cuba's independence; explosion of battleship *Maine*; the Philippines; August 12, 1898; a world power

Changes at Home and Abroad Atlantic and Pacific Oceans; ten years; that the government and citizens could make life better; prejudice; W. E. B. DuBois; Civil

Lesson 2 World War I, p. 197

Causes of World War I Allied Powers, Central Powers; Germany sank American ships.

Fighting the War trench warfare, machine guns, barbed wire, tanks, poison gas, airplanes

The War at Home government took over parts of industries; more opportunities for women and African Americans

The Effects of the War President Wilson's idea, United States did not join; gave women the right to vote

Lesson 3 Good Times and Hard Times, p. 201

The Good Times produced new consumer goods, automobiles industry and other industries grew

New Art Forms jazz, Harlem Renaissance, radio programs

The End of the Good Times stock market crashed, factories and banks closed

Hard Times the Great Depression, Dust Bowl in Midwest

The New Deal federal agencies such as the TVA, CCC, and WPA; gave people hope, gave federal government more authority and made it larger

Lesson 4 World War II, p. 205

Before the War economic troubles; to solve problems by force

A Global Conflict 1939; German troops invaded Poland; much of Europe under German control

The United States Enters the War Japanese planes attacked Pearl Harbor; December 7, 1941

Americans and the War made weapons and war supplies, rationing; put in internment camps

The War in Europe and Africa Students' charts should include events for 1942; 1943; June 6, 1944; May 2, 1945; May 8, 1945.

The War in the Pacific Students' charts should include events for 1942; 1942–1943 (Guadalcanal); 1945 (Iwo Jima, Okinawa); April 1945; August 6, 1945; August 9, 1945.

Lesson 5 The Effects of the War, p. 209

The Holocaust concentration camps; genocide, to kill all Jewish people; murder of more than six million Jewish people; brought to trial, sentenced to death

A Hard Peace April 1945; New York City; to promote cooperation among nations; the Soviets set up communist governments; blocked travel between Berlin and West Germany; started the Berlin Airlift to get supplies to West Berlin

Chapter 13

Lesson 1 The 1950s, p. 213

The Korean War June 1950; South Korea; the United Nations; cease-fire in 1953

A Growing Economy huge new suburbs; interstate highways; created more jobs

Television Brings Changes entertainment, how Americans spent free time; politics and government

The Cold War two different systems of government; the United States and the Soviet Union; Sputnik; NASA; 1958

Lesson 2 The 1960s, p. 217

A New Decade the Peace Corps; land an astronaut on the moon

Trouble in Cuba October 1962; Soviet missles in Cuba; 13 days; Soviet Union took missiles out of Cuba

Changes at Home Head Start, Medicaid, Medicare; July 16, 1969

The Vietnam War to help South Vietnam; sent more soldiers to South Vietnam; protests; 1973; peace talks, cease-fire

Lesson 3 Equal Rights for All, p. 221

A Supreme Court Ruling to go to school with other children in her neighborhood; an end to segregation in public schools

A National Movement African Americans; their civil rights; Rosa Parks arrested for not going to the back of a bus; Supreme Court ruled that segregation had to end on all public transportation; Martin Luther King, Jr.; nonviolence; Malcolm X; change to happen faster

Civil Rights for All the Civil Rights Act; 1964; migrant farm workers, women

Lesson 4 The 1970s and 1980s, p. 225

President Richard M. Nixon Cold War tensions; the Watergate scandal

Global Challenges nation's economy slowed, unemployment rose, fuel shortages; inflation; Israel and Egypt

President Ronald Reagan the government should be less involved in the economy and public life

Ending the Cold War Gorbachev; Berlin Wall; November 1989; communism; early 1990s; civil wars

Lesson 5 The 1990s, p. 229

Challenges for a New President George H. W. Bush; 1988; recession

The Persian Gulf War August 1990; Iraq invaded Kuwait; 33; the United States; Allied forces defeated Iraq

Changes at Home Bill Clinton; 1992; economic growth; national budget; controversy

Facing New Dangers 1993; World Trade Center in New York City; 1995; Oklahoma City, Oklahoma; 1998; African countries of Kenya and Tanzania, USS *Cole*

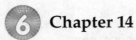 **Chapter 14**

Lesson 1 New Challenges, p. 233

Events Shape the Nation election too close to call; Supreme Court ruled in Bush's favor; September 11, 2001; terrorists flew planes into the World Trade Center and Pentagon

Modern Challenges October 2001; Afghanistan; United States and allies defeated Taliban government; 2003; Iraq; government fell, but violence continued; Department of Homeland Security; strong hurricanes damaged many areas of the Southeast.

Lesson 2 Our Nation's Economy, p. 237

Free Enterprise what to produce; how to produce; for whom to produce; human resources; natural resources; capital goods

Using Scarce Resources command economy; market economy

Prices in a Market Economy demand; supply; competition

Productivity an educated workforce, capital goods, specialization; natural resources, finished products, services

Lesson 3 A Global Economy, p. 241

A Changing Economy agriculture; manufacturing; the United States economy; services to other people; the 1970s; high-tech industries

Free Trade modern transportation and communication systems; free-trade agreements; Mexico, Canada, the United States; the world market in which companies from different countries buy and sell goods and services

Lesson 4 Growth and the Environment, p. 245

The Effects of Growth 248 million people; more than 296 million people; population growth; more cars, more traffic, air pollution

Changing the Environment allows travel and transport but affects plants and animals; improved shipping but affects plants and animals; getting enough water for irrigation; that a certain amount of water must reach Mexico.

contiguous Unit 1, Chapter 1, Lesson 1	**climate** Unit 1, Chapter 1, Lesson 2
region Unit 1, Chapter 1, Lesson 1	**mountain range** Unit 1, Chapter 1, Lesson 2
relative location Unit 1, Chapter 1, Lesson 1	**erosion** Unit 1, Chapter 1, Lesson 2
continent Unit 1, Chapter 1, Lesson 1	**prairie** Unit 1, Chapter 1, Lesson 2
population Unit 1, Chapter 1, Lesson 1	**environment** Unit 1, Chapter 1, Lesson 2
landform region Unit 1, Chapter 1, Lesson 2	**inlet** Unit 1, Chapter 1, Lesson 3

The kind of weather a place has over a long time.	Next to each other.
A group of connected mountains.	An area in which many features are similar.
The gradual wearing away of the Earth's surface.	The position of one place compared to other places.
An area of flat or rolling land covered mostly by grasses.	One of Earth's seven largest land masses.
The surroundings in which people, plants, and animals live.	The number of people who live in an area.
Any area of water extending into the land from a larger body of water.	A region that has similar landforms throughout.

gulf Unit 1, Chapter 1, Lesson 3	**elevation** Unit 1, Chapter 1, Lesson 4
sound Unit 1, Chapter 1, Lesson 3	**natural vegetation** Unit 1, Chapter 1, Lesson 4
tributary Unit 1, Chapter 1, Lesson 3	**arid** Unit 1, Chapter 1, Lesson 4
river system Unit 1, Chapter 1, Lesson 3	**tundra** Unit 1, Chapter 1, Lesson 4
drainage basin Unit 1, Chapter 1, Lesson 3	**land use** Unit 1, Chapter 1, Lesson 5
fall line Unit 1, Chapter 1, Lesson 3	**natural resource** Unit 1, Chapter 1, Lesson 5

The height of land in relation to sea level.	A large inlet.
The plant life that grows naturally in a place.	A long inlet that separates offshore islands from the mainland.
Dry.	A stream or river that flows into a larger stream or river.
A cold, dry region where trees cannot grow.	A river and its tributaries.
How the land is used.	The land drained by a river system.
Something found in nature, such as soil, plants, water, or minerals that people can use to meet their needs.	A place where the land drops sharply, causing rivers to form waterfalls or rapids.

renewable resource Unit 1, Chapter 1, Lesson 5	
nonrenewable resource Unit 1, Chapter 1, Lesson 5	
modify Unit 1, Chapter 1, Lesson 5	
irrigation Unit 1, Chapter 1, Lesson 5	
efficiency Unit 1, Chapter 1, Lesson 5	

	Resources that can be made again by people or nature.
	Resources that cannot be made again by people or nature.
	To change.
	The use of canals, ditches, or pipes to move water.
	Using less energy to do the same tasks.

ancestor Unit 1, Chapter 2, Lesson 1	**class** Unit 1, Chapter 2, Lesson 1
theory Unit 1, Chapter 2, Lesson 1	**division of labor** Unit 1, Chapter 2, Lesson 2
migration Unit 1, Chapter 2, Lesson 1	**palisade** Unit 1, Chapter 2, Lesson 2
artifact Unit 1, Chapter 2, Lesson 1	**longhouse** Unit 1, Chapter 2, Lesson 2
civilization Unit 1, Chapter 2, Lesson 1	**wampum** Unit 1, Chapter 2, Lesson 2
tradition Unit 1, Chapter 2, Lesson 1	**confederation** Unit 1, Chapter 2, Lesson 2

A group of people in a society who have something in common.	An early family member.
Work that is divided so that it is possible to produce more goods.	An idea based on study and research.
A wall made of tall wooden poles to protect a village from enemies.	The movement of people.
A long wooden building in which several families could live.	An object made by a person.
Beads cut from seashells to make designs that showed important decisions, events, or stories, or traded and exchanged for goods.	A group of people with ways of life, religion, and learning.
A loose group of governments working together.	A way of life or an idea handed down from the past.

wigwam Unit 1, Chapter 2, Lesson 2	**council** Unit 1, Chapter 2, Lesson 3
lodge Unit 1, Chapter 2, Lesson 3	**ceremony** Unit 1, Chapter 2, Lesson 3
sod Unit 1, Chapter 2, Lesson 3	**adapt** Unit 1, Chapter 2, Lesson 4
scarce Unit 1, Chapter 2, Lesson 3	**staple** Unit 1, Chapter 2, Lesson 4
tepee Unit 1, Chapter 2, Lesson 3	**surplus** Unit 1, Chapter 2, Lesson 4
travois Unit 1, Chapter 2, Lesson 3	**adobe** Unit 1, Chapter 2, Lesson 4

A group of leaders who meet to make decisions.	A round, bark-covered shelter.
A celebration to honor a cultural or religious event.	A large round earthen house used by Central Plains Native Americans.
To adjust way of living to land and resources.	A layer of soil held together by the roots of grasses.
Something that is always needed and used.	In short supply.
An extra amount.	A cone-shaped tent made from wooden poles and buffalo skins.
A brick or building material made of sun-dried earth and straw.	A device made of two poles fastened to a dog's harness, used to carry goods.

hogan Unit 1, Chapter 2, Lesson 4	**potlatch** Unit 1, Chapter 2, Lesson 5
trade network Unit 1, Chapter 2, Lesson 4	**kayak** Unit 1, Chapter 2, Lesson 5
harpoon Unit 1, Chapter 2, Lesson 5	**igloo** Unit 1, Chapter 2, Lesson 5
clan Unit 1, Chapter 2, Lesson 5	
economy Unit 1, Chapter 2, Lesson 5	
barter Unit 1, Chapter 2, Lesson 5	

A Native American celebration meant to show wealth and divide properly among the people.	A cone-shaped Navajo shelter built by covering a log frame with mud or adobe.
A one-person canoe made of waterproof skins stretched over wood or bone.	A system that allows people to get goods from faraway places.
A house made of snow or ice.	A long spear with a sharp shell point.
	An extended group of family members.
	The way people of a state, region, or country use resources to meet their needs.
	To exchange goods.

technology Unit 2, Chapter 3, Lesson 1	**benefit** Unit 2, Chapter 3, Lesson 1
navigation Unit 2, Chapter 3, Lesson 1	**Reconquista** Unit 2, Chapter 3, Lesson 1
expedition Unit 2, Chapter 3, Lesson 1	**isthmus** Unit 2, Chapter 3, Lesson 2
empire Unit 2, Chapter 3, Lesson 1	**treaty** Unit 2, Chapter 3, Lesson 2
entrepreneur Unit 2, Chapter 3, Lesson 1	**grant** Unit 2, Chapter 3, Lesson 3
cost Unit 2, Chapter 3, Lesson 1	**conquistador** Unit 2, Chapter 3, Lesson 3

A reward that is gained.	The use of scientific knowledge and tools to make or do something.
The movement to make Spain all Catholic; also called the Reconquest.	The science of planning and following a route.
A narrow strip of land that connects two larger land areas.	A trip taken with the goal of exploring.
An agreement between two countries about peace, trade, or other matters.	A collection of lands ruled by the nation that won control of them.
A sum of money or other payment given for a particular purpose.	A person who sets up and runs a business.
Any of the Spanish conquerors in the Americas during the early 1500s.	The effort made to achieve or gain something.

reform Unit 2, Chapter 3, Lesson 3	
Reformation Unit 2, Chapter 3, Lesson 3	
Counter-Reformation Unit 2, Chapter 3, Lesson 3	
missionary Unit 2, Chapter 3, Lesson 3	
Northwest Passage Unit 2, Chapter 3, Lesson 4	
mutiny Unit 2, Chapter 3, Lesson 4	

	To change for the better.
	A Christian movement that began in sixteenth-century Europe as an attempt to reform the Catholic Church; resulted in the founding of Protestantism.
	A time when the Catholic church banned books and used its courts to punish people who protested Catholic ways.
	The religious teacher sent out by a church to spread its religion.
	A waterway in North America thought to connect the Atlantic Ocean and the Pacific Ocean.
	Rebellion against the leader of one's group.

colony Unit 2, Chapter 4, Lesson 1	**hacienda** Unit 2, Chapter 4, Lesson 1
plantation Unit 2, Chapter 4, Lesson 1	**raw material** Unit 2, Chapter 4, Lesson 2
slavery Unit 2, Chapter 4, Lesson 1	**stock** Unit 2, Chapter 4, Lesson 2
borderlands Unit 2, Chapter 4, Lesson 1	**cash crop** Unit 2, Chapter 4, Lesson 2
presidio Unit 2, Chapter 4, Lesson 1	**profit** Unit 2, Chapter 4, Lesson 2
mission Unit 2, Chapter 4, Lesson 1	**indentured servant** Unit 2, Chapter 4, Lesson 2

A large estate or home where cattle and sheep are raised.	A land ruled by another country.
A resource that can be used to make a product.	A large farm.
Part ownership in a business.	The practice of holding people against their will and making them work without pay.
A crop that people grow to sell.	Areas of land on or near the borders between countries, colonies, or regions.
The money left over after all costs have been paid.	A Spanish fort.
A person who agreed to work for another person without pay for a certain length of time in exchange for passage to North America.	A small religious settlement.

legislature Unit 2, Chapter 4, Lesson 2	**majority rule** Unit 2, Chapter 4, Lesson 3
represent Unit 2, Chapter 4, Lesson 2	**demand** Unit 2, Chapter 4, Lesson 4
royal colony Unit 2, Chapter 4, Lesson 2	**supply** Unit 2, Chapter 4, Lesson 4
pilgrim Unit 2, Chapter 4, Lesson 3	**ally** Unit 2, Chapter 4, Lesson 4
compact Unit 2, Chapter 4, Lesson 3	**proprietary colony** Unit 2, Chapter 4, Lesson 4
self-government Unit 2, Chapter 4, Lesson 3	

The political idea that the majority of an organized group should have the power to make decisions for the whole group.	The lawmaking branch of a government.
A need or a desire for a good or service by people willing to pay for it.	To speak for.
An amount of a good that is offered for sale.	A colony ruled directly by a monarchy.
A partner.	A person who makes a journey for religious reasons.
A colony owned and ruled by one person who was chosen by a king or queen.	An agreement.
	A system of government in which people make their own laws.

dissent Unit 2, Chapter 5, Lesson 1	**Middle Passage** Unit 2, Chapter 5, Lesson 1
expel Unit 2, Chapter 5, Lesson 1	**refuge** Unit 2, Chapter 5, Lesson 2
industry Unit 2, Chapter 5, Lesson 1	**proprietor** Unit 2, Chapter 5, Lesson 2
import Unit 2, Chapter 5, Lesson 1	**trial by jury** Unit 2, Chapter 5, Lesson 2
export Unit 2, Chapter 5, Lesson 1	**immigrant** Unit 2, Chapter 5, Lesson 2
triangular trade route Unit 2, Chapter 5, Lesson 1	**diversity** Unit 2, Chapter 5, Lesson 2

The journey millions of enslaved Africans were forced to travel across the Atlantic Ocean from Africa to the West Indies.	**Disagreement.**
A safe place.	**To force to leave.**
An owner.	**All the businesses that make one kind of product or offer one kind of service.**
The right of a person to be tried by a jury, or a group, of citizens to decide if the person is guilty or innocent of committing a crime.	**A product brought into a country.**
A person who comes into a country to make a new home there.	**A product that leaves a country.**
A group of people from many parts of the world.	**Shipping routes that connected England, the English colonies, and Africa.**

religious toleration Unit 2, Chapter 5, Lesson 2	**broker** Unit 2, Chapter 5, Lesson 3
apprentice Unit 2, Chapter 5, Lesson 2	**naval stores** Unit 2, Chapter 5, Lesson 3
constitution Unit 2, Chapter 5, Lesson 3	
debtor Unit 2, Chapter 5, Lesson 3	
planter Unit 2, Chapter 5, Lesson 3	
indigo Unit 2, Chapter 5, Lesson 3	

A person who is paid to buy and sell for someone else.	Acceptance of religious differences.
Products used to build ships.	A person who lived and worked with an artisan's family for several years, learning a skill in order to earn a living.
	A written plan of government.
	A person who was put in prison for owing money.
	A plantation owner.
	A plant from which a blue dye can be produced.

alliance Unit 3, Chapter 6, Lesson 1	**treason** Unit 3, Chapter 6, Lesson 2
delegate Unit 3, Chapter 6, Lesson 1	**congress** Unit 3, Chapter 6, Lesson 2
Parliament Unit 3, Chapter 6, Lesson 1	**boycott** Unit 3, Chapter 6, Lesson 2
proclamation Unit 3, Chapter 6, Lesson 1	**repeal** Unit 3, Chapter 6, Lesson 2
budget Unit 3, Chapter 6, Lesson 1	**imperial policy** Unit 3, Chapter 6, Lesson 2
representation Unit 3, Chapter 6, Lesson 2	**protest** Unit 3, Chapter 6, Lesson 2

The act of working against one's own government.	A formal agreement among groups or individuals.
A formal meeting of government representatives.	A representative.
To refuse to buy or use goods or services.	The lawmaking branch of the British government.
The cancel, or undo, a law.	A public announcement.
Laws and orders issued by the British government.	A plan for spending money.
To work against or object to a certain policy.	To have someone speak or act for you.

monopoly Unit 3, Chapter 6, Lesson 3	**commander in chief** Unit 3, Chapter 6, Lesson 4
blockade Unit 3, Chapter 6, Lesson 3	**earthwork** Unit 3, Chapter 6, Lesson 4
quarter Unit 3, Chapter 6, Lesson 3	**olive branch** Unit 3, Chapter 6, Lesson 4
petition Unit 3, Chapter 6, Lesson 3	**independence** Unit 3, Chapter 6, Lesson 5
Minutemen Unit 3, Chapter 6, Lesson 3	**resolution** Unit 3, Chapter 6, Lesson 5
revolution Unit 3, Chapter 6, Lesson 3	**declaration** Unit 3, Chapter 6, Lesson 5

A person who is in control of all the armed forces of a nation.	The complete control of a product or good by one person or group.
A wall made of earth and stone.	To use warships to prevent other ships from entering or leaving a harbor.
An ancient symbol of peace.	To provide or pay for housing.
The freedom to govern on one's own.	A signed request made to an official person or organization.
A formal group statement.	A member of the Massachusetts colony militia who could quickly be ready to fight the British.
An official statement.	A sudden, complete change, such as the overthrow of an established government.

preamble

Unit 3, Chapter 6, Lesson 5

grievance

Unit 3, Chapter 6, Lesson 5

	An introduction; first part.
	A complaint.

Patriot Unit 3, Chapter 7, Lesson 1	**enlist** Unit 3, Chapter 7, Lesson 2
Loyalist Unit 3, Chapter 7, Lesson 1	**mercenary** Unit 3, Chapter 7, Lesson 2
neutral Unit 3, Chapter 7, Lesson 1	**campaign** Unit 3, Chapter 7, Lesson 2
inflation Unit 3, Chapter 7, Lesson 1	**turning point** Unit 3, Chapter 7, Lesson 2
profiteering Unit 3, Chapter 7, Lesson 1	**negotiate** Unit 3, Chapter 7, Lesson 2
veteran Unit 3, Chapter 7, Lesson 1	**civilian** Unit 3, Chapter 7, Lesson 3

To sign up or to join.	A colonist who was against British rule and supported the rebel cause in the American colonies.
A soldier who serves for pay in the military of a foreign nation.	A person who remained loyal to the British king.
A series of military actions carried out for a certain goal.	Not choosing a side in a disagreement.
An event that causes an important change.	An economic condition which results in an increase in the price of goods.
To try to reach an agreement among different people.	Charging an extra-high price for a good or service.
A person who is not in the military.	A person who has served in the military.

traitor

Unit 3, Chapter 7, Lesson 3

abolitionist

Unit 3, Chapter 7, Lesson 4

abolish

Unit 3, Chapter 7, Lesson 4

territory

Unit 3, Chapter 7, Lesson 4

ordinance

Unit 3, Chapter 7, Lesson 4

	Someone who acts against his or her own government.
	A person who wanted to end slavery.
	To end.
	Land that belongs to a nation but is not a state and is not represented in the national government.
	A law or set of laws.

arsenal Unit 4, Chapter 8, Lesson 1	**legislative branch** Unit 4, Chapter 8, Lesson 2
federal system Unit 4, Chapter 8, Lesson 1	**executive branch** Unit 4, Chapter 8, Lesson 2
republic Unit 4, Chapter 8, Lesson 1	**electoral college** Unit 4, Chapter 8, Lesson 2
compromise Unit 4, Chapter 8, Lesson 1	**veto** Unit 4, Chapter 8, Lesson 2
bill Unit 4, Chapter 8, Lesson 1	**impeach** Unit 4, Chapter 8, Lesson 2
separation of powers Unit 4, Chapter 8, Lesson 2	**judicial branch** Unit 4, Chapter 8, Lesson 2

The branch of government that makes the laws.	A weapons storehouse.
The branch of government that has the power to enforce the laws.	A system of government in which the power to govern is shared by the national and state governments.
A group chosen by citizens to vote for the President.	A form of government in which people elect representatives to run the government.
To reject.	To give up some of what you want in order to reach an agreement.
To accuse a government official of a crime.	An idea for a new law.
The court system, which is the branch of government that decides whether laws are working fairly.	The division of powers among the three branches of the national government.

justice Unit 4, Chapter 8, Lesson 2	**due process of law** Unit 4, Chapter 8, Lesson 3
rule of law Unit 4, Chapter 8, Lesson 2	**reserved powers** Unit 4, Chapter 8, Lesson 3
amendment Unit 4, Chapter 8, Lesson 2	**Cabinet** Unit 4, Chapter 8, Lesson 3
ratify Unit 4, Chapter 8, Lesson 3	**political party** Unit 4, Chapter 8, Lesson 3
Federalists Unit 4, Chapter 8, Lesson 3	**checks and balances** Unit 4, Chapter 8, Lesson 4
Anti-Federalists Unit 4, Chapter 8, Lesson 3	**union** Unit 4, Chapter 8, Lesson 4

The principle that guarantees that people have the right to a fair trial by jury.	A judge.
Authority that belongs to the states or to the people.	The principle that every member of a society, even a ruler, must follow the law.
A group of the President's most important advisers.	A change.
A group that tries to elect officials who will support its policies.	To approve.
A system that keeps each branch of government from becoming too powerful or misusing its authority.	Citizens who were in favor of ratifying the Constitution.
An alliance that works to reach common goals.	Citizens who were against ratification of the Constitution.

popular sovereignty Unit 4, Chapter 8, Lesson 4	**gap** Unit 4, Chapter 9, Lesson 1
democracy Unit 4, Chapter 8, Lesson 4	**pioneer** Unit 4, Chapter 9, Lesson 1
public agenda Unit 4, Chapter 8, Lesson 4	**consequence** Unit 4, Chapter 9, Lesson 1
suffrage Unit 4, Chapter 8, Lesson 4	**impressment** Unit 4, Chapter 9, Lesson 2
civic virtue Unit 4, Chapter 8, Lesson 4	**national anthem** Unit 4, Chapter 9, Lesson 2
naturalization Unit 4, Chapter 8, Lesson 4	**nationalism** Unit 4, Chapter 9, Lesson 2

A low place between mountains.	The idea that government gets its power from the people.
An early settler of an area.	A form of government in which the people rule and are free to make choices about their lives and their government.
Something that happens because of an action.	What the people need and want from the government.
The taking of workers against their will.	The right to vote.
The official song of a country.	Qualities that add to a healthy democracy.
Pride in one's country.	The process of becoming a legal citizen of the United States.

assimilate	gold rush
Unit 4, Chapter 9, Lesson 2	Unit 4, Chapter 9, Lesson 3
dictator	forty-niners
Unit 4, Chapter 9, Lesson 3	Unit 4, Chapter 9, Lesson 3
annex	canal
Unit 4, Chapter 9, Lesson 3	Unit 4, Chapter 9, Lesson 4
ford	lock
Unit 4, Chapter 9, Lesson 3	Unit 4, Chapter 9, Lesson 4
manifest destiny	locomotive
Unit 4, Chapter 9, Lesson 3	Unit 4, Chapter 9, Lesson 4
cession	Industrial Revolution
Unit 4, Chapter 9, Lesson 3	Unit 4, Chapter 9, Lesson 4

A sudden rush of people to an area where gold has been found.	Adopted.
A gold seeker who arrived in California in 1849.	A leader who has complete control of the government.
A human-made waterway that connects bodies of water.	To add to.
A part of a canal in which the water level can be raised or lowered to bring ships to the level of the next part of the canal	To cross.
A railroad engine.	Certain future.
The period of time during the 1800s when machines took the place of hand tools to manufacture goods.	Something that is given up, such as land.

cotton gin

Unit 4, Chapter 9, Lesson 4

interchangeable parts

Unit 4, Chapter 9, Lesson 4

	A machine that could quickly remove the seeds from cotton.
	Parts that can be made exactly alike by machines.

sectionalism Unit 5, Chapter 10, Lesson 1	**fugitive** Unit 5, Chapter 10, Lesson 1
diverse economy Unit 5, Chapter 10, Lesson 1	**Underground Railroad** Unit 5, Chapter 10, Lesson 2
free state Unit 5, Chapter 10, Lesson 1	**secede** Unit 5, Chapter 10, Lesson 3
slave state Unit 5, Chapter 10, Lesson 1	**Confederacy** Unit 5, Chapter 10, Lesson 3
tariff Unit 5, Chapter 10, Lesson 1	**border state** Unit 5, Chapter 10, Lesson 3
states' rights Unit 5, Chapter 10, Lesson 1	**artillery** Unit 5, Chapter 10, Lesson 3

Someone who escapes from the law.	Regional loyalty.
A system of secret escape routes that led enslaved people to free land.	An economy that is based on many industries rather than just a few.
To leave.	A state that did not allow slavery before the Civil War.
The states that left the Union to form their on national government called the Confederate States of America.	A state that allowed slavery before the Civil War.
A state located between the North and the South that permitted slavery but had not seceded.	A tax on imports.
Large mounted guns such as a cannon.	The idea that the states, not the national government, should have the final say on all laws.

civil war Unit 5, Chapter 10, Lesson 3	**Reconstruction** Unit 5, Chapter 11, Lesson 1
strategy Unit 5, Chapter 10, Lesson 4	**black codes** Unit 5, Chapter 11, Lesson 1
emancipate Unit 5, Chapter 10, Lesson 4	**acquit** Unit 5, Chapter 11, Lesson 1
prejudice Unit 5, Chapter 10, Lesson 4	**freedmen** Unit 5, Chapter 11, Lesson 1
address Unit 5, Chapter 10, Lesson 5	**sharecropping** Unit 5, Chapter 11, Lesson 1
assassinate Unit 5, Chapter 10, Lesson 5	**secret ballot** Unit 5, Chapter 11, Lesson 1

Rebuilding.	A war between people in the same country.
Laws limiting the rights of former enslaved people.	A long-range plan made to reach a goal.
Not guilty.	To free.
Men, women, and children who had been enslaved.	An unfair feeling of dislike for members of a certain group because of their background, race, or religion.
A system of working the land in which the worker was paid by letting them keep a share of the crops they harvested.	A short speech.
A voting method that does not allow anyone to know how a person has voted.	Murdered in a sudden or secret attack.

segregation Unit 5, Chapter 11, Lesson 1	**transcontinental railroad** Unit 5, Chapter 11, Lesson 3
prospector Unit 5, Chapter 11, Lesson 2	**skyscraper** Unit 5, Chapter 11, Lesson 3
boom Unit 5, Chapter 11, Lesson 2	**petroleum** Unit 5, Chapter 11, Lesson 3
bust Unit 5, Chapter 11, Lesson 2	**labor union** Unit 5, Chapter 11, Lesson 3
homesteader Unit 5, Chapter 11, Lesson 2	**strike** Unit 5, Chapter 11, Lesson 3
reservation Unit 5, Chapter 11, Lesson 2	**collective bargaining** Unit 5, Chapter 11, Lesson 3

The railroad that crossed North America.	The practice of keeping people in separate groups based on their race or culture.
A very tall steel-framed building.	A person who searches for gold, silver, or other mineral resources.
Oil.	A time of fast economic or population growth.
A workers group that fights for better working conditions and pay.	A time of fast economic decline.
The stopping of work to make employers meet worker's demands.	A person who settled on the land granted by the government.
A process that allows employers and workers to discuss and agree on working conditions.	Land set aside by the government for use by Native Americans.

tenement	
Unit 5, Chapter 11, Lesson 4	
reformer	
Unit 5, Chapter 11, Lesson 4	
settlement house	
Unit 5, Chapter 11, Lesson 4	

	A poorly built apartment building.
	A person who tries to improve society.
	A place that provided food, healthcare, and classes for immigrants.

armistice Unit 6, Chapter 12, Lesson 1	**consumer good** Unit 6, Chapter 12, Lesson 3
progressive Unit 6, Chapter 12, Lesson 1	**assembly line** Unit 6, Chapter 12, Lesson 3
conservation Unit 6, Chapter 12, Lesson 1	**stock market** Unit 6, Chapter 12, Lesson 3
military draft Unit 6, Chapter 12, Lesson 2	**depression** Unit 6, Chapter 12, Lesson 3
trench warfare Unit 6, Chapter 12, Lesson 2	**bureaucracy** Unit 6, Chapter 12, Lesson 3
no-man's land Unit 6, Chapter 12, Lesson 2	**rationing** Unit 6, Chapter 12, Lesson 4

A product made for personal use.	An agreement to stop fighting.
A system of mass production where products are put together as they move past a line of workers.	A person who worked to improve live for those who were not wealthy.
A place where people can buy or sell stocks or shares in companies.	The wise use and protection of natural resources.
A time when the economy does not grow and people lose jobs and have little money.	A way to bring people into the military.
The workers and groups that run government programs.	A type of fighting that takes place in deep trenches, dug in the ground.
Limiting what people can buy.	During war, the area between the trenches.

internment camp Unit 6, Chapter 12, Lesson 4	**cease-fire** Unit 6, Chapter 13, Lesson 1
concentration camp Unit 6, Chapter 12, Lesson 5	**suburb** Unit 6, Chapter 13, Lesson 1
genocide Unit 6, Chapter 12, Lesson 5	**cold war** Unit 6, Chapter 13, Lesson 1
Holocaust Unit 6, Chapter 12, Lesson 5	**arms race** Unit 6, Chapter 13, Lesson 1
communism Unit 6, Chapter 12, Lesson 5	**satellite** Unit 6, Chapter 13, Lesson 1
free world Unit 6, Chapter 12, Lesson 5	**developing country** Unit 6, Chapter 13, Lesson 2

A temporary end to a conflict.	An enclosed camp used in the United States during World War II to hold Japanese Americans.
A community or neighborhood that lies outside a city.	A prison camp.
A war fought mostly with words and money rather than soldiers and weapons.	A planned attempt to kill an entire people.
A competition of adding new weapons.	The mass murder of Jews during World War II.
An object that circles a planet.	A political and economic system in which the government owns all industries and property.
A country whose economy is still being built.	The United States and its allies.

crisis	deficit
Unit 6, Chapter 13, Lesson 2	Unit 6, Chapter 13, Lesson 4
integration	recession
Unit 6, Chapter 13, Lesson 3	Unit 6, Chapter 13, Lesson 5
civil rights	coalition
Unit 6, Chapter 13, Lesson 3	Unit 6, Chapter 13, Lesson 5
nonviolence	terrorism
Unit 6, Chapter 13, Lesson 3	Unit 6, Chapter 13, Lesson 5
arms control	
Unit 6, Chapter 13, Lesson 4	
scandal	
Unit 6, Chapter 13, Lesson 4	

A shortage.	A difficult situation.
A time of slow economic activity.	The bringing together of people of all races.
An alliance or group united around a common goal.	The rights guaranteed to all citizens by the Constitution.
The use of violence to promote a cause.	The use of peaceful ways to bring about change.
	A competition of adding new weapons.
	An action that brings disgrace.

hijack Unit 6, Chapter 14, Lesson 1	**market economy** Unit 6, Chapter 14, Lesson 2
free enterprise Unit 6, Chapter 14, Lesson 2	**competition** Unit 6, Chapter 14, Lesson 2
human resource Unit 6, Chapter 14, Lesson 2	**productivity** Unit 6, Chapter 14, Lesson 2
capital goods Unit 6, Chapter 14, Lesson 2	**specialization** Unit 6, Chapter 14, Lesson 2
scarcity Unit 6, Chapter 14, Lesson 2	**interdependent** Unit 6, Chapter 14, Lesson 2
command economy Unit 6, Chapter 14, Lesson 2	**service industry** Unit 6, Chapter 14, Lesson 3

An economic system in which producers buy resources for a certain price.	To illegally take control of a vehicle.
The contest among companies to get the most customers or sell the most goods.	An economic system in which people are able to start and run their own businesses with little control by the government.
A measure of how many resources are needed to produce goods and services.	A worker who brings his or her own ideas to a job.
Becoming skilled at one kind of job.	Buildings, machines, technology, and tools needed to produce goods and services.
Depending on other states and regions for natural resources, goods, and services.	When people want more than their resources can provide.
An industry that provides services to other people.	An economic system in which the government owns all the resources and controls businesses.

high-tech Unit 6, Chapter 14, Lesson 3	
globalization Unit 6, Chapter 14, Lesson 3	
urban sprawl Unit 6, Chapter 14, Lesson 4	

	Based on computers and other kinds of electronic equipment.
	The growth of a global economy.
	Developing land for cities or housing.